Game Guns and Rifles

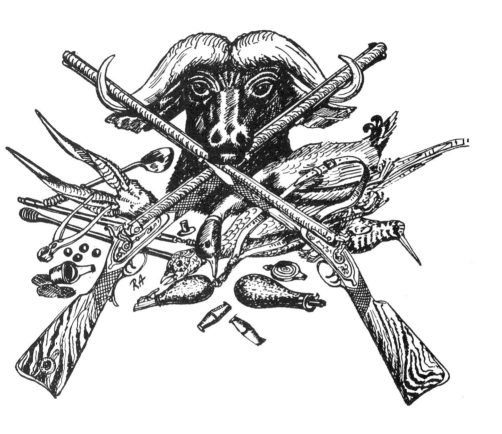

GAME GUNS
AND RIFLES

PERCUSSION TO HAMMERLESS EJECTOR
IN BRITAIN

Richard Akehurst

° THE °
SPORTSMAN'S
PRESS
LONDON

TO
MY DEAR WIFE
SARAH

Published by The Sportsman's Press 1992

© Richard Akehurst 1992

First published 1969, second impression 1985, third impression 1992

A catalogue record of this book is available from the British Library

ISBN 0-948253-61-4

Printed in Great Britain by
Redwood Press Limited, Melksham, Wiltshire

Contents

8   BREECH-LOADING GAME RIFLES

9   GUNMAKING IN THE BREECH-LOADING ERA UP TO 1900

powders—necessary research by cartridge makers—'chamberless' guns and the thin brass case—Dr C. J. Heath—conversion of guns for the thin brass case—attempts to standardize cartridge and chamber sizes.
ALTERATIONS TO RULES OF PROOF: Alterations made necessary to take account of breech-loaders—the Gun Barrel Proof Act of 1868—new rules applying to sporting guns and rifles—Gunmakers' Company (London) and The Guardians (Birmingham): proof marks—new rules to cover choke bores—supplementary proof for nitro powders and first 'Nitro Proof' marks—further alterations to take account of express rifles and rifled choke guns.

Preliminary notes—histories, gun numbers and dates:
Henry Atkin—Frederick Beesley—Thomas Bland & Sons—Boss & Co.—Churchill Ltd—Cogswell & Harrison—John Dickson & Son—George Gibbs of Bristol—Stephen Grant—W. W. Greener—Holland and Holland—Charles Lancaster—Joseph Lang—John Manton—Joseph Manton—James Purdey & Sons Ltd—John Rigby and Co.—Webley & Scott Ltd—Westley Richards and Co. Ltd—John Wilkes—James Woodward.
Mr W. R. H. Robson's notes on gunmakers:
Adams, Andrews, Baker, Barton, Beattie, Blanch, Bozard, Breech Loading Armoury Co Ltd, Colt, Daw, Dougall, D. & J. Egg, Evans, Fairman, Forsyth, Gye & Moncrieff, Hancock, Harrison & Hussey, Harriss, Hellis, Henry, Hussey, Jeffrey, Ling, Little, London Armoury Co., Maleham, Manchester Ordnance and Rifle Co., Moore & Grey, Morris, Jackson, Murcott, Needham, Nock, Parkin, Paton, Perkes, Pritchett, Reilly, Riviere, Searle, Silver, Smith, Staudenmayer, Storm's Breech Loading Arms Depot, Sylven, Tatham, Thorn, Tolley, Wallis, Watson, Whitworth, Wilkinson, Wilson. Provincial Gunmakers c. 1900 listed by G. T. Teasdale-Buckell.

Safety precautions—re-proof—loads and loading for shotguns and rifles—cleaning—useful equipment—early breech-loaders—safety and proof—black powder and nitro proof—Explosives Licence for black powder, Firearms Certificate for rifles.

List of Plates and Figures

PLATES

FIGURES

Preface

Since this book was first published in 1969, there has been a greatly increased interest in the period and subject matter covered. That interest has been reflected in a widespread demand for this book, which is now happily met with this reprinting.

The last fifteen years have seen further well-known gunmakers ceasing to trade and an increased tendency for lower and middle priced guns to be imported. The making of 'best' guns, still using many of the traditional craft skills, continues to flourish but at a very much increased cost.

The aim of this book is to interest both shooters and collectors in what must surely be one of the most exciting periods in the whole history of gunmaking, and to serve as a basis of study for those who wish to explore further. The word 'game' in the title has been used broadly to describe all hunted birds and beasts and the guns and rifles developed for their pursuit.

Following chapters on the development and perfecting of the percussion gun and rifle, the book goes on to describe the tremendous surge of activity and invention throughout the rest of the century, during which the early breech-loaders were transformed into the modern game gun and rifle. Also considered are the changes in game shooting, wildfowling, trap pigeon and wild pigeon shooting, and the robust early days of big game shooting with muzzle-loaders are contrasted with later changes brought about by the tremendous power and accuracy of high velocity breech-loading rifles and easier travelling facilities.

Traditional craft methods of gunmaking have been described, and particular attention has been paid to those superb examples of forging artistry, Damascus barrels. With the complicated breech-loading actions came the increased use of machinery, and with the moderately priced gun came the beginnings of the use of large-scale production methods, while in contrast so far as 'best' guns were concerned the craft tradition remained firmly entrenched.

Within the scope of this book it is obviously not possible to cover every patent gun and rifle action, so precedence has been given to the main stream of development. Rather less space in proportion to breech-loading guns has been given to breech-loading rifles because of the difficulty of collecting these items in Britain with its firearm restrictions.

The short histories and the notes on gunmakers of the period are given for their interest and help in the dating of guns. Some notes are also included to help those who may wish to shoot with their muzzle- or early breech-loading guns.

CHAPTER ONE
Percussion Cap Guns

B Y about 1830 the percussion gun primed with a copper cap was firmly established (plate 2). The simplicity of the system combined with greater speed and certainty of ignition had caused the long reign of the flintlock to come to an end. John and Joseph Manton who had done so much to perfect the Regency flintlock (plate 1) were, in common with all the leading gunmakers of their day, quick to appreciate the advantages of the new system. Though at first, as with most innovations, there were those who had their doubts or those who stoutly championed the flintlock which they had used for so long and understood so well, the great majority of sportsmen either had percussion guns made or had their flint guns converted. The most popular method of conversion was by means of a side plug and nipple screwed into the side of the breech in the place of the touchhole and the flint cock was then replaced by the familiar percussion hammer. A better method was to fit a new breech and percussion lock.

At last the sportsman had in his hands a gun which, when well constructed and, quite as important, suitably loaded, threw its shot load hard and fast without perceptible delay between the pulling of the trigger and discharge. This opened up the possibility of shooting birds flying fast at all angles with a reasonable chance of a successful shot. In the days of the flint gun a steady shot at a going away bird walked up with the aid of pointers was the most favoured one. With the percussion gun some took to having their game driven towards them, where at their stand with a pair or more of guns and loaders they fired many shots in a short time trying to perfect the art of shooting and prove it by the size of bag. The tendency towards the driving of game was gradual at first, for it depended for success on good management in the preservation and rearing of game and the skill with which the birds were put over the guns. Until the coming of the breech-loader walking up with the aid of dogs was still for the majority the usual means of bringing game to bag.

The typical game gun (plate 4) in use for normal game shooting was double-barrelled, the barrels being of a variety of twist, of 12 to 16 bore and of 30 inches in length. The breeches retained platinum plugs with vent holes at the side and had the nipples set well in to connect the flash of the cap as directly as possible with the rear of the patent breech. The ribs, mostly broad and of a slight U form, were elevated to some extent, to cause the centre of the shot pattern to strike above the point of aim, this being an aid when taking a rising bird. The stocks are rarely to be found at this period with much cast off or on and have less bend than was the case in the 18th century. This straighter stock also aided a shooter to give enough lead on a rising bird. It should be mentioned that the fashion for ribs and stocks designed to cause the shot to be thrown above the point of aim came about to some extent as a result of interest in pigeon match shooting in which this was a desirable quality.

The stocks were mostly of walnut, figured to a greater or lesser extent, but in the early years of the percussion gun there was a fashion for birdseye maple stocks, which although attractive to look at, were so difficult for the stockers to work that gunmakers were at some pains to persuade their customers away from them. Forward action locks (plate 7) in which the mainspring was positioned in front of the hammer were fitted to most best quality guns, for they were considered to act more quickly and smoothly than back action locks. A considerable number of guns, some of high quality, notably those by Rigby of Dublin, were however fitted with back action locks (plate 8), though these do not give quite the balance of line and elegance to a gun as a forward action lock. The trigger guards and heel plates were of swaff iron, charcoal blued. In the engraving of various parts floral scrolls dominated, but sometimes game scenes were added.

There were, of course, numbers of guns at this period that varied from this general pattern of the game gun but there were also some built to suit the needs of particular sports, such as pigeon match shooting and wildfowling.

The sport of shooting pigeons sprung from traps, often for large prizes or wagers, had started in Regency times in a rough and ready manner. The 'Old Hats' public house on the Uxbridge Road at Ealing near London is said to have obtained its name from the fact that the pigeons used for the matches were placed in holes in the ground, and were covered with old hats which were pulled off by means of cords to release the birds. Later wooden or iron traps were used, which flung open, also on the pulling of a cord from a point behind the shooter. Trap shooting became popular and more organised, notable bona fide pigeon clubs being formed at Hornesy Wood House and the Red House, Battersea. Many of the best game shots tried their skill at the traps and with both money and reputation at stake they took care to have built powerful guns designed to throw heavy loads of shot hard and well distributed high of the point of aim, so as to ensure as far as was possible that no truly aimed shot should fail to 'grass' their bird.

In the first instance these special pigeon guns were single-barrelled and of large bore (10, 8 and even 6), some using the tube type of detonator which was thought to give quicker and more certain ignition than the copper cap. These large bore guns can usually be distinguished from wildfowl guns by their shorter 30 to 32-inch barrels and by the lack of provision for a ramrod; a loading rod being carried in the gun case with the remainder of the equipment. Also it will be seen that pigeon guns are often finished in a superior manner. It should be noted that these large bore guns were not necessarily used with their full loads, it being known that, say, 1½ oz would be shot more efficiently by an 8 bore than by a 10 bore and better still by a 6 bore, the shot column being shorter the bigger the bore.

In the late percussion and breech-loading period the pigeon gun was limited to a double gun of 11 bore or smaller. Some of these double guns are also to be found without provision for a ramrod and they are rather heavier than the normal game gun. This was both for steadiness and to minimise the recoil of heavy charges, 1¼ oz of shot being the standard load for a 12 bore pigeon gun. Many percussion pigeon guns were made well into the breech loading period (plate 7).

'Marksman' in his book *The Dead Shot*, 1862, writes that the customary gauge of a pigeon gun is of 12 bore, and none larger than 10 bore should be permitted. He warns the country sportsman against shooting matches with 'professional' pigeon shots who may well have guns of 6 bore firing a load of 5 drams of power and 2 or more ounces of shot. For the 12 bore, although there was no restriction as to powder, the usual charge was from 2¾ to 3 drams and that of the shot from 1 to 1½ oz. The size of shot varied from No 5, 6, 7, to 8 and it was usual for all to load from the same bowl any size and charge of shot agreed on. In some matches shooters were allowed a larger charge if they moved back from the trap one yard for every eighth of an ounce of extra shot.

'Marksman', after remarking on the disgraceful tricks resorted to by 'professionals', such as including extra shot concealed in paper wadding, goes on to write: 'Strange to say until the publication of the first edition of this work, there were no other printed or authorised rules in regard to pigeon shooting, than those of the old Battersea school; and though some of those are useful, they are quite inadequate to the requirements of the present day. In the event of any difficulty or dispute arising at a shooting match, it has been usual to refer the matter to the editors of *Bell's Life in London*, whose decisions thereon have generally been sound and good.'

Prizes of guns, rifles, gold and silver cups and tankards as well as money prizes were contended for by the shooters but as considerable prestige attached also to the winning guns, gunmakers were quick to see the advantages of having their guns excel in public. Soon the leading gun manufacturers were to be found in attendance at the fashionable pigeon clubs, which became for them something of an unofficial gun trial with much custom to be gained by the winning makers.

Popular amongst countrymen were starling and sparrow shooting matches using No 8 and No 10 shot. These matches were often shot behind country public houses, the range at which they were shot being shorter than was the case with pigeons.

Col. Peter Hawker in his famed book *Instructions to young sportsmen in all that relates to guns and shooting* had done much to make wild-fowling more popular as a sport, so that like-minded enthusiasts, attracted to the wild and solitary stretches of salt marsh, had guns made which were suited to the longer ranges at which shots at duck or geese might be obtained on these coverless expanses. Leaving aside the heavy artillery of the punt gunner, the shore shooter armed himself with either a double gun of 8 or 10 bore with 32 to 34 inch barrels or took to a great long single barrelled 4- or 6-bore gun suited to throwing a heavy load of large shot at long range at numbers of sitting or flying ducks or geese (plate 8). Because of the rugged nature of wildfowling and the subjection of man and gun to mud and salt water, a strong, durable and plainly finished gun was most in demand, though some are to be found as finely finished and stocked as the best game guns.

The percussion lock was a great help to the wildfowler for in the days of flint the flash of the powder in the pan could cause diving ducks to dive, 'ducking the flash', or flying birds to swerve before the gun fired, especially was this so if the gun hung fire from the powder in the pan having got damp, as it often did in the misty air of dawn or dusk. A misfire on such occasions was a frequent occurrence giving much disappointment in circumstances where good chances were seldom obtained. The percussion cap, although not entirely proof against damp or wet, was a great improvement in this respect and of course the flash of the pan and the delayed fire were no longer a problem.

When shooting at sitting wildfowl there was in fact some advantage in the flintlock, for the slight delay between the flash of the pan and the firing of the charge was just sufficient to put the birds up, when they presented with their opened wings a better target for the shot pattern. A percussion gunner sometimes gave a shout a moment before firing, to achieve the same object.

The importance of loading to suit the gun has been mentioned and should therefore be examined in greater detail. For each gun there will be found an ideal load that will be fitting for the weight, bore and length of barrels of the gun and also a correct proportion of powder to shot. Too much shot to powder will give weak shooting and a considerable drop at forty yards, though the shot should give a reasonable pattern. Too much powder to shot will give strength but tend to scatter the shot widely, and for this reason this type of load was sometimes used for covert or rabbit shooting. There was great temptation after missing a few birds to increase the powder and shot load, but even if the recoil was not unpleasant it is unlikely that better pattern and penetration would be the result. It is generally true that the longer the shot column becomes beyond an ideal proportion of length to width of bore, the less efficiently will the shot be thrown.

The average proportions for various bores which have been arrived at as a result of practical experience and trials by notable sportsmen and gunmakers alike are given below, together with the appropriate size of powder. As a general rule the heavier the load and the longer the barrel the bigger should be the size of black powder grain used. Also the larger the bore the thicker the wad should be.

20 bore, 30-inch barrel, 2 drams No 2 or 4 powder, $\frac{3}{4}$-oz shot
16 bore, 30-inch barrel, $2\frac{1}{2}$ drams No 2 or 4 powder, $\frac{7}{8}$-oz shot
15 bore, 30-inch barrel, $2\frac{3}{4}$ drams No 2 or 4 powder, 1-oz shot
14 bore, 30-inch barrel, $2\frac{7}{8}$ drams No 2 or 4 powder, $1\frac{1}{16}$-oz shot
12 bore, 30-inch barrel, 3 drams No 2 or 4 powder, $1\frac{1}{8}$-oz shot
10 bore 32–34-inch barrel, 4 drams No 4 or 6 powder, $1\frac{1}{2}$-oz shot
8 bore, 34–36-inch barrel, 6 drams No 6 powder, 2-oz shot
4 bore, 36+-inch barrel, 9 drams No 8 powder, 3-oz shot

Slight variations might be used with advantage to suit particular guns but any major departure from these proportions would not give good results. Where advantage can be gained is in using slightly lighter loads of powder and shot. For instance a very effective load in a light 12 bore is $2\frac{3}{4}$ drams No 2 powder and 1 oz of No 6 or 7 shot. Where loads of shot are below 1 oz it is advisable to use No 7 shot with 340 pellets per ounce rather than No 6 at 272, for more birds are lost through the pattern being too open than for want of penetration at normal sporting ranges particularly in cylinder bored guns, as all were at this time.

The sportsman setting out to shoot with his percussion muzzle loader had quite a number of pieces of equipment to remember. Also he had to ensure that his gun was ready for use by wiping excess of oil from the barrel and by firing off caps to clear the nipples and breech of oil; in achieving this a little loose powder put into the barrel and tapped well down was a help.

His gun ready for loading, he next filled his capacious pockets with his powder flask adjusted to the appropriate measure, thick felt wads oiled or greased at the edges in one pocket and thin card top wads with a hole in to let the air through in another. Across his shoulder he hung a shot flask or belt. In one waistcoat pocket he put his cap dispenser, in another his nipple key with spare nipples and pricker for cleaning out the hole in same, and perhaps a powder measure in another pocket.

Now, with his equipment on him, he proceeded to load. He would then be aware of any item he had forgotten as he proceeded to pour the measure of powder down both barrels, tapping the butt to shake it well down the breech to the nipples, then he placed his two felt wads over the barrel ends, drew his ramrod and rammed them home lightly but firmly. Next the shot load was put down and the thin top card wads rammed home; the ramrod was then replaced. The hammers were now drawn to half cock, the caps placed on the nipples, and our sportsman was ready to proceed in search of game, bringing the hammers to full cock when a shot seemed likely. If he wished to render his gun safe at any time he would remove the percussion caps.

A particular danger in a muzzle-loading gun, especially after firing the first shot, was that a piece of tow, left in the breech after cleaning, might still be smouldering when the next powder charge was poured down. It could ignite the powder, which in its turn could explode the flask in the hand. To guard against this patent fire-proof flasks were made but the safest method was to pour the powder first into a powder measure so that this only was held over the barrel. Great care had also to be taken to ensure that both powder and shot loads were put into the correct barrels, it being easy in the heat of the moment to double load with one or the other. A simple check was to mark the ramrod at the place it should show above the muzzle when the barrel was correctly loaded. The percussion cap of the other barrel should always have been removed while one barrel only was being reloaded. As an aid to quick loading steel double ended shot chargers and sometimes powder and shot chargers were used; these were safe and simple but would be rather heavy and bulky if many were carried in place of powder and shot flasks; however two or three in a waistcoat pocket could be very handy.

On returning from a day's shooting it was customary to fire off the loaded barrels or to withdraw the top wad with the worm end of the ramrod and tip the shot out into the hand; it was wise of course to remove the percussion caps before doing this and then put them on again to fire off the powder.

For cleaning, the barrels were removed from the stock by sliding back the 'side nail' or bolt that secured the loop under the barrels to the fore part of the stock. The breech ends of the barrels were placed in a bucket of cold water and a rod, with a tow-wrapped jag on the end, was worked up and down piston fashion until all the fouling had been expelled. If the barrel was very foul the nipples were removed to make the clearing of the fouling easier. Next near boiling water was poured through the barrels which were held with a cloth and then while still hot the surplus moisture was wiped out with a newly towed jag and as much moisture as possible blown out at the breech end by the pumping movement of the rod. The barrels were then left in a warm place until there was no doubt about their dryness before they were oiled. If the barrels were leaded, a brass turk's head would assist in removing this or any persistent fouling. Next, the nipples and the hammer head were cleaned and oiled, special tools were provided for this purpose, one of which was a tiny cone shaped jag which was wound with tow for cleaning the cup of the hammer and the other a hollow brass tool with a castellated bottom edge that fitted over the nipple for cleaning round its base.

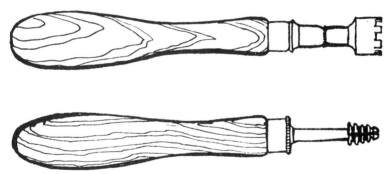

Figure 1. *Top*, tool with castellated top for cleaning round the base of the nipples; *bottom*, miniature jag for cleaning the inside of the hammer cup.

When a pair or more of guns were used the loaders were provided with loading rods slung from a leather retainer. These rods had a round ball at the top and were much more pleasant than a ramrod when a lot of loading had to be done in fouled barrels.

An incident occurred at a partridge drive when Earl de Grey was shooting in the next butt to Lord Walsingham with muzzle loaders. De Grey suddenly saw a flash, Walsingham was covered by a dense cloud of smoke, and the butt caught fire. It seemed that the loader was pouring black powder from one canister to another when a spark from the gun ignited it. Walsingham was a bit singed and the loaders too, but no one was seriously hurt.

Lord de Grey, later Lord Ripon, and Lord Walsingham, the Hon. Thomas de Grey before he succeeded, were two of the greatest game shots of the century, about whom there will be more to say in the chapters on the breech-loading period. Lord de Grey expressed the opinion that the best shot he had ever seen was Lord Walsingham with regard to both rapidity and accuracy. Also he said that with three guns and two skilled loaders it was extraordinary how quickly one could shoot with muzzle-loading guns, a worthwhile opinion from one who regularly took two grouse or partridges before and two behind.

The railways had made travel relatively easy, so that wherever sport was to be found, whether in the turnip fields of Norfolk or the moors of Yorkshire or Scotland, it was just a matter of gathering together guns, equipment and clothes and driving to the nearest railway station. One of the effects of this situation was that the 'crack' shots of the day tended to be invited to great estates for the sake of prestige and in the hope that record bags would be made, whilst in the past these had been the preserve of the local shots. To meet the needs of travel it became usual for good quality guns to be provided with strong mahogany or oak cases, often brass-bound and with leather covers to protect the wood. Within these cases were to be found all that a sportsman could desire in the way of equipment to load, clean and maintain his gun in remote places (plates 5, 6).

There could be in the case: the powder flask and shot flask, a spare ramrod, felt and card wads and a wad cutter, a tin of caps and a cap dispenser, a few shot chargers, a nipple key with spare nipples and pricker, a cleaning rod with jag, turk's head, worm and wool mop, some tow, a turnscrew and sometimes even spare springs and a spare lock screw. The case would have in the lid the finely engraved trade label of the gunmaker and also, most interesting to us now, the recommended load of powder and shot.

Of great assistance in quick-loading and long-range shooting were the Eley shot cartridges which were much used in the 1840s, 50s and 60s. These were of two types, the first being 'Eley's Universal Shot Cartridges' which had a top card wad and a load of shot packed in bone dust and wrapped in a thin paper. The gauge of the bore was shown on the orange red label on the bottom and the size of shot on a label on the top wad. The shot cartridge was wrapped, for protection before use, in a cartridge paper cover which was stripped off with the aid of a tape.

The second type was Eley's 'Patent Wire Cartridges for long distances', often green in colour, which were much the same as the above but with the addition of a wire cage open at the front and with a mesh slightly larger than the shot size, which could be as large as

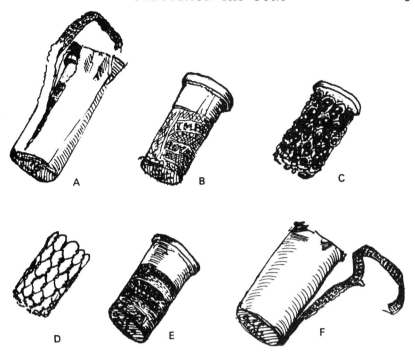

Figure 2. Eley long range wire cartridge and shot cartridge for muzzle-loaders.
Left to right:

A. Cartridge in outer covering which is opened by the tape.
B. The cartridge ready for loading with top wad.
C. With thin paper removed showing wire cage, top wad and shot packed in fine bonedust.
D. The wire cage open in front and closed in behind.
E. The shot cartridge ready for loading containing shot packed in fine bone-dust.
F. Outside paper case showing tape opener.

SG. The wire cage held the shot packed in bone dust together for some distance after they had left the barrel and as the top wad and the bone dust was blown away the shot began to break out of the wire cage and give a spread pattern. This system not only kept the shot from spreading too widely at long range but also by keeping all together for some distance it helped to maintain velocity at long distance.

These cartridges were designed to be used without a thick felt wad on top of the powder, the shot packed in bone dust expanding to make a gas-tight seal behind the top wad. The bone dust packing also assisted in maintaining the round shape of the pellets.

Colonel Peter Hawker records in his diary for November 1848: 'The birds would not let us get into the same field with them. Determined to "serve them out", I loaded "Big Joe" with Eley, started at five in the evening in the cart and was in again by half past six with ten first rate young partridges. Nothing like a duck gun from a horse and cart on the road to fill a bag when all popgunning becomes a wild goose chase!'

Also in January 1851 a further entry records: 'Sadly in want of a brace of birds, so took out my duck gun, "Big Joe" at dusk, crawled up to three partridges that were feeding, and floored the trio at 95 yards with a four ounce Eley cartridge. This may be called poaching, but show me the gent who would not chuckle at such an extraordinary shot.'

'The Old Shekarry' (the pen name of H. A. Leveson) in *The Hunting Grounds of the Old World* refers to 'loading his gun with a couple of Eley's green long-range cartridges' with which he bagged a fine pair of bustard with a right and left.

These wire cartridges continued to be used into the breech-loading period. A leaflet put out by Eley Bros. in the 1860s refers to: 'Eley's cylindrical wire cartridges for breech-loading cases', with instructions for loading: 'Put the charge of powder into the case, and place the cartridge with the red end on the powder. No wadding need be put between the powder and the cartridge. If a wadding is employed it should be a thin one.'

The use of concentrators in cartridge cases tended to lessen the use of wire cartridges in breech-loaders, because this simply involved the placing of a card ring about half an inch in depth round the top part of the shot and in contact with the top wad. Later choke boring was to render both unnecessary.

CHAPTER TWO

Percussion Cap Rifles

BETTER travel facilities had opened up many new hunting grounds abroad, which drew to them travellers and sportsmen from home seeking adventure and those sporting soldiers and officials whose duty placed them within easy reach. At home Scotland had become accessible by means of a comfortable railway journey while Queen Victoria and Prince Albert had done much to make the highlands, and the sport found there, fashionable. Queen Victoria records in her diaries her pleasure at being allowed to accompany her dear Albert on stalking expeditions, during which she proudly sketched the stags he shot. The enjoyment of highland life by the royal couple was echoed by many sportsmen who were attracted by the grandeur of the country and the wonderful stalking. The greatly increased interest in deer stalking at home and the pursuit of a wide variety of game abroad acted as a stimulus to the further development of game rifles.

In the early percussion era the typical rifle followed much the same general lines as the flintlock, that is, it was single-barrelled, this being of stub twist forging and octagonal external section. The rifling was multigroove of about a three-quarter turn in thirty inches. The rifle would be half stocked with a cheek piece towards the face and a circular patch box set in flush on the other side. The lock would usually be a forward action one with a sliding safety and a set trigger that gave a very light pull. The furniture would be of swaff iron, the trigger guard finished with a curved iron hand grip and the engraving, in the form of floral scrolls, would often be enlivened with delightful miniatures of animals of the chase. The ramrod, with a horn ball end, was a good strong one to stand up to the ramming of a tightly patched ball (plate 15, top).

The size and bore of these rifles varied considerably according to the type of game they were designed to be used against but the overall pattern was much the same. For smaller bore rook and rabbit rifles fine multigroove or hair rifling was sometimes used. These smaller bores were rarely much less than about 70 bore or roughly ·400 because of the difficulty of loading narrow bores, especially when foul, with a thin ramrod and because a ball of smaller diameter would be too light. The barrel would normally take a ball of rather less diameter than the bore to allow for the thickness of the patch. These rook and rabbit rifles would be used with a charge of around ¾ of a dram of powder and would rarely be used at ranges beyond 50 to 75 yards.

The medium size of rifle most popular for deer shooting was of 16 bore (·662), firing an ounce ball (plate 14) propelled by 1½ to 2 drams of powder. Though sighted up to 250 yards, in practice they would not often be used at more than 100 to 150 yards.

For big game, rifles of from 12 to 4 bore were made, but these too had to be used with relatively light charges, 2½ to 3 drams in the case of a 12 bore to about 6 to 8 drams in the case of a 4 bore.

The reason for the relatively light charges was that if the load of powder was increased the patched ball would strip across the rifling. It was therefore necessary to make up for the lack of velocity by using a heavy ball which even at a lower velocity would give reasonable striking energy. Because of the tendency to strip, it was particularly necessary to use a moderately slow burning grain of powder, number 6 for medium and light rifles and a larger grain for large bore, long-barrelled rifles, to give the ball a slower start and progressive propulsion.

In an attempt to key the ball well into the grooves, rifles were designed with deep rifling and a tight fitting ball which when patched had to be started down the barrel with a starter, a short wooden rod with a brass concave end which was placed over the ball and hammered down the first few inches with a leather faced wooden mallet and then forced down the remainder with a stout ramrod. It was most important to see that the ball was rammed well down on to the powder however difficult this was in a barrel fouled with use, because if a rifle were fired with the ball not in contact with the powder, at the least a very great strain would be exerted on the breech by the rapidly expanding gases being suddenly checked on meeting the ball. The ball would in any case be likely to be propelled in an erratic manner.

These single-barrelled rifles were very accurate at moderate ranges, if well made and correctly loaded, but the time it took to reload was a very great handicap if a second shot was required. This was bad enough if it allowed a deer to escape for want of a quick second shot but with dangerous game it could be a fatal misfortune. To meet the hunter's need, double rifles were made which gave him that often vital second shot. In the 1830s and 40s the double rifle took its place as the number one game rifle (plate 13), but single rifles were still used in the largest bores when a second gun would be carried by a bearer, and light single rook and rabbit rifles continued to be made.

The double rifle was the summit of the rifle maker's art, for while it was comparatively easy to sight in a single barrel, it becomes a very difficult task indeed to align two barrels precisely to the one set of sights. A factor that needed to be taken into account was that if the barrels were parallel the right barrel would throw to the right and the left barrel to the left. This was corrected by making them converge at the muzzle, the degree of convergence depending on the range at which the barrels were to zero, usually 100 yards. Another factor was that if the rifle was to shoot correctly the load and bullet for which it was designed and sighted must be kept constant. For instance, an increased charge in the right barrel would cause the rifle to shoot high and to the right, and the lighter the rifle in relation to the charge the stronger this tendency would be.

These double rifles were in many respects similar to the single rifles except that the barrels are almost always circular in section with a broad flat rib into which the sights are set: leaf sights with a platinum centre line which hinge up for the various ranges, and a foresight generally of the fine bead type. Where the stock was not formed into a semi pistol grip the effect was achieved by a curved hand grip that extended from the rear of the trigger guard. Usually in a double rifle the fore trigger only will have a set trigger, for the second trigger if too light could easily be prematurely pulled in the heat of the moment or jarred off by the first barrel. Other rifles had both triggers normal but with very smooth trigger pulls. A set trigger is one that has a spring which is compressed and lightly caught by pushing the trigger forwards, this on the lightest of pulls flicks up the sear releasing the hammer. The operation is so light that a small movable piece known as a 'detent' is required to ride the sear smoothly past the half cock bent.

Hunters who expected to face dangerous game at close quarters wanted and needed a rifle with a crushing 'knock down' potential, but being denied this in the case of the average double rifle, they took to powerful ball guns (plate 12) and some sportsmen even had their rifles bored out smooth. These ball guns were smooth bores, accurate up to about fifty yards and designed to be shot with very large charges of powder. Sir Samuel White Baker, author of *Rifle and Hound in Ceylon*, had made for him ball guns which were of 10 bore, weighed 15 lb, and were designed for a load of 10 drams of No 6 powder. Such guns at close range would, with their blunt round ball, give a tremendous knock down blow, but as Baker said it was most annoying to be unable to take shots at 100 yards or more because he was carrying a ball gun whose accuracy at that range could not be relied upon.

The compromise solution to the problem was to a large extent provided by the two-groove rifle (plate 15 lower). This enabled heavy charges to be used without stripping, giving higher velocity, a lower trajectory and reasonable accuracy at normal sporting ranges. The

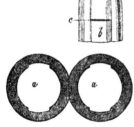

Figure 3. Section of two-groove Purdey rifle and conical bullet with two step wings.

bullets, both ball and conical, relied upon projections fitting into the two grooves of the barrel for their ability to hold the rifling when under very severe strain (plate 17). To help the bullets in this respect they were cast in hardened lead; pewter which contained tin, was added to lead for this purpose.

The great friction caused in these two-groove rifles was largely the result of the theory current with both sportsmen and rifle makers that a three-quarter turn in 30 inches was essential to accuracy; this theory, which had been established in the days of multi-groove rifling, was continued into the period dominated by the two-groove.

So far as sportsmen were concerned the two-groove system gave them most of the desired capabilities, provided they loaded according to the needs of the game expected, for although the conical bullet gave greater accuracy at long range its effect was considerably lessened because of its passing through the animal, therefore its striking energy was only partly absorbed by the animal. For large or dangerous game the blunt belted ball was best as this transmitted the full striking energy, velocity plus the weight of the ball, to the animal, the ball spreading on impact and therefore usually staying in the animal. The shock of impact would stop a charging animal even though not placed in a fatal spot, allowing time for an aimed second shot. Some hunters favoured hardened bullets for thick-skinned animals to ensure penetration.

A particular problem facing the hunter in the breathless, humid heat of dense tropical bush or forest was that, on firing his first barrel, the black powder would put such a smoke screen between him and a charging animal that there was an agonising wait for the smoke to clear before he saw either the beast stretched before him or found it bursting through on top of him. 'The Old Shekarry' in his book *The Hunting Grounds of the Old World* (1868) relates the story of his hunt for a notorious man-eating tiger, in which he acts as bait by walking at dusk down the road where its many victims have been killed: 'Then I heard a loud purring sound, and saw something twitching backwards and forwards behind a clump of low bush and long grass about eight or ten paces from me, and a little to the rear. I stepped back a couple of paces in order to get a better view, which action probably saved my life, for immediately the brute sprang into the middle of the road alighting about six feet from the place where I was standing. I fired a hurried shot ere he could gather himself for a second spring, and when the smoke had cleared away I saw him rolling over and over in the dusty road, writhing in his death agony, for my shot had entered the neck and gone downwards into his chest. I stepped on one side and gave him my second barrel behind the ear, a slight tremor passed over all his limbs and all was still. The man-eater was dead and his victims avenged.'

Baker also refers to the danger, when shooting in thick jungle, of the obscurity caused by the firing of the first barrel, the smoke hanging around and often preventing a clear aim being taken with the second, as the following incident illustrates.

'A cloud of smoke hung over me for a second and throwing my empty gun on one side, I put my hand behind me for a spare rifle. I felt the welcome barrel pushed into my hand at the same moment that I saw the infuriated head of the elephant with ears cocked charging through the smoke! It was the work of an instant. I just had time to cock the two-ounce rifle and take a steady aim. The next moment we were in a cloud of smoke, but as I fired, I felt certain of her. The smoke cleared from the thick bushes and she lay dead at six feet from the spot where I stood. The ball was in the centre of her forehead. Had she been missed I should have fired my last shot.'

The following letter from this renowned hunter Sir Samuel White Baker to the West Country rifle maker George Gibbs of Bristol is interesting:

30 August, 1887

About forty-six years ago your firm made for me the first rifle I ever planned. This was entirely my own idea at a time when rifle shooting was but little understood. I was only twenty years of age, but having taken a peculiar interest in the subject I was sure that a heavy charge of powder was the first necessity to procure a high velocity, and consequently a low trajectory. Your firm made for me a rifle weighing 22 lbs to carry a two-groove belted ball of 3 ozs, with a charge of 1 oz (16 drams) of powder. This was the first heavy rifle that ever was introduced to Ceylon, and it is referred to in my first work, 'The Rifle and Hound in Ceylon', as a very wonderful weapon. The rifle was made according to drawings submitted by myself. As you made the first large bore that I ever had, which was the most successful, I have no doubt that you would achieve a like success with the small-bore high express 125 grains of powder.

Yours faithfully,

Samuel Baker

In his preface to the 1892 edition of *The Rifle and Hound* Baker states his opinion that the best weapon for a hunter of average strength is a double rifle weighing 15 lb, of No 10 calibre. This should carry a charge of 10 drams of No 6 powder of coarse grain. Rather surprisingly he goes on to say that in former days he used 6 or 7 drams of the finest grained powder with the old muzzle-loader (a two-groove). This would be a pretty drastic load and it is as well that his rifles were made with great strength. However, he concludes by acknowledging that it is well known that the rim of the breech-loading cartridge is liable to burst with a heavy charge of the fine grain powder, therefore No 6 is best adapted for the rifle.

He concedes that a diversity of calibres is a serious drawback to a hunter in wild countries but unavoidable as there is no rifle that will combine the requirements of a great variety of game: the elephant requiring the heavy bullet, while for the deer the small-bore suffices.

Baker recommends the following equipment for hunting every species of game in wild tropical countries:

'One single-barrel rifle to carry a half pound projectile or a four ounce, according to the strength of the hunter. Three double-barrelled No 10 rifles, to carry ten drams No 6 powder. One double-barrelled small bore rifle, sighted most accurately for deer shooting. Express to carry 5 or 6 drams, but with hardened solid bullet. Two double-barrelled No 10 smooth-bores to carry shot or ball; the latter to be the exact size for the No 10 rifles. For many years I have been supplied with first rate No 10 rifles by Messrs Reilly & Co of Oxford Street, London, which have never become in the slightest degree deranged during the rough work of wild hunting. Mr Reilly was most successful in the manufacture of explosive shells from my design; these were of cast-iron coated with lead, and their effect was terrific.'

James Purdey the elder showed great interest in his later years in the making and shooting of double rifles. These were in the first instance of 16 bore shooting $1\frac{1}{2}$ drams of No 6 powder and a 1 oz ball. They had deep multigroove rifling of ten grooves and although of a relatively low velocity they shot with great accuracy. Later he experimented with 32 bores, using $2\frac{1}{4}$ to $2\frac{1}{2}$ drams of powder and firing a short pointed conical bullet, some cast with raised bumps at the base of the bullet which coincided with the ten grooves of the rifling. He is said to have tried out these rifles at small plaster casts made to resemble butterflies.

His son, James Purdey the younger, turned his attention to two-groove rifles of 40 bore (about ·500 in) shooting 4 drams of powder and 50 bores (about ·450 in) shooting $4\frac{1}{2}$ drams. To rifles of this type he gave the name of 'Express train' and since that date, 1856, the term 'Express' has come into general use in describing a rifle designed to give a long point-blank range and low trajectory. Later he made 70 bores (about ·408 in) and 100 bores (about ·360 in) shooting proportionately larger powder charges.

Other types of rifling were used in sporting rifles of the late percussion era, principally the oval bore of Charles Lancaster, which was in effect a wide and shallow version of the two-groove with a corresponding moulded oval bullet. This had the advantage of ease of loading and cleaning. Also worthy of notice were those rifles with shallow multigroove rifling and a bullet with an expanding hollow base which either expanded with the aid of a wooden wedge as in the case of that invented by W. Greener or was simply forced apart by the action of the gas pressure on the base of the bullet. Both methods ensured that the bullet keyed tightly into the rifling.

A number of capping breech-loaders were used for sporting purposes, two of the most popular being Prince's rifle and Calisher and Terry's rifle, some of the latter being double-barrelled.

Prince's rifle (plate 24) had a single short screw breech which was unscrewed by means of an arm projecting from a slot under the breech, this arm was then moved forward to open the breech. Into the breech was placed the very simple paper cartridge pasted round the base of the ball and screwed up at the other end. The breech was then securely closed by reversing the opening process, and the charge fired by means of the special percussion cap on the nipple, the cap being sufficiently strong to strike through the paper and ignite the charge. A specially prepared 'explosive' paper was recommended but other papers capable of being pierced by the percussion cap could also be used.

Skin cartridges were invited by Captain M. Hayes, R.N., the sausage skin type of membrane being protected until required, by a cartridge paper cover which was opened by a red tape. These cartridges were made and sold by Messrs Brough & Moll, London.

Callisher and Terry's rifle (plate 27) had a breech that was opened by the backward movement of a bolt, after it had made a right-angle turn. To accomplish this turn a lever, sprung and hinged from the end of the bolt, was first swung out from its position beside the bolt, and then used as a lever to turn the bolt 90° until the lever was in an upright position, the bolt now freed was moved back to its full extent, exposing the breech for loading the cartridge.

The cartridge for this rifle was made of strong brown paper secured to the ball by an adhesive and having glued to the back end a wad, saturated in tallow to minimise fouling after repeated use of the gun. The nipple was so placed that the flash from the cap came in the centre of the charge; this caused the wad to be pressed firmly against the rear of the breech to prevent the escape of gas as the bullet moved forward. The wad remained in the breech and was pushed forward as the next cartridge was put in. The nipple used was of the type that was more open at the top, tapering downwards, thus projecting the full force of the cap in such a way that it could not fail to pierce the paper cartridge.

A few over-and-under rifle and shot guns were made, notably by Rigby and Walsh of Dublin. Typical is the deeply etched damascus-barrelled type made by Rigby, having for instance the top barrel of 38 bore rifled and the bottom barrel of 14 bore for shot; the separate ramrods were stowed on either side of the barrels, the locks being back action.

A number of seven-barrelled goose rifles were made which were of small bore and multigroove rifling. The barrels fired together and were designed to throw the seven balls in a moderate group at around 100 yards (plate 22). A few rifles mostly of the lighter kind were made on the superimposed load system with a lock and hammer which slid back to strike the nipples in turn. Most accurate loading was of course essential to place the ignition behind each load. Lancaster made some four-barrelled rifles on the turn over system (plate 21).

In parts of the world remote from gunmakers it was essential that the hunter should be self sufficient and to this end the best quality rifles were provided with fitted cases containing all that would be needed to cast bullets, load, clean and maintain the rifle. The following equipment may well be found in these cases: bullet moulds for ball and conical bullets, a powder flask and powder measures, a patch cutter and patch box to hold the greased patches, a nipple key complete with pricker and spare nipples (leather cases were provided for carrying these in the field), turnscrews, a main spring clamp, sometimes spare mainsprings and sear springs and a spare ramrod. For cleaning the rifle there would be cleaning rods, brass 'turks' heads', jags, wool mops and worms for withdrawing a ball. The hunter would of course take with him quantities of soft and hardened lead, linen for patches, grease, oil, tow for cleaning and sealed canisters of black powder of the required grain sizes. Some of these items or substitutes could often be obtained locally but it was best if possible to keep to the materials that had stood the test of trial and experience and could be relied upon.

As a specimen of the varied outfit a traveller required in the 1840s we may note some of the contents of the wagons of George Gordon Cumming's five-year hunting expedition in South Africa and Bechuanaland in 1843. Besides weapons numerous and good, he carried lead ladles of various sizes, a whole host of bullet moulds, loading rods, shot belts and powder flasks, 3 hundredweight of lead, 50 pounds of pewter for hardening the balls to be used against large game, 10,000 prepared lead bullets, bags of shot of all sizes, 100 pounds of fine sporting powder, 300 pounds of coarse gunpowder, about 50,000 best percussion caps, 2,000 gun flints, greased patches and cloth for the same.

For the wagons, spare yokes, yoke-skeys, whip-sticks, rheims (leather traces) and straps, and two sets of spare linch-pins.

For provisions the country was depended on to a large extent. Accordingly the reserve constituted mainly of 300 pounds of coffee, 4 quarter-chests of tea, 300 pounds of sugar, 300 pounds of rice, 180 pounds of maize meal, 100 pounds of flour, 100 pounds of salt, a keg of vinegar, several large jars of pepper, half a dozen hams and cheeses, 2 cases of gin, an anker of brandy and half an 'aam' (17 gallons) of the potent brandy known as 'Cape Smoke'. In addition, simple cooking utensils, water casks and tar to mix with grease for lubricating the wagon-wheels were taken.

As presents for the natives there were 6 dozen pocket knives, 24 boxes of snuff, 50 pounds of tobacco, 300 pounds of mixed beads, 3 dozen tinder boxes, and a hundredweight of brass and copper wire for wrist and leg ornaments.

Also stored in the capacious wagons were two dozen sickles, a set of carpenter's tools, a gross of awls, a gross of sail needles, 50 hanks of twine, 2 bolts of sail cloth, 2 dozen gown pieces, 117 dozen Malay handerchiefs, thread, needles and buttons, ready made jackets and trousers, several dozen cotton shirts, Scots bonnets and 'cocker-nonys', a few medicines, some arsenical and ordinary soap and about £200 in cash.

They also carried pickaxes and spades, for a great deal of shooting was done by water holes beside which the hunters lay concealed in holes dug for them and from which they could shoot with comparative safety.

One great advantage in those days was that with a mixed battery of rifles a hunter could cast such bullets as were in most demand at the time, there being no need as in the breech-loading era to carry large quantities of heavy cartridges for all calibres just in case of need.

As Samuel Baker discovered, there are times when desperate situations require most unorthodox substitutes for bullets. In Ceylon, he had waded into the water to meet a buffalo and, after firing twice, found himself face to face with a wounded and furious bull. He dared not retreat, so there he stood unloaded with his last bullet fired. However, with great presence of mind he hastily grabbed a handful of loose change from his pocket, twisted it together in a piece torn from his shirt, and quickly ramming the coins down the barrel was just in time to fire the loose change at the head of the buffalo as it charged. While the bull stopped temporarily stunned, he beat a hasty retreat before the animal recovered.

Some idea of the range and power of Baker's heavy single two-groove rifle, firing a belted ball weighing 3 ounces, can be gained from his description of the shooting of a buffalo at 600 yards; the ball, which was propelled by 16 drams of powder, passed right through the beast at this great range. The conical bullet for this rifle weighed a little more than 4 ounces. Baker mentions that he frequently used 16 drams of powder with this rifle but the recoil was very severe, the normal load being 12 drams, but he goes on to say that with 16 drams and a 4 ounce steel-tipped conical bullet the effect was tremendous.

It was usual for hunters to fire off their rifles at the end of the day before returning to camp so that they could be cleaned and made ready for the following day; the firing off of the guns a mile or so from camp was a useful signal that the hunters were returning, so that all could be made ready to receive them (plate 20).

The washing out and careful cleaning of the guns was a vital task that could not be left to servants, for a dirty breech on the morrow could be a life or death matter, so however tired the hunter might be the 'right sort' saw their guns clean before retiring.

There is in the Badminton Library *Big Game Shooting* of 1894 a most interesting and informative account of hunting methods employed by a great explorer and sportsman, William Cotton Oswell, for whom Sir Samuel White Baker, who wrote the biographical sketch had the highest esteem. In those early and middle years of the 19th century, when much of Africa remained unknown, it fell to such as Oswell to see the mighty hosts of animals on land where no European foot had trod before. Those days have passed, but the thrill of them may still be recalled in the many gripping accounts to be found in the 19th century sporting books. In the rifles of this period too, something of the romance of those days still lingers.

Baker writes of Oswell:

'He was a first-rate horseman, and all his shooting was from the saddle, or by dismounting for the shot after he had run his game to bay.

'In 1861, when I was about to start on an expedition towards the Nile sources, Oswell, who had then retired from the field to the repose of his much-loved home, lent me his favourite gun, with which he had killed almost every animal during his five years' hunting in South Africa. This gun was a silent witness to what its owner had accomplished. In exterior it looked like an ordinary double-barrelled rifle, weighing exactly ten pounds; in reality it was a smooth-bore of great solidity, constructed specially by Messrs Purdey & Co for Mr Oswell. This useful gun was sighted like a rifle, and carried a spherical ball of the calibre No 10; the charge was six drachms of fine-grained powder. There were no breech-loaders in those days, and the object of a smooth-bore was easy loading, which was especially necessary when shooting from the saddle. The spherical ball was generally wrapped in either waxed kid or linen patch; this was rolled rapidly between the hands with the utmost pressure; the folds were then cut off close to the metal with scissors, and the bullet was again rolled as before. The effect was complete; the covering adhered tightly to the metal, which was now ready for ramming direct upon the powder-charge, without wads or other substance intervening. In this manner a smooth-bore could be loaded with great rapidity, provided that the powder-charge was made up separately in the form of a paper cartridge, the end of which could be bitten off, and the contents thrust into the barrel, together with the paper covering. The ball would be placed above, and the whole could be rammed down by a single movement with a powerful loading rod if great expedition should be necessary. Although the actual loading could thus be accomplished easily, the great trouble was the adjustment of the cap upon the nipple, which with an unsteady horse was a work of difficulty.

'This grand old gun exhibited in an unmistakable degree the style of hunting which distinguished its determined owner. The hard walnut stock was completely eaten away for an inch of surface; the loss of wood suggests that rats had gnawed it, as there were minute traces of apparent teeth. This appearance might perhaps have been produced by an exceedingly coarse rasp. The fore-portion of the stock into which the ramrod was inserted was so completely worn through by the same destructive action, that the brass end of the rod was exposed to view. The whole of this wear and tear was the result of friction with the 'wait-a-bit' thorns!

'Oswell invariably carried his gun across the pommel of his saddle when following an animal at speed. In this manner at a gallop he was obliged to face the low scrubby 'wait-a-bits', and dash through these unsparing thorns, regardless of punishment and consequences, if he were to keep the game in view, which was absolutely essential if the animal were to be ridden down by superior pace and endurance. The walnut stock thus brought into hasty contact with sharp thorns became a gauge, through the continual friction, which afforded a most interesting proof of the untiring perseverance of the owner, and of the immense distances that he must have traversed at the highest speed during five years' unremitting pursuit of game upon the virgin hunting-grounds of Southern Africa. I took the greatest care of this gun, and entrusted it to a very dependable follower throughout my expedition of more than four years. Although I returned the gun in good condition, the ramrod was lost during a great emergency. My man (a native) was attacked, and being mobbed during the act of loading, he was obliged to fire at the most prominent assailant before he had time to withdraw his ramrod. This passed through the attacker's body, and was gone beyond hope of recovery.

'There could not have been a better form of muzzle-loader than this No 10 double-barrel smooth-bore. It was very accurate at fifty yards, and the recoil was trifling with the considerable charge of six drams of powder. This could be increased if necessary, but Oswell always remained satisfied, and condemned himself, but not his gun, whenever a shot was unsatisfactory. He frequently assured me that, although he seldom fired at a female elephant, one bullet was sufficient to kill, and generally two bullets for a large bull of the same species.'

While on the subject of shooting in Africa it is interesting to note what W. W. Greener has to say regarding the development of rifles suited to the longer ranges required for the plains of South Africa. He refers to a rifle termed the 'Cape Rifle' of the 1850s with a calibre of 40 or 52 bore, the rifling being of the deep two-groove type with one turn in twenty inches to fire a heavy charge (plate 26). These rifles weighed about twelve pounds and were sighted up to 1,200 yards. He also refers to Mr Purdey's 'Express' rifles, two-groove with long point-blank range and low trajectory. The qualities of these sporting rifles and the high standards of long range accuracy set by the hexagonal bore rifles of Sir Joseph Whitworth were to mark the direction for the perfecting of the 'Express' game rifle as a breech-loader.

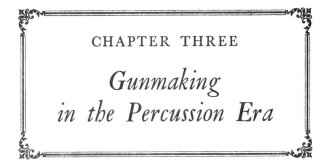

CHAPTER THREE

Gunmaking
in the Percussion Era

B Y the time the percussion gun had become established, the main
source of the production of components in the rough, from which
both London and provincial makers built their guns, was Birmingham. This situation had evolved through the economic need for
specialisation. For instance it was not possible, at an economic cost,
for London makers to forge their own twist barrels; W. Fullerd, of
Clerkenwell was the last in London who specialised and excelled
in the art, carrying on the unequal struggle until his death in 1833.

In Birmingham they had the advantage of being in the centre of
the iron and steel industry with access to cheap coal and coke and a
plentiful supply of skilled labour. Also so far as barrel forging was
concerned, it was only possible to make the best barrels when the
forge had been brought into proper trim for a few hours in the middle
of the day, the forge time before and after being used for the making
of inferior barrels for which the best gun-makers would have no use.

In Birmingham therefore, by large-scale production of a variety
of barrels, full use was made of forge and man hours thus enabling
best barrels to be supplied to the London and provincial trade at a
lower cost than they could produce them themselves.

The same tendency applied also to the production of rough forgings for the many parts of the gun from locks to furniture; the gunmakers designed the particular gun or rifle, ordered the necessary
components in the rough, finished them according to their requirements and finally fitted them to a stock shaped to suit the customer.
The highly skilled men required for this best work tended to move to
London where payment was highest or to those provincial makers
of the greatest reputation for fine work. Certain other provincial
makers were little more than gun sellers and repairers, who sold guns
that were ready-made in Birmingham, upon which their names

were engraved, or partially finished guns which they finished according to the desires of their customers.

Looking at the gun trade of these times in greater detail, starting with the most important part of the gun, the barrel, it is to that now extinct body of men the forgers of twist barrels that we must pay tribute. Without their skill, and the perfecting of the forging techniques necessary, the percussion gun would not have had the advantage of relatively light, strong and resilient barrels.

Stub twist barrels were originally made from old horse and mule shoe nails, fused together and forged out into ribbon-like lengths (plate 30, top). These were then wound round a mandril at red heat, brought up to welding heat, part welded by 'jumping' or banging down on end to bring the edges together and finished by bringing about three inches at a time to welding heat and completing the welds by hammering on to a hardened mandril over a U-shaped anvil. Then the whole barrel was cold hammered in the most thorough manner in order to condense, toughen and harden the metal. W. Greener was of the opinion that a few jars of ale at this stage provided the best means of producing well finished barrels by causing the hammers to swing with a mighty good will.

It was desirable that the barrel should be forged close to its final proportions so that the toughened dense skin produced by the hammering should not be filed away when the barrel was brought to its final proportions.

It was then essential to see that the goodness of the hammering was not dissipated by brazing the barrels together. The brazing heat

Figure 4. Wood engraving of barrel welding 1850s.

would certainly soften the iron reducing its strength and resilience. Soft solder if well applied was quite strong enough and the heat necessary was insufficient to harm the iron.

When browned, the barrel was distinguished by streaks of brown that followed the direction of the ribbon of metal round the barrel.

It was held for many years, in the flintlock era, that stub twist barrels of pure iron made from horse shoe nails were the best and only barrels of worth. These nails were supposed to have attained a special quality from having been pounded on the roads for many a mile, but in fact their true value lay in the high quality of the iron from which they were made. This is borne out by the fact that barrel forgers in this country obtained their old nails from the continent, for our own being made from inferior iron were unsuitable for barrel making.

However in the percussion era it was appreciated that it was desirable to add a proportion of steel varying from one quarter to three quarters; this was usually steel scrap made from pieces of old coach springs. When old nails were in short supply the best wrought iron scrap was used instead. Swedish iron was of particularly high quality. Where this iron and steel mixture has been used it becomes apparent in the marked distinction between the lighter steel streaks and the darker iron (plate 4).

The stub twist barrels were, towards the end of the percussion era, largely succeeded by the delicately patterned barrels known generally as 'Damascus'. As the name suggests they owe their origin to the pattern welded barrels of the Middle East and India. J. Rigby of Dublin was amongst the first, around 1818, to forge barrels of this type and it is interesting to note that he finished them by deep etching to bring out the contours of the iron and steel in the manner of some of the Eastern barrels.

The Birmingham barrel forgers soon became proficient in the technique of forging these barrels and, although there were variations, the following description is that of one of the main methods: Six thin rods of best iron and six of mild steel were arranged alternately and welded to form a rod $\frac{3}{8}$ of an inch square and 4 to 6 feet in length. The rod was then heated to red heat, the ends fixed into a twisting machine, one end being fixed and the other turned by hand by means of a handle attached to a large iron wheel. Another man held the rod from place to place with tongs ensuring that the twists were even and until it had between 12 to 14 twists to the inch. The rod of 6 feet was by this means reduced to about 3 feet and doubled in thickness; it was then round with the thin edges of the iron and steel layers to the outside. Three of these twisted rods were placed together with the twists running opposite ways and were welded into one with hammer strikes at white heat. This three-in-one

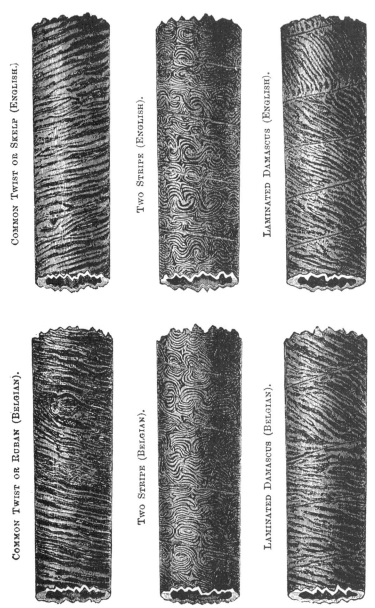

COMMON TWIST OR SKELP (ENGLISH).

TWO STRIPE (ENGLISH).

LAMINATED DAMASCUS (ENGLISH).

COMMON TWIST OR RUBAN (BELGIAN).

TWO STRIPE (BELGIAN).

LAMINATED DAMASCUS (BELGIAN).

Figure 5. Figures shown by Belgian and English barrels.

rod of about $\frac{3}{4}$ inch width was then rolled out to thicknesses depending on the part of the barrel for which it was intended: $\frac{1}{4}$ inch for the breech, $\frac{3}{16}$ of an inch for the centre and $\frac{1}{8}$ inch for the muzzle (plate 30, bottom).

For coiling the iron was heated to a bright red heat and one end was fixed to the end of a taper mandril and turned to a coil. Further lengths of the strip were added by tapering the ends with a hammer and neatly welding the heated overlapping ends with a smart tap of the hammer. When the whole length had been wound on, it was brought to welding heat and 'jumped' while on the mandril to part weld it. The welding was then completed by bringing about three inches at a time to welding heat and hammering on to a U-shaped anvil with the mandril inside. The mandril was of course taken out when the barrel was in the fire. The whole length of the barrel was finally cold hammered (plate 29).

About three-quarters of the material was cut away in the course of making a pair of 12 bore barrels. About 16 lb of iron and steel would be reduced to only 3 to 4 lb when the barrels were finished.

The welding completed, the barrels were bored to size, filed to shape and the figure produced by the process of browning, to show the fine wire-like curls of alternate iron and steel.

Wilkinson and Son, at the Great Exhibition of 1851, showed a series of exhibits demonstrating the forging of barrels and including Damascus twist made from 21 alternate bars of iron and steel which were then welded, drawn out by rolling to a square rod, twisted and then flattened; two or three rods were then welded together, wound round a mandril and forged as before. They also showed a specimen composed of two bars of 48 alternations of iron and steel, a specimen called 'chain twist', another called 'steel Damascus' and a finished barrel composed of seven different kinds of twist. There is an almost infinite variety of patterns both practical and decorative that can be formed and though in general practical considerations took precedence in England, one can feel the fascination in forging iron and steel together to make such patterns. On the continent the Belgian smiths were particularly noted for the fineness and intricate nature of their patterns and also for the cunning practice of 'veneering' a thin coat of Damascus over a common iron barrel. In other countries such as Germany, Austria and France barrels with extraordinary decorative effects were produced.

Laminated steel barrels, which were particularly enthused over by W. Greener in the 1850s, were made from best quality steel scrap which was cleaned in a revolving drum, mixed with a small proportion of charcoal iron, heated in a furnace, puddled into a ball and worked up under a forge hammer. This working up if conscientiously done, meant forging out the metal, cutting it into short lengths,

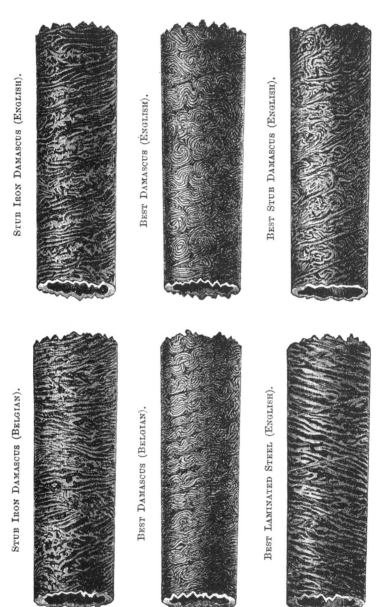

STUB IRON DAMASCUS (ENGLISH).

BEST DAMASCUS (ENGLISH).

BEST STUB DAMASCUS (ENGLISH).

STUB IRON DAMASCUS (BELGIAN).

BEST DAMASCUS (BELGIAN).

BEST LAMINATED STEEL (ENGLISH).

Figure 6. Figures shown by Belgian and English barrels.

faggoting these together and forging out again until the metal had the desired close and even grain required, with the fibres of the metal drawn out lengthwise. The metal in this state was rolled out to the required length, width and thickness and thereafter treated as for any twist barrel. When browned these barrels lacked the elegance of pattern of Damascus metal, but when well made were strong and durable. While on the subject of Damascus barrels it is as well to draw attention to the distinction between pattern-welded barrels both Eastern and Western, which were forged from two distinct types of metal, and the so-called 'Damascus' sword blades of the East, which were forged from the famous steel ingots produced notably in the Hyderabad district of India. In this steel the pattern is in the nature of the ingot of the metal, the contrast of light and dark pattern being caused by the light 'grain' of the globular cementite within the darker matrix of the pearlite. The contrast in colour is brought out by the action of acids. It was thought in the 19th century that the pattern in these blades was achieved by some sort of pattern welding akin to that used in barrel making. Confusion was caused by the use of the term 'Damascus' for both; and further confusion was sometimes caused by the loose use of the term 'Damascening' which normally refers to the hammering of gold or silver in designs on to a prepared surface, usually on iron.

There were two further interesting types of metal used for good quality barrels. The first was named 'Stub Damascus' and was made from a quantity of old files, heated red hot and rendered hard and brittle by quenching in cold water, after which they were pounded to the size of No 5 shot and a proportion of 15 lb of these added to 25 lb of stubs. The mixture was fused together on the bed of an air-furnace, hammered to condense the metal and rolled into rods $\frac{3}{8}$ inch square. These rods were twisted and treated as for Damascus, the effect being of a mottled twist.

The second type was a fancy steel twist giving a 'herring-bone' pattern. Three parts of steel to two of iron were intermixed and two rods twisted opposite ways, after which they were again dealt with as in the case of Damascus.

There were a number of barrels of inferior quality made by the twist method but employing iron made up from second or third quality scrap termed 'Threepenny skelp iron' and 'Twopenny' or 'Wednesbury skelp'. Because of the spongy nature of these irons they were capable of considerable improvement by good rolling and hammering, so that when well forged they were reasonably service-able with moderate charges.

Next we have an iron of the poorest quality, the name 'Sham damn skelp' being adequately descriptive of the fact. These common barrels welded along the length were originally painted with great cunning to imitate good twist barrels but later, when forgers learnt to veneer these common barrels with a thin twist of Damascus iron, the deception became much more difficult to detect.

William Greener refers to a case in which best quality heavy rifle barrels which he ordered to be of solid Damascus, were found when received to be plated with Damascus over common iron. This amounted to fraud, for Greener was charged the full cost of Damascus. He subsequently discovered that such practice was not uncommon, especially in the case of heavy rifle barrels. The saving by using mostly common iron as against Damascus was considerable and a great temptation.

When the barrels had been forged, they were bored and then ground or turned to size. For a description of these processes it would be hard to better that given by W. Greener in his book *Gunnery In 1858*:

'Boring and grinding gun-barrels generally take place under the same roof; the borer occupying a very small shop, the grinder a large one. Two men and two boys are generally found in a shop. There are four benches, to each a spindle, in which there is an oblong hole to receive the end of the boring bit. The barrel is secured on a sort of carriage, which is at liberty to traverse the whole length of the bench. A boring bit is then selected of suitable size; it is put into the spindle, and the point introduced into the end of the barrel. A sort of lever is then taken and hooked on to a kind of staple, or a piece of hooked iron (a number of which are fixed in one side of the bench the whole length), and passed behind the carriage to force it up to the bit; this is removed and fixed again, until, by forcing up the carriage, the boring bit has passed through the whole of the barrel. During this operation a stream of water is kept playing on the barrel to keep it cool. A bit, of larger dimensions, is next introduced and passed through; then others of still larger dimensions, until the whole of the scales or blacks are entirely bored out; or until the barrel has become so large in the bore, as to preclude any further boring with safety. If the scales are of great extent, the fault is the forger's, and the loss will consequently be his. If the barrels be found perfect, they are sent back to the filer, or he comes to inspect them, in order to ascertain whether they be perfectly straight in the inside; if not, to make them so.

'The necessity of great care and attention to this point, must be very obvious; for, if not perfectly correct at this stage, it will require more skill and time to get it correct afterwards than the generality of barrel-makers are inclined to bestow.

'When the inside has been found to be all right, the barrel is ready for grinding. Many barrel-makers turn their barrels entirely by self-acting lathes, and thus obtain a correct taper from breech end to muzzle. Experience has clearly convinced us that this is not the best shape, but slightly hollow towards the muzzle is preferable, as additional weight there is decidedly injurious, and the shooting of barrels of lighter construction is decidedly better.

'The generality of Birmingham barrels are ground to the size required on large stones, which revolve at a terrific rate. The skill acquired by many of the workmen is astonishing. Over and over again, have we seen barrels coming from the mill put into the lathe, and found almost as true as if they had been turned. They have a method of allowing the barrel to revolve in their hands at half the rate of the stone, and by this means they grind them so fine that many would be puzzled to determine whether they had been turned or ground, were the barrel smoothed lengthways merely to take out the marks of the stone. We have seen the squares of a rifle barrel ground to as perfect an octagon as the eye could assist in forming. Best barrels are generally turned after they are ground. Inferior barrels are struck up with a large rubber, or smooth, by boys; in some instances by women.

'There is one advantage derived from grinding barrels, namely, that the friction of the stone being continuous, the temper of the barrel is not so much affected as where the tool in the slide-rest is cutting a considerable portion at once; for all barrels are best, and superior to their compeers, which require least metal to be either ground or turned off their surface, as there is a density on the outer which is not in the interior portion. The harder the material, the less the extent of this objection.

'To obtain the true form, it is important that they should be turned. The way of fixing them in the lathe is by having a number of plugs or mandrils, which are perfectly true, and of various sizes, to fit different bores; these are centred and put in the lathe; a carrier is then secured on a part of the plug that projects out of the breech-end of the barrel, and then put into the face-plate of the lathe, which carries it round. The leading screw that travels the slide-rest, is then set in the angle to which the barrel is to be turned (though some lathes have not the power of alteration, but turn all barrels in one angle); the slide is next adjusted to the thickness of the muzzle wanted, and, when all is ready, the lathe is set going; the leading screw is turned at the same moment by the machinery connected, which keeps the tool cutting sufficiently keen to turn a barrel in about twenty-five minutes. This being done, nothing more is required than a fine smooth file to remove the marks of the tool.'

William Fullerd of Compton Street, Clerkenwell and Charles Lancaster of Tichfield Street were both famed for the fine barrels they supplied to the leading gunmakers, such as John and Joseph Manton and, in his early years as a gunmaker, James Purdey. William Fullerd forged as well as bored and filed his barrels, while Charles Lancaster selected his from the best forged in the Birmingham area, which he then bored and filed in a superior manner. Numerous best guns of the early percussion period may be found to have the initials W.F. or C.L. beside the proof marks on their barrels. Colonel Peter Hawker who had the highest opinion of these two men, quotes the boring of a double fourteen bore gun with barrels by Lancaster as being tight for the first six inches, cylinder for one foot nine inches and relieved for the last five inches. Another method of boring—more common in percussion guns—was to open the barrel slightly at the breech and muzzle. The general idea behind these boring methods was that friction should hold back the charge until it had obtained the fullest degree of thrust from the powder and then, by releasing this friction towards the end of the barrel, to throw the shot at a high velocity. Sometimes the boring rings were left rough near the breech to cause added friction. Close shooting and even pattern, that is comparatively for a cylinder, were very much the result of trial and error and particular methods were arrived at as a result of much experience. There is no doubt that some of these barrels shoot better than others, probably when the many factors, including loading, achieve a near perfect relative proportion. Certainly a great deal of mystery and conjecture surrounded the problem of just how to make a barrel throw shot hard, close and evenly spaced. Objective study of the scientific principles involved were not helped by legends, created by sportsmen after a few lucky long range shots, of guns that shot hard and killed dead at twice normal ranges.

Hawker gives the cost of a best Damascus barrel in Birmingham as:

Forging ...	£1	10	0
Boring and grinding ...	£0	5	0
Filing and patent breech ...	£0	11	0
Proof ...	£0	1	6
	£2	7	6

and best stub twist barrels at about sixteen shillings each.

Barrels were submitted for proof either at the Birmingham or at the London Proof House, according to the terms of the proof Act of 1815. This proof act was capable of a certain laxity of interpretation and matters were tidied up in the Gun Barrel Proof Act of 1855 by which powers were strengthened and the principle established that all barrels could be proved in the rough but must again be proved when soldered together, breeched and percussioned

Thus the barrel in its final proportions was again tested, as also was the soundness of the breeching and the screwing in of the nipples.

Some idea of the laxity of proof under the 1815 Act can be gained from the fact that the bore was often not stamped on the barrel. It would seem that considerable discretion was allowed or taken by gunmakers to alter the bore after proof.

Hawker describes a visit to the Proof House: 'Went to the Proof House and was present at the proving of an immense number of barrels. The proof, as ordered by the late act of parliament, is to one ounce ball (i.e. for a 16 bore) thirteen drams and a half of the best cartridge powder, with some very stiff wadding of paper on each; and so on, more or less according to whatever ball will tightly fit the calibre.'

Figure 7. Wood engraving of provisional proof of barrels 1850s.

The provisional proof involved fitting a temporary plug or 'hut' to the breech end, loading with ball and a heavy charge according to the size of bore, laying out a hundred or more on a bench, running a trail of powder under the breeches and firing the trail from outside the building. The barrels discharged in a continuous roar into a sandbank and recoiled into another opposite, the ventilators were then opened to clear the smoke and the barrels gathered for examination. Those found to be perfect were marked with the provisional proof mark of London or Birmingham and after the proof Act of 1855 with the bore at which they were proved. This enabled a check to be made as to how much a barrel had been bored out after proof. The Rules of Proof were further strengthened and regularised as between London and Birmingham, by the Gun Barrel Proof Act of 1868. For definitive proof the guns were handled separately in small rooms.

W. Greener gives the number of barrels provisionally proved at Birmingham in 1857 as 416,194 of which 136,804 were twisted barrels. He further writes that in the region of 200,000 are proved by the London Proof House, which were all welded, bored and ground in Birmingham before being sent to London.

A fine gunlock with its clean, graceful, functional shapes and highly polished surfaces is a beautiful thing to behold but the goodness of it may also be felt in the crisp fluency of its movement. The parts comprising the best locks were filed to shape from pieces most skilfully forged. The ability to file the graceful curves and to file flat and square came only after long years of dedicated apprenticeship. These men were specialists working largely in Birmingham and the Black Country. Perhaps the most famed were Joseph and other members of the Brazier family of Wolverhampton who supplied the finest quality locks to leading gunmakers. J. and R. Brazier exhibited locks and fittings at the Great Exhibition of 1851 (plate 49 top).

After about 1830, the parts of cheaper locks were die stamped instead of being forged. It would seem that although most of the leading London makers employed lock filers and achieved the highest reputation for their locks, they found it necessary to augment their production with that of the best specialists, who supplied locks to the gunmakers' specifications, when they were unable to keep pace with the quantity required.

Percussion cap locks needed to have strong main springs and consequently strong hammers to ensure the complete firing of the cap and also that the hammer was not blown upwards by pressure from the nipple when a gun was heavily loaded. This could be dangerous as it was in these circumstances that pieces of cap were most likely to fly about. Extra strong springs are often found on two groove rifle locks where the barrel pressures were likely to be high.

The dolphin hammer head, which seems to have been the design used with the earliest copper cap locks, remained the most popular design throughout. The shank of the hammer varied considerably from heavy and cumbersome to strong but graceful. The cup-shaped shield on the hammer head opened to the front to give a forward outlet to the explosive force of the cap.

The best gun furniture was forged from swaff iron and that of common quality was cast. The swaff, consisting of turnings, filings and chippings, was swept up in the workshops of Birmingham and was a source of beer money for the workmen when sold to the swaff forgers. The swaff was immersed in dilute sulphuric acid, which was then drained off. It was then placed in an iron pan, in a hot place,

1   Flintlock gun by John Manton, No. 7569, of 1820, built for the 6th Duke of Bedford. A good example of the last phase of the flintlock, with its spur cock, V-shaped flash-pan with a platinum strip along its base and with an inset and cut-away breech. Quick and reliable though it was, the ignition was not comparable to that of a good percussion gun.

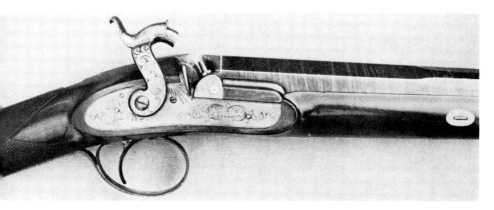

2   Early percussion gun by James Purdey, No. 483, c. 1821–3. 30-in. 11 bore barrel by Charles Lancaster. Typical Purdey engraving of this period—note the coiled dragon on the hammer.

3   Top view of gun No. 483, by James Purdey, showing on top of the breech the platinum inset, PURDEY LONDON, and the graceful engraving behind the breech.

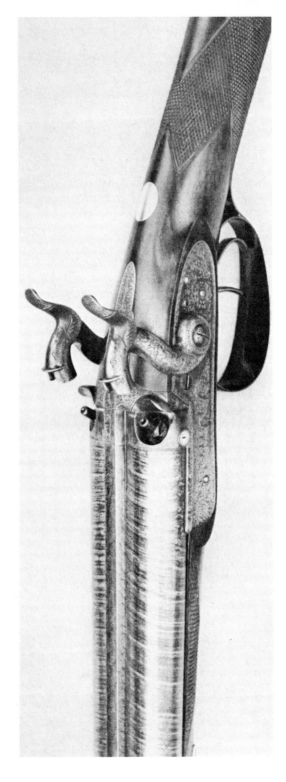

4 Double 15 bore gun, No. 2966 by James Purdey, 1837, with 30-in. skelp twist barrels. Weight, 6¼ lb. Label in case states charge: 2½ drams No. 2 powder and 1 oz shot.

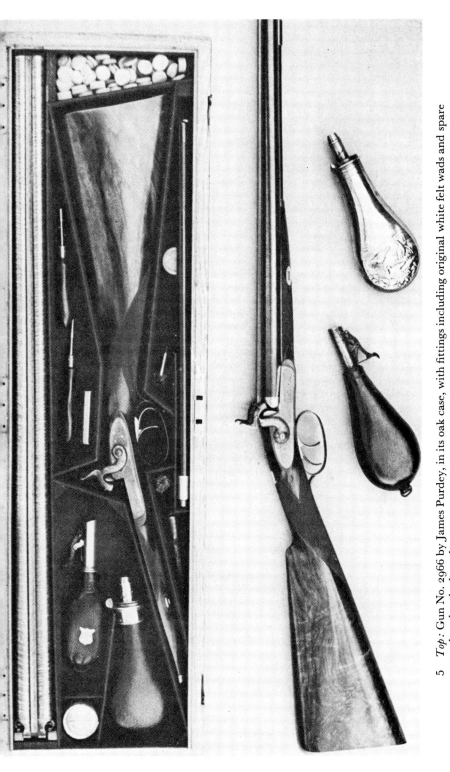

5 *Top*: Gun No. 2966 by James Purdey, in its oak case, with fittings including original white felt wads and spare ramrod under the barrels.

Bottom: Double 15 bore gun, No. 1558, by Charles Lancaster, c.1843, with 31-in. Damascus barrels. Weight, 7¼ lb. Charge: 2 drams No. 2 powder and 1 oz of shot, and throw of shot stated to be 156 No. 6 shot in a 30-in. circle at 40 yards. One of the pair shown in double case.

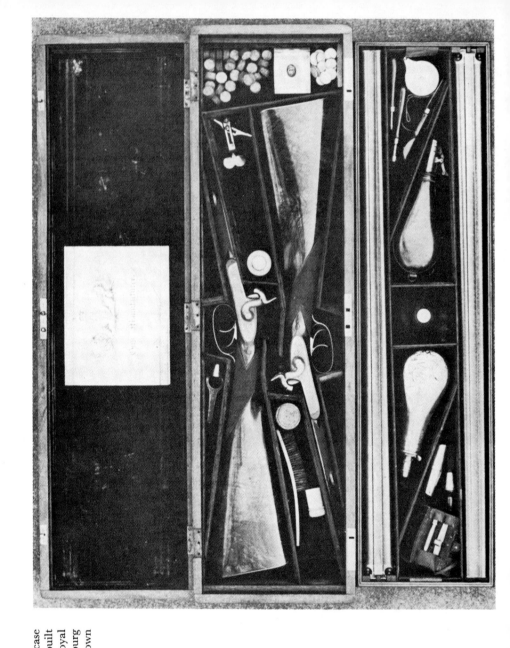

6 Fine blue velvet-lined mahogany case containing guns Nos. 1558 and 1559, built by Charles Lancaster, c.1843, for His Royal Highness, Prince Albert of Saxe-Coburg Gotha, Consort to Queen Victoria. Shown with the barrel tray lifted out.

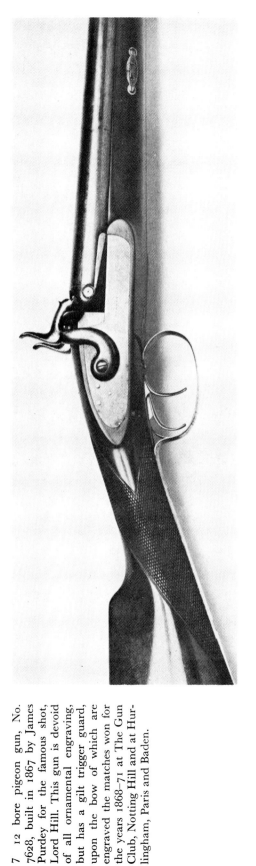

7 12 bore pigeon gun, No. 7628, built in 1867 by James Purdey for the famous shot, Lord Hill. This gun is devoid of all ornamental engraving, but has a gilt trigger guard, upon the bow of which are engraved the matches won for the years 1868–71 at The Gun Club, Notting Hill and at Hurlingham, Paris and Baden.

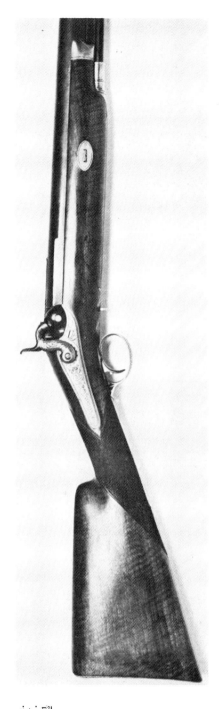

8 4 bore duck gun with 54-in. twist barrel, No. 8293, by W. & J. Rigby, 1838. Weight, 18½ lb.

9 Double percussion gun by Pritchard of Manchester, 1835, with English Damascus barrels of exceptional quality.

10 Detail of the extraordinary barrels of the percussion gun by Pritchard.

11 Adams six-chambered revolving percussion shot gun of 20 gauge.

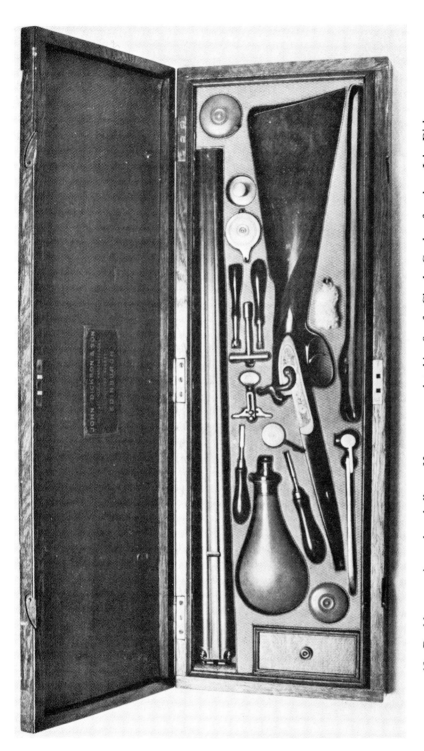

12 Double percussion 12 bore ball gun, No. 4572, completed in 1893 for Charles Gordon, for whom John Dickson & Son built large numbers of muzzle-loading guns around this late date. This gun weighs 10½ lb and the 30-in. barrels 7 lb 2 oz. The lavishly fitted case is typical of the ones specially made for Charles Gordon.

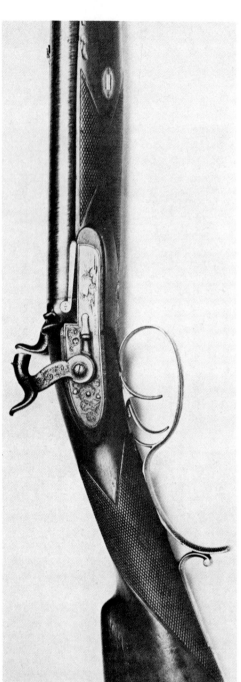

13 Double-barrelled percussion 16 bore rifle by James Purdey, No. 2619, built 1834. Deep ten-groove rifling.

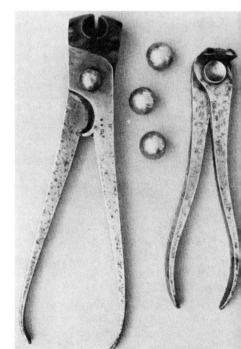

14 16 bore bullet mould for rifle No. 2044, together with tang clippers for cutting off the tag in a manner that leaves the ball spherical.

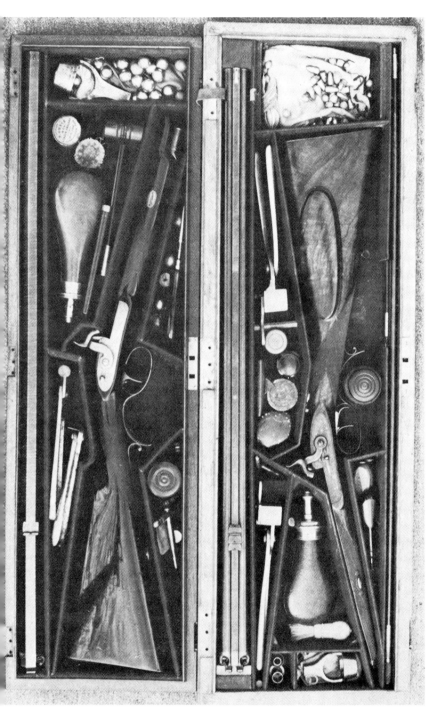

15 *Top*: Single-barrelled 16 bore rifle by James Purdey, No. 2044, built 1831. Deep ten-groove rifling, in its case with its fittings.

Bottom: Double-barrelled percussion 95 bore two-groove rifle of the Express type, No. 7044, built 1865, by James Purdey for the famous sportsman Lord Henry Bentinck, who once stalked a stag for two days and a night. James Purdey wrote under Lord Henry's photograph, 'My first and best customer'.

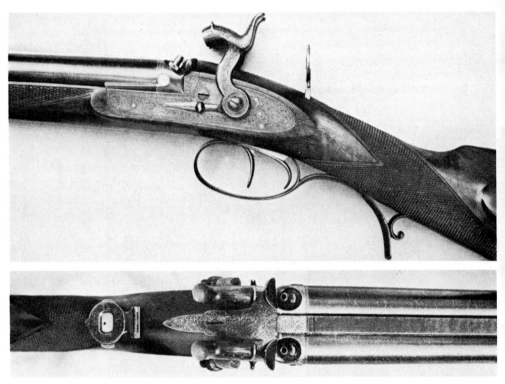

16 *Top:* Double percussion 95 bore rifle by James Purdey, No. 7044, built 1865. Heavy barrels with two-groove rifling, 'winged' conical bullet or belted ball. Detail showing raised peep sight.

Bottom: Detail of Purdey rifle No. 7044, showing top of breech, folding peep sight, file-cut rib, and nipples placed well to the centre of the breeches. Note nipples have the larger hole at the top, with small platinum bushed hole at bottom.

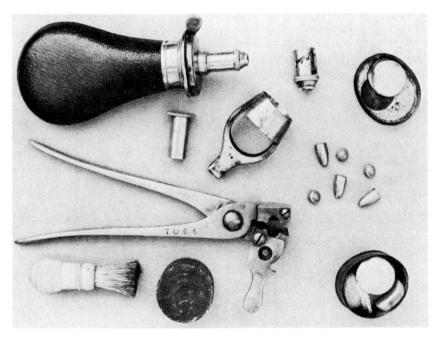

17 Equipment for Purdey rifle No. 7044, showing powder flask with extra top for increased measures, powder measure for 1½ drams, bullet mould for conical bullets, brush for cleaning round the nipples, tin of percussion caps, patch cutter, conical and belted ball bullets, greased patches in tin.

18 Hunting the African rhinoceros on horseback with a double-barrelled ball gun. The after rider followed to hold the hunter's horse when necessary. From *Sport in many Lands* by H. A. Leveson.

19 Detail of patch box on Purdey rifle No. 7044.

20 Hunters' camp in India, c.1850, showing, on left, harness and belt for carrying powder and ball; on right, washing barrels through with the breech ends in a tub; and centre, skin pegged out for preliminary drying, scraping and curing. From *Tiger Shooting in India*, by Lieut. W. Rice, 1857.

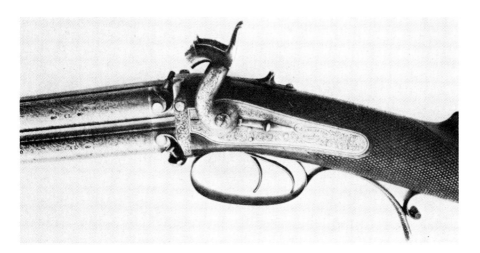

21 Four-barrelled ·500 calibre oval-bore rifle by Charles Lancaster, No. 2800, c.1857. The barrels turn over by hand on drawing back the top lever.

22 Seven-barrelled volley rifle by Henry Nock. Converted from flintlock to percussion. Used for volley shots at geese beyond the range of a gun.

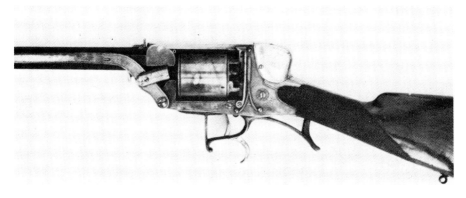

23 Tranter six-chambered, ·577 calibre revolving percussion rifle. Note the cowl round the hammer to protect the eye, which was close behind the cap and nipple in the firing position.

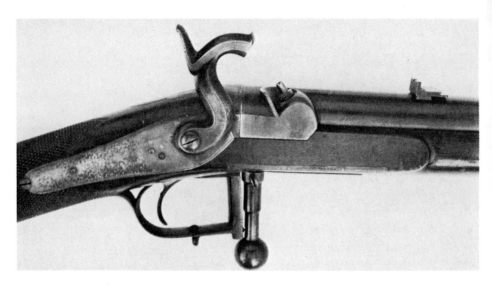

24 Prince's patent capping breech-loading rifle of 32 bore, made by Prince and Green, showing action closed.

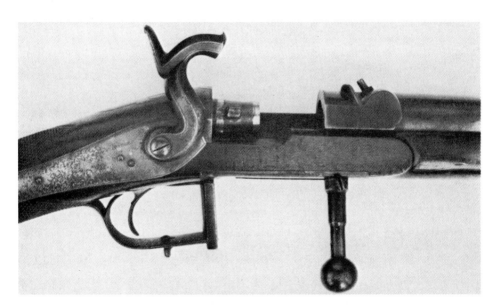

25 Prince's patent capping breech-loader, showing action open.

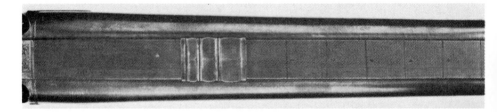

26 'Cape Rifle' for ball and shot by Deans of London, showing very wide rib with measure in inches and sights for 100, 200 and 300 yards.

27 Calisher and Terry double capping, breech-loading, 32 bore rifle, shown with the action closed.

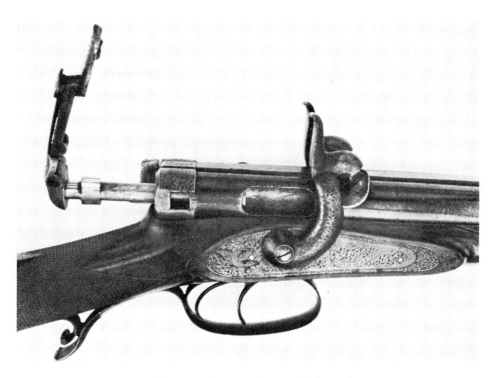

28 The Calisher and Terry, shown with the action open.

29 W. W. Greener in the barrel-welding workshop at St Mary's works, watching Damascus rods being twisted and the coils of a Damascus barrel being forge-welded. The foreman indicates with his small hammer where the blows from the heavy hammers are required to fall. From W. W. Greener's *The Gun* 1881.

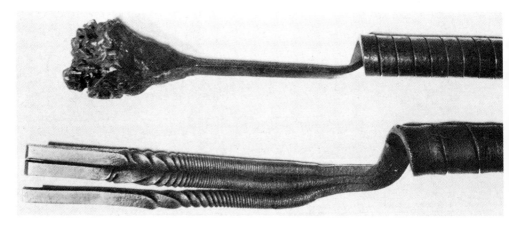

30 *Top*: Skelp twist barrel, showing the lump of horseshoe nail stubs from which the ribbon is formed and the beginning of the coil.

Bottom: Damascus forged from three square rods of alternate iron and steel showing tight twist, combination into a three-stripe ribbon, and the beginning of the coil.

to cause the pieces to be quickly rusted together. It was then tipped out, heated to welding heat in an air furnace and forged into bars by three men beating it with light hammers. The iron was then sold to gun work forgers for working into patent breeches, lockplates and furniture. The interesting grain of this swaff iron can be seen on these parts of guns, especially if they have become rusted at some time the softer parts of the iron being eaten away more than the harder parts of this mixed metal.

Silver furniture was not common in the percussion era but where it was used the work was put out to such silversmiths as specialised in it.

For stocking, walnut (*Juglans regia*) was and is the most suitable wood. English walnut though of good quality lacks the beauty of grain that so enhances a fine stock. Figured walnut blanks now come from France, but in the 19th century exceptionally fine Circassian walnut was still available and this had the desirable qualities of strength, closeness of grain, freedom from faults and remarkable grain effects in which the rick dark veins were contrasted with lighter areas. The finest stocks were cut from the base of the tree where it curves out into the root wood. The grain of the wood follows the curve of the grip and continues straight through to the fore-end, while at the butt end the grain disports itself in those fantastic patterns which so delight the eye.

In the 1820s and 1830s birdseye maple stocks were used to some extent but never by any means rivalled walnut. These birdseye maple stocks are often stained or flame darkened a dark blackish colour and were heartily disliked by the stockers who found the grain most awkward to work. James Purdey made rifles in the 1830s with 'ebonised' stocks, the effect of ebony being achieved by a kind of black lacquered finish on a stock of common walnut. By far the larger number of stocks of this period were straight, without cast off or on and they were mostly finished with a thick coat of hard varnish.

According to W. W. Greener, stockers in Birmingham did only that job, while in London and in the country the stocker also screwed and sometimes finished the gun.

When the stocker received the stock blank, he first roughed it into shape and fitted the false breech. It was then passed to the screwer who let in the trigger plate and fitted the breech pin or screw. Next, the locks having been stripped, the stocker let in the lock plates, after which, when the locks had been re-assembled, the wood was carefully removed until the lock was exactly set in place, while able to function freely. The stock was then shaped, rounded up and rasp-filed.

The screwing further involved the making and fitting of the pins which held the iron to the woodwork, including the bolt that held the barrels to the fore-end of the stock.

The percussioner dealt with the important task of fitting the nipple, drilling and plugging the vent hole, shaping the fences and fitting the hammers or cocks as they were then called, the name carried over from the flint cock. The best hammers were filed up from forgings and the others from stampings. The percussioner first drilled a hole in the hammer, which was squared to the precise size of the square shank of the tumbler by means of a series of square drifts which gradually opened and squared the hole by condensing the metal around it. This method helped to ensure that the hammer would not loosen. The noses of the hammers were then filed until they struck the face of the nipple evenly. This done the hammers were filed up, care being taken to see that they were both exactly alike and that they stood together at half and full cock.

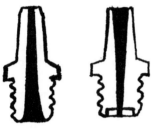

Figure 8. Two types of nipples: left, with the larger opening at the bottom commonly used in fowling pieces; right, with the larger opening at the top and a platinum bushed small hole at the bottom, commonly used for rifles where the breech pressures were greater.

When the gun was percussioned and the barrels fine-bored, shot for pattern and smoothed ready for browning, the gun was sent to the finisher. The finisher checked that the gun conformed to its specification and that matters such as the balance and the shaping and measurements of the stock were correct. Next the iron work was smoothed and the wood after being finally shaped was cleansed by wetting it and rubbing it down when dry several times, to ensure that the grain would not raise should the stock get wet during use. The whole gun was then buffed over with a leather buff-stick, pumice stone and rotten stone. The stock was then chequered and the iron work sent for polishing, engraving and hardening. When these had been done all was put together again, final adjustments were made, the stock varnished and the gun completed for its final inspection. The finisher co-ordinated and brought into harmony the work on the many parts that went to building the completed gun; he therefore had to have an extensive knowledge of the art and science of gun-making.

The polisher had to see that all traces of the file were removed from the ironwork and this was accomplished by a series of emery bobs and sticks. All ironwork that was intended for blueing was burnished over after polishing to close the grain of the iron and give a fine finish to the blue.

The polished work was next sent to be engraved and when this had been done the false-breech, hammers, trigger and lock plates, bridles, triggers, bolt and escutcheons and screws were hardened.

The work to be hardened was placed in a cast-iron pot and covered with bone dust obtained from bone and ivory turners; sometimes burnt leather from old shoes was used as a substitute. The pot was then placed in a bright coal fire, where it remained at a worm-red colour, from one to one-and-a-half hours according to the size of the piece to be hardened. When it was ready the work was removed from the pot and plunged into cold water. The iron at red heat absorbed the carbon and on being suddenly cooled the surface became very hard and at the same time took on the mottled colouring that was so desirable. Iron in this state could still be bent or set as the hardening was on the surface only.

The blue colour on the furniture was obtained by putting the objects in a pan, covering them with finely powdered charcoal and heating them on a fire. The pieces were removed from time to time and rubbed with tow or powdered chalk to remove any grease and keep a high gloss on them. The colour first attained was a pale straw colour, then light blue, purple, dark blue, red, white and lastly a very dark purple blue, the darkest blue taking about 20 to 25 minutes.

The engraving of the ironwork was done with a hard steel burin or graver. Fine fern-like tendrils curling in rhythmic designs were the basis of most ornament though on some guns, game and dogs were depicted in addition.

It was customary for some gunmakers who sold a variety of qualities of gun, to scale the quantity and quality of the engraving accordingly. This gave rise to the idea that a gun could be judged by its engraving and that engraving was expensive. In fact the cost of engraving would rarely exceed five per cent of the gun's total cost. There was therefore a temptation on the part of the less scrupulous, to beguile the unknowing with extravagant engraving, at the expense of qualities less obvious.

There were on the other hand guns and rifles of the highest quality, often those designed for use abroad, which were finished without, or with little engraving. These could however look very bare when the case-hardening and blueing colours wore off.

The quality of engraving can be recognised by the clean strength and precision of the lines cut by the burin and by the sensitive placing of ornament in relation to the shape to be enriched. Fussy design or the misguided filling of all space with ornament was best avoided. The most attractive effects were most likely to be obtained where there was a subtle interplay between engraved and plain areas.

Barrel browning was quite an art in itself for without the skill of the browner, the work of the barrel forger would not have been seen to such effect. The browning involved a controlled rusting of the surface of the barrels which rendered the barrels less likely to rust by natural means, as well as showing up the pattern.

The barrels for browning were first highly polished, then plugged with tight fitting wooden pegs by which they were handled during the process. The barrels were covered with damp whiting which was brushed off when dry to remove all grease. Next a browning mixture was applied with a piece of flannel and the barrels were left in a humid room for twelve to eighteen hours, by which time they were covered with surface rust. They were then scratched off with a steel wire brush and the process repeated except that the time needed was shortened and the room temperature raised. The continual scratching off and re-rusting was necessary to prevent uneven rusting and also to achieve this end great care had to be taken to see that all applications of browning mixture and all scratching off were evenly done.

When the barrels were dark enough they were boiled for a few minutes in a trough of soft water in which logwood chips and a little soda, or sometimes sulphate of copper had been placed. The object of this last process was to halt and cure the rusting. The barrels were wiped dry and if they had been well done the distinction between the dark iron and the lighter steel would be seen as a clear, sharp contrast.

A browning mixture recommended by W. Greener was as follows:

1 oz muriate tincture of steel, 1 oz spirits of wine, $\frac{1}{4}$ oz muriate of mercury, $\frac{1}{4}$ oz strong nitric acid, $\frac{1}{8}$ ounce sulphate of copper and 1 quart of distilled water, which should be allowed to stand for a few days before use.

Gun cases were usually made up by specialist case makers, to take a particular gun or rifle and the fittings for it. The fittings themselves, powder and shot flasks, bullet moulds, cleaning rods, turnscrews and a host of other small items were supplied to the trade by specialist firms large and small, prominent amongst which were such well known firms as C. & J. W. Hawksley, James Dixon and Sons of Sheffield, and Sykes.

Colonel Hawker writes that: 'All shooting articles in Birmingham are usually sold, or to use the term of the trade 'put in' by the dozen at a mere nothing in comparison with the retail price. One of the best shops at which I stocked myself was that of Messrs Allen and Reneaud of No 7, Whittal Street, who supply many of the gunmakers with all kinds of turnscrews, brushes, tools, etc., and almost everything that can be required in the sporting way, at about one fifth of the price you pay in London.'

Hawker gives the price of a John Manton double gun as fifty-five guineas and sixty-five in the case of Joseph Manton but mentions that Mr Bishop of 170, New Bond St will usually have some of the best guns, entirely new, at reduced prices upon which some gentleman has 'raised the wind'. This was the celebrated 'Bishop' of

Bond Street, agent for Westley Richards, who, complete with white apron, top hat, and his pug Tiny was one of the most colourful of London characters.

Having noted the cost of the best guns it is revealing to read the cost and also the breakdown into the various items and work entailed in making guns of 'Twopenny iron' and 'Sham Damn Iron' as given by W. Greener.

Cost of Material and Workmen's Prices for making Double and Single Guns, with 'Twopenny' or 'Wednesbury Skelp Iron' Twist Barrels.

DOUBLE GUNS	s.	d.	SINGLE GUNS	s.	d.
Double barrels, twist, patent breeched	12	0	Single barrel, twist, etc.	5	9
Pair of locks	2	0	Lock	1	0
Wood for stock	0	6	Wood for stock	0	6
Set of cast furniture	0	5	Set of cast furniture	0	4
Stocking	2	0	Stocking	1	0
Screwing together	3	0	Screwing together	2	0
Percussioning	2	0	Percussioning	1	0
Polishing and engraving	1	0	Polishing and engraving	0	8
Varnishing (including painting)	0	6	Stock varnishing and painting	0	4
Browning	0	6	Barrel browning	0	4
Finishing	3	0	Finishing	2	0
Ramrod, tip, and worm	0	6	Ramrod, tip, and worm	0	6
Small work, nails, escutcheons, wood, screws, etc.	1	0	Small work, etc.	0	8
	£1 8	5		16	1

COST OF GUNS MADE OF SHAM DAMN IRON

DOUBLE GUNS	s.	d.	SINGLE GUNS	s.	d.
Double barrels, plain iron, with side huts, per pair	7	0	Single barrel, ribbed and breeched	3	8
Locks	1	6	Lock	0	9
Wood for stock	0	6	Wood for stock	0	6
Stocking	1	2	Stocking	0	8
Furniture	0	5	Furniture	0	4
Screwing together	2	0	Screwing together	1	4
Percussioning	1	4	Percussioning	0	9
Polishing and engraving	0	9	Polishing and engraving	0	6
Varnishing and painting stock	0	4	Varnishing and painting stock	0	4
Painting twist barrels	0	4	Painting twisted barrel	0	3
Rod, tip, worm	0	4	Rod, tip, worm	0	4
Small work	0	7	Small work	0	4
	16	3		9	9

Iron and steel played a large part in industrial development during the reign of Queen Victoria. It was fitting therefore that the beauty and character of these metals should have been shown to such effect in the guns of the period. These qualities were revealed in the intricate pattern of intertwined iron and steel in the russet brown barrels, the rich purple-blue of the highly polished, charcoal-blued furniture and the delicate yellows, blues and purples of the case-hardened locks, the insides of which were finished to mirror-brightness.

Apart from fine and unobtrusive engraving both wood and metal were allowed to speak for themselves and the clean lines of these gracefully functional objects show a restraint that was remarkable in an age surfeited with over abundant ornament.

CHAPTER FOUR

The Pinfire Breech-loader

HALF-WAY through the nineteenth century there appeared in England for the first time a type of breech-loading gun that was destined to set gunmakers on a course of incredible activity and inventiveness for the remainder of the century. The barrels of the gun, which was originated by the Paris gunmaker Lefaucheux, hinged down to open when the side swing of the forward lever released a hook from a single slot in the lump.

Into the breech was set an expanding gas-tight cartridge developed by Houllier, also of Paris, in 1850. The cartridge was fired by means of an overhead hammer striking the brass pin that projected from the base of the cartridge, the other end of this pin connecting with an internal percussion cap. A groove in the top breech end of the barrel allowed the pin to fit between the barrel and the breech face. The pin also served as the implement for extracting the cartridge from the breech with thumb and finger. In the event of its sticking a small instrument was provided to hook over the pin to pull it out.

The gun and cartridge as seen at the Great Exhibition of 1851 left a great deal to be improved but, much to his credit, Joseph Lang was quick to appreciate the potentials of both gun and cartridge and within a few months of the closure of the Exhibition he brought out his own version of the pinfire gun, stronger in construction and more English in character (plate 31). Some gunmakers followed the lead and soon brought out guns with a variety of ingenious actions, while others stood their ground in vain against the tide of change. First we will examine the development of the pinfire and the varieties of actions, and then we will look at the arguments for and against as they were put by champions of the muzzle-loader on the one hand and the breech-loader on the other.

The various systems that followed Lang's version of the Lefaucheux gun were directed in the main to improving the strength of the action, the efficiency of the closure method, and substituting for the thumb and finger a mechanical extractor which was of great assistance in removing sticking cartridges which were then a common nuisance.

An important method of closure which became the most widely used in pinfire guns was, according to W. W. Greener, the invention

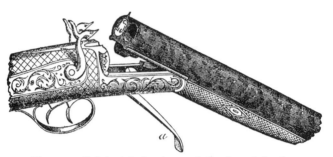

Figure 9. Original Lefaucheux pinfire breech-loader.

of a Birmingham gunmaker who omitted to patent it. The system was operated by means of a lever swung round and under the trigger guard from the open position at right angles to the gun. The two twist grooves in the cylinder at the head of the lever engaged two flanges on the lump, and as the lever was drawn back to its position under the guard the powerful screw action secured the barrels to the action body. The robust simplicity and strength of this grip led to its continued use far into the centre-fire period in a semi-snap version.

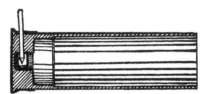

Figure 10. Pinfire cartridge case.

Bastin Lepage designed a system by which the barrels were slid forward, by means of a lever under the fore-end, until there was sufficient space to load and extract a cartridge (plate 38). On pushing the lever forward again the barrels were wedged tight against the standing breech.

A very sound action that combined the forward movement with the drop down hinged movement was that known as Dougall's lock-fast (plate 40). In this action the hinge pin was eccentric and on depressing the side lever the barrels first moved forward from the standing breech to clear the bosses that engaged the ends of the chambers, and then hinged down in the familiar manner. It was the intention that these disc-shaped bosses should prevent side to side movement developing in the course of normal usage. This sound but unnecessarily complicated action continued to be used on some centre-fire hammer guns.

The turn over principle was tried with side by side barrels which pivoted on a screw pin fixed to the standing breech, the barrels swinging out to the side to load and unload, and being secured in the firing position by a bolt entering the end of the rib. This principle did not facilitate the working in of extractors and therefore was not continued.

Mr Jeffries of Norwich invented in about 1862 a side motion breech mechanism in which the barrels were swung out sideways on a vertical pivot in the action body by means of an under lever. Though it was a sound action it was not able to challenge successfully the drop down principle.

One of the awkward features of early pinfire guns was the fact that the hammers had to be drawn back to half cock before they cleared the breech ends of the barrels and allowed the gun to open. Needham's side lever mechanism of 1862 is remarkable for the self-cocking device which raised the hammers automatically to half cock and also for being the first of the snap-actions in which the bolt that holds the barrels down is sprung into the lump slots on closure instead of being levered manually. W. W. Greener in 1864 brought out a self half-cocker on the drop down principle that was secured when closed by a bolt that engaged a slot below the end of the rib from its position near the top of the standing breech.

Westley Richards in 1862 produced an interesting snap action using for the first time a thumb-operated top lever (plate 37) which on being pulled back, and in a later edition pressed to the right, caused a wedge-shaped retainer to disengage the slot in the doll's head extension projecting from, and brazed to, the top breech ends of the barrels. There were other unusual features in this gun, it being fitted with bar-locks (forward action) unusual in a pinfire as also was the bar in wood which not only came forward under the locks but also covered the hinge bolt with a wooden joint. Another interesting feature of this gun was that the bottom breech ends of the barrels were left rounded and not finished with the customary flats; these rounded breech ends bedded down on to a similarly rounded action body. This Westley Richards action proved to be sound and durable and was continued in use into the centre-fire period, in which form the author used one with every satisfaction for some time. By an ingenious arrangement some of these guns were made dual purpose to fire either pin or centre-fire cartridges, the breast of the hammers connecting with the centre-fire strikers while the hammer heads dealt with the pinfire cartridges (plate 44).

Some of the pinfire guns built by James Purdey in the 1860s were fitted with a form of sliding bar snap action worked by a lever set into an opening in the front of the trigger guard which was pushed forward by pressure from the thumb. This thumb operated snap action, sometimes called the 'Purdey' (plate 46), was the fore-runner of the famous top lever operated Purdey bolt of 1867 which will be described later in connection with the centre-fire gun.

In addition to guns made as breech-loaders there were a number that were converted from muzzle-loaders, though this could only be done in a satisfactory manner in a minority of cases. First, the barrels had to be thick enough at the breech to stand the loss of metal necessary for chambering and also possible loss of strength due to the heat involved in brazing on the lumps and possible weakening caused by drilling the holes for the extractor slides; especially was this the case if these holes were not drilled with the utmost care. The barrels had to be fine bored, thus slightly increasing their size, and after all this stand proof.

A further condition necessary to conversion was that the cartridge for which the barrels were chambered had to be two sizes larger than the bore and some sizes of bore did not suit the available cartridge sizes. In converting rifles it was rarely that the bore and cartridge were exactly suited.

Generally it was better to order a new gun rather than risk spoil-ing a good muzzle-loader and collectors of fine percussion guns must be thankful that this was so. The above remarks regarding conversion apply equally to pin and centre-fire guns.

It was not long after the introduction of breech-loaders that it was considered advisable to use stronger barrels and especially to thicken them in the region of the cartridge chambers. These stronger barrels were of the Damascus type already described but using a higher per-centage of steel than before, and the lump instead of being just brazed on to the undersides of the barrels was neatly dovetailed into the breech ends in all the best quality guns. The fore-ends of pinfire guns and indeed the early centre-fire guns were held in place by the side nail or bolt familiar on muzzle-loaders.

There was no sudden abandonment of the muzzle-loader during the pinfire period, on the contrary many continued to be made particularly for pigeon trap shooting. The advocates of muzzle- and breech-loading were fiercely divided and the battle of words raged in the sporting papers and magazines. One of the most ardent cham-pions of the muzzle-loader was W. Greener, father of W. W. Greener who was to devote himself so enthusiastically to the development of the breech-loader. W. Greener has summarised his objections to the breech-loader in his book *Gunnery* 1858, a book which was an attempt to bring a more scientific attitude to the practice of gun-making.

There can be no denying W. Greener's prejudice against the new breech-loader; but it is interesting to look at the newcomer through the eyes of contemporary opinion and to see how much these opinions were justified. It is well to remember that both the breech-loading gun and cartridge in these early days left much to be desired, while the percussion muzzle-loader had reached the height of perfection.

Some idea of the strength of W. Greener's views and the reasons put forward for the superiority of the muzzle-loader can be gained from the following passage from his book:

'The French system of breech-loading fire-arms is a specious pretence, the supposed advantages of which have been loudly boasted of; but none of these advantages have as yet been established by its most strenuous advocates. How it is that the British sportsman has become the dupe of certain men who set themselves up for reputable gunmakers I know not. It is certain, however, that by these acts they have forfeited all claims to the confidence of their too confiding customers, and that they never could have tested the shooting properties of their guns. With regard to the safety of these guns, they display an utter want of the most ordinary judgment; and this is abundant proof that they considered neither their safety, nor (what is also of importance) the economy of the whole arrangement, as regards their manufacture or their use.

'Guns are perfect only so long as they possess the power of shooting strong and close, with the least available charges. The period has passed when barrels were bored by rule of thumb, without any well-defined intention; the workman being ignorant as to whether he would have the bore of the barrel cylindrical, or (as was frequently the case) in the form of two inverted cones, and thus he continued to bore the barrel until it was utterly useless, or until by chance he hit upon a tidy shooting bore. Barrels are now constructed so nearly alike, that it is no stretch of truth to assert that ninety-six or ninety-eight barrels out of a hundred can be made so nearly alike in their shooting, as to render it very difficult to discover the real difference between them. Yet, in the face of this high state of perfection certain English gunmakers introduce and recommend to their patrons as an improvement, a description of gun possessing the following negative qualities: First, there is no possibility of a breech-loader ever shooting equal to a well-constructed muzzle-loader; secondly, the gun is unsafe, and becomes more and more unsafe from the first time it is used; and, thirdly it is a very costly affair, both as regards the gun and ammunition. Nor are these negative qualities at all compensated for by any of the advantages claimed for these guns by their advocates this assertion I now proceed to establish. . . .

'The time was, when guns were so imperfectly constructed, that the recoil and friction of the charge against the barrel destroyed more than half the force generated by the explosion of the gunpowder; and this loss of force having been obviated, by finely polishing the interior of the barrel, as well as by improving the metal of the gun, has rendered English guns superior in their performance to those manufactured in any other country. Breeches of a conical form offer the greatest resistance to the action of aeriform bodies in a direct line; this is the principle of what is best known as "the patent breech": to speak of which would be a waste of time, as nothing more is required to support its superiority than the fact, that in well constructed artillery of every country, the interior form of the breech or chamber is more or less conical. Thus we see that by adopting the crutch gun, we have to give up one of the oldest and most universally acknowledged principles in lessening recoil—namely, the conical form of the breech—and to adopt the very reverse of this: namely, the old right-angled, flat-faced breech, upon which recoil can exert its utmost force with the certainty of its reaching the shoulder of the unfortunate user.

'Secondly, to enable the gun to be loaded with a cartridge which shall keep its place, a complicated arrangement is necessary. On inspection of the barrel, it will be perceived that a cavity has been formed larger than the bore of the barrel, and that this in some cases only tapers toward the further end. This cavity exactly receives the cartridge, and the gunpowder is inflamed in a space much larger than the barrel, which it has afterwards to pass through. The charge of shot is also started in a larger space than that which it afterwards has to traverse, and the column must of necessity become contracted and elongated before it can escape from the barrel. The first consideration is at what cost of force is all this effected? Thirty per cent would certainly be a shrewd guess; and who is there conversant with the nature of gunpowder hardy enough to gainsay the fact?

'I here present the reader with the measurement of a pair of barrels—bore 12, diameter of the cavity 10, or two sizes difference—tried at the celebrated trial of Breech- versus Muzzle-loading firearms, which took place in April last, in the court at Cremorne. The following are the results of the trial:

'Class 1 comprised twelve bore double guns, not exceeding $7\frac{1}{2}$ lb in weight; the charge for the breech-loaders was three drams of powder, and one ounce and a quarter of shot; that for the muzzle-loaders, two and three-quarter drams of powder, and an ounce and a quarter of shot. The question will be asked why were both not charged alike? and the answer is, because the advocates for breech-loaders well knew the loss of power caused by the enlarged breech end would require a larger quantity of powder; yet, with this advantage, the result was a verdict in favour of the muzzle-loaders of nearly two to one. I quote from the "Field". The aggregate numbers of pellets in the targets from breech-loaders was 170, the penetration 19. The aggregate number of pellets put in by the muzzle-loaders was 231, the penetration 48; and this was effected with a quarter of a dram of powder less. . . .

'Another question is, can breech-loading guns, be used longer than muzzle-loaders, without cleaning? My opinion is THEY CANNOT. At the trial already spoken of, after twenty-two shots had been fired from the breech-loaders, the cartridge-cases had to be extracted from the barrels with a hook, and in several cases it was necessary to cut them out with a knife; whilst a muzzle-loading gun without friction would have gone on to a hundred shots without being wiped out. . . .

'No fear need be entertained that the use of breech-loaders will become general. . . .

'The majority of guns on this principle merely abut against a false breech; and, from the fact of there being no connection either by hook or by cohesion, the explosion causes a separation between the barrel and the breech to an extent which would scarcely be credited. This may, however, be satisfactorily demonstrated by binding a small string of gutta percha round the joint, when after explosion the string will be found to have fallen in between the barrel and the breech; thus showing that the muzzle droops in the act of being discharged, which must materially influence the correctness of fire.

'The recoil of an ordinary 12 bore gun, loaded at the muzzle, varies from forty to forty-eight pounds, seldom exceeding the latter; that of a breech-loader varies from sixty-eight to seventy-six! And this quite independently of the enormous force which is exerted on the sides of these enlarged breech guns. The shoulder left in the barrel, too, is a formidable barrier for the charge to pass by; and, in doing this, the circle of shot in immediate contact with the barrel becomes disfigured and misshaped, so as to ensure its flight only to a very short distance. In the muzzle-loader an average of 180 shots strike a target of two feet six inches diameter; but breech-loaders of the same calibre will rarely put in 120 shots; showing a clear loss of 60 pellets. This is due to the enormous jamming they have undergone in passing from the greater to the lesser area of the barrel. It is said that the paper of the cartridge fills up this enlargement; but anyone who knows what the force of gunpowder is, must also know that paper intervening between the charge and the sides of the barrel would be condensed at the moment of explosion to one-fourth its original thickness.'

W. Greener's catalogue of faults to be found in the early breech-loaders was quite formidable but within a few years these early imperfections were to be overcome by improvements to both gun and cartridge. W. Greener's prejudice against the gun as it was prevented him from seeing its potential for improvement.

A second and more comprehensive trial took place in 1859 which again showed the muzzle-loader guns to be best in each class but by a small margin. It was of note that in all the best guns there was considerable variation between the patterns of right and left barrels.

The guns selected fired Lawrence's No 2 powder and No 6 shot (290 to the ounce). The results are summarised in the following table showing the best three breech- and best three muzzle-loaders. It will be noticed that the breech-loaders used an extra $\frac{1}{4}$ dram of powder, also they were heavier than the muzzle-loaders.

THE FIELD GUN TRIAL, 1859

Name of maker	Kind of gun	Charge of powder (drams)	Charge of shot (oz)	Average of pattern		Average of penetration	
				Rt	Lt	Rt	Lt
Pape	Muzzle-loader (12 bore) 6 lb 11 oz	2¾	1¼	158	118	28	33
Prince & Green	Muzzle-loader (12 bore) 6 lb	2¾	1¼	148	98	28	22
Pape	Muzzle-loader (12 bore) 6 lb 8 oz	2¾	1¼	116	129	25	28
Egan	Breech-loader (12 bore) 7 lb 8 oz	3	1¼	144	90	28	30
Prince & Green	Breech-loader (12 bore) 7 lb 2 oz	3	1¼	103	93	24	31
Pape	Breech-loader (12 bore) 7 lb	3	1¼	132	93	26	33

Where, as in pigeon trap shooting, quickness and ease of loading were of little consequence compared to shooting qualities, the participators in this exacting sport were in no doubt as to which gun shot best, for muzzle-loaders were used by them well into the 1860s. This, apart from *The Field* trials, puts beyond doubt the fact that the early breech-loaders could not compete on equal terms with the muzzle-loaders so far as shooting powers were concerned; however in turning to look at their use in the field we find that their shortcomings so far as shooting was concerned were in great measure compensated for in other ways.

Looking at these compensations through the eyes of H. A. Leveson, that sportsman of wide experience who wrote under the name of

'The Old Shekarry', we find in his book *Hunting Grounds of the Old World* 1868, his views on the breech-loading gun:

'All our first-class gunmakers, amongst whom I may enumerate Purdey, Lancaster, Lang, Westley Richards, Boss, Moore, Terry, Needham, Whitton and Daw, and Leetch, are manufacturing small-arms (both guns and rifles) that load at the breech, of one description or another. Lancaster, Westley Richards, Terry, and Leetch have peculiar systems of their own invention, but most of the others have adopted that of Lefaucheux, which, although it has been invented for upwards of five-and-twenty years, was very little known in this country until that excellent shot and practical mechanic Mr Lang, of "Old Red House" notoriety, took it up; and it is to him that we are indebted for the efficient carrying out and improvement of a principle, which is almost as great an era in gun-making as the invention of the copper cap.

'The following are some of the great advantages that the new system has over the old for fowling-pieces.

'I shall begin with the extreme facility and quickness in the loading, whereby any person armed with a breech-loader can load and fire at least six shots in the same time that another with a common gun takes to load and fire two, with much greater comparative safety, as with a breech-loader the muzzle of the gun can never by any chance be directed towards the person of the loader; no mistake can be made, such as putting two charges of powder or shot into one barrel; there is no chance of losing a hand by pouring powder from a flask down the muzzle of a gun recently discharged, in which, perhaps, a bit of lighted tow, or, what is oftener the case, a small piece of cork (got among the powder in opening the canister) may remain—an accident which may happen to the most careful sportsman. Again, one is always able to see clearly through the barrels, and can be certain that no dirt or obstruction has got in, which is a great advantage, as many people have been injured by guns bursting from the muzzle being accidently plugged up with clay, which may have got in whilst jumping a ditch, climbing over a fence, or stumbling in an uneven turnip-field. The sportsman can never meet with an accident by loading one barrel whilst the other is on full-cock, which the ramming down of a wad or the catching of a twig might cause to go off; and when game is abundant, in the hurry of reloading or the excitement of the moment, accidents from this cause frequently occur: also there is no danger of an unlucky cap flying and endangering the eye-sight—not a very uncommon occurrence.

'As to the pleasantness of shooting, both to self and company, there can be no doubt; for what an advantage it is for sportsmen, when beating country, to be able to load without halting or breaking the line, and making all the rest of the company wait until the operation is finished. Who has not been put off his shooting by having to wait whilst some nervous, fidgety old gentleman hunts in a dozen different pockets to find his powder-flask, wadding, shot-bag, and caps, which are all dispensed with by using a breech-loader? What an advantage it is, when shooting in fens or swamps, to be able to load without putting the butt of your gun in the mud or water, whereby you soil your clothes when you put it up to the shoulder and make yourself uncomfortable for the rest of the day. Also, what sportsman, after a heavy day's shooting, has not found his hands blackened and sticky from exploded gun-powder, and sometimes raw and blistered from constantly ramming down the charge? And in cold weather who has not found loading with a common gun, and putting on the caps, distress him beyond measure, more especially if he has been obliged to pull off his warm gloves before he is able to effect it at last?

'Another great advantage is to be able to change the charge in a moment, according to the game to be met with, instead of the old tedious method of drawing the shot with the screw of the ramrod; and also to be able to load without noise, as, when game is plentiful, the noise of ramming down an obstinate wad frequently puts up birds on all sides.

'A sportsman armed with a breech-loader can re-load almost as soon as a keeper can hand him a second gun and receive the one discharged, which does away with the necessity of having a man at one's heels with a loaded gun—an objectionable practice, as a trip or stumble might so easily occasion an accident.

'Breech-loaders foul very little, as the thick elastic mercurial waddings which enter the breech are fully a size larger than the bore of the muzzle; consequently, being forcibly driven through the barrel with the force of the powder, each discharge carries away any refuse or accumulation that may have been left by the ones previous, and at the end of a long day's shooting the barrel is just as free from foulness as at the beginning; also, the explosion of the charge does not take place in the breech, but in the paper cartridge, which comes out uninjured, containing the debris of the burnt powder, which in the ordinary gun is driven into the chamber and nipple every time it is reloaded, until the latter becomes clogged up, and miss-fires are the consequence.

'The ease of cleaning is also very apparent, for nothing is required but the passing of a little tow through the barrel once or twice, and afterwards wiping with an oiled rod; whereas, with an ordinary gun, the dirt is forced in the breech and through the nipple, and frequent washing out of the barrels is required, which is never the case with a breech-loader.

'There is less recoil in a breech-loader than in a muzzle-loader of the same size and weight, which I account for by its construction rendering it necessary to have more weight of metal at the breech; and also because at the bottom of the cartridge of the breech-loader there is a tight roll of paper, about one-eighth of an inch in thickness which (like the buffer of a railway carriage) gives with the action of the powder and lessens the recoil.

'After five years' experience with breech-loaders during which I have made a series of practical experiments, I have come to the conclusion that they shoot rather harder than ordinary muzzle-loaders; and my way of accounting for this fact is, that all windage is prevented (by the wadding used being a size larger than the bore); besides which, I think they will burn more powder, and of a larger grain than that in general use for percussion-guns, which is stronger, because there is more air that facilitates combustion between the grains. I also consider that they shoot quicker, because there is no long communication (the nipple) between the point of ignition and the charge, the explosion of the cap taking place in the centre of the powder, which is inflamed almost simultaneously; for it is an error to suppose that gunpowder explodes instantaneously, as, however rapid its progress, it takes a certain time in travelling from the first grain to the last.

'The sportsman can easily make up his own cartridges at the rate of about half a gross in an hour, or, if he prefers it, he can purchase them all ready from any gunmaker.

'When all the advantages of the breech-loader are contrasted with the known disadvantages of the muzzle-loader, it is difficult to account for the prejudice that has existed against them for years; for, notwithstanding that the present system was introduced by Lefaucheux a quarter of a century ago, it is only lately that it has come into general use amongst sportsmen. Numerous objections have been urged against the system, but none appear to have had any substantial foundation; and I shall not enter into them, although I am aware that there are many sportsmen of the old school who, from prejudice, will not even deign to give it a trial: with them arguments and facts are both equally lost.

'In the pursuit of large game, breech-loading arms are infinitely preferable; for until the last few years the hunter was always obliged, when waging war with the denizens of the forest, to keep up a battery of several guns and rifles, which, to say nothing of the expense of the first outlay, and the continual wear and tear, was attended by several serious disadvantages, some half-dozen of which I shall enumerate. In the first place, two or three gun-bearers are required to each sportsman, whose duty it is to pass up the spare guns as fast as those in hand are discharged: now it is a great disadvantage for a hunter, when on trail or stalking, to have a number of persons at his heels, on account of the extra noise they must necessarily make in forcing their way through cover, which often gives alarm to the game and prevents him from getting a shot. Secondly, it is a great drawback, when in the pursuit of some dangerous animal, when a faux pas might be attended with fatal consequences, to have another than yourself to look after. Thirdly, it is not pleasant to have loaded firearms carried in the rear by inexperienced hands, with whom an accident from carelessness is as likely to occur as not. Fourthly, it is not a comfortable feeling to have to depend upon the coolness and courage of your followers; and many a sportsman has found himself in an awkward position by his sub-bearers having been seized with a panic, and bolted, leaving him, with both barrels discharged, in the presence of a wounded and infuriated animal, when nothing but some lucky chance can prevent a catastrophe. Fifthly, it frequently happens, in hunting in different parts of the country, that the sportsman (if he does not keep in his pay a shekar-gang of his own, which is expensive work) has to intrust his spare guns to men of whom he knows nothing, who may be tempted to decamp with them—not a very unfrequent occurrence. Sixthly, it is a great annoyance to a tired sportsman, after a hard day's fag, to have to clean four or five double guns and rifles, which task he dare not intrust his followers to perform, as there are times when a miss-fire might be attended with the most serious consequences. Happily for the sportsman of the present day, all these disagreeable contingencies may now be avoided by making use of rifles on the breech-loading system. Now, independent of gun-bearers, he may roam through the forest alone, careless as to what animal he may meet, for he knows that, should his first shots not take deadly effect, he can reload in the twinkling of an eye, and keep up a running fire, against which nothing can stand, instead of having to bolt under cover to reload (in case a spare gun is not to hand) returning breathless, and often with unsteady hand, from having to use sheer force in jamming an obstinate ball down a foul barrel. When mounted, a rifle on the breech-loading system has immense advantages, as it can be easily reloaded, without in any way interfering with the management of the horse; whereas with the old muzzle-loader the sportsman was entirely powerless whilst drawing his ramrod and ramming home the bullet. He who has once used a breech-loading gun or rifle will no more think of going back to a muzzle-loader, than the crack marksman at Hythe would return to old "Brown Bess".'

Leveson's account of the advantages of breech-loaders was certainly a glowing one and if in his enthusiasm he overstated the case in one or two respects we must remember that his practical experience in the field enabled him to recognise all the desirable qualities of breech-loading in a variety of situations. He was in fact in error when he considered that there was less recoil to a breech-loader, though this may have been so because the extra weight of his gun absorbed the extra recoil. Weight of gun and charge being equal, there was more recoil in a breech-loader. His feeling that the breech-loader shot harder was also not borne out by practical experiment but obviously some early breech-loaders shot better than others and some cartridges must have been more suitably loaded than others.

As a good example of what could be done with good quality pin-fire guns we can do no better than read Sir Frederick Milbank's account of a memorable day's grouse shooting on Wemmergill Moor in 1872 when he killed 364 brace of grouse:

'The charge was $2\frac{3}{4}$ drs black powder and $\frac{7}{8}$ oz of No 6 shot. My three guns were 12-bore pinfire, by Westley Richards. All the three guns I used in the great drive, in which I killed 95 brace of grouse, were so hot that on laying two of them down on a mossy wet bank close to the "stand" it made it "smoke". It must, however, be remembered that the drive only lasted twenty-three minutes. It may be asked how I know this? It was in this way. At the very first shot I had, the hammer of my gun caught the watch chain, which drew the watch out of my pocket, and I then saw the time; and after my last shot I purposely took the time, as I then knew what an extra-ordinary drive I had had. I think you will say it was sufficient to make guns hot! For the last five or six minutes I was obliged to shoot from the "trigger guard", owing to the heat of the barrels. I have to ask, would some of the new powders we read of have stood this heat without exploding? It may be the whole firing was so extraordinarily quick, from the first shot to the last, that there was no time for the heat to get through the cartridge case.'

One drawback to the pinfire cartridge was the safety factor, an accidental knock or a fall on to a pocket full of cartridges could cause an explosion, because the cartridges were charged with black powder. For this reason special cases were made to carry pinfire cartridges in the field in such a way that the pins were protected from an acci-dental knock. A long metal tray with a hinged lid was incorporated into some gun cases and also these cases contained the tools for loading the cases, which were, in many instances, sold capped but uncharged. Sportsmen had their favourite loads acquired through experience in muzzle-loading days and of course liked to vary the loads according to the sport offered (plates 33, 34, 35).

It was rarely that the pinfire guns achieved the balance and ele-gance of the best muzzle-loaders. Their back action locks with large cumbersome hammers, angular fences and rather graceless breech actions tended towards this lack of elegance and, although the scroll engraving lightened the effect, it was rarely integrated with the shape of the surface to be enriched to the extent that it had been on percussion muzzle-loaders, or was to be on the centre-fire hammer gun. The iron heel plate on the stock was generally retained, although there was no longer need to place the butt on the ground when re-loading. The custom of fitting heel plates was not discontinued until the centre-fire hammer gun was well established.

Pairs of pinfire guns are comparatively rare as also are those with exceptionally finely figured stocks, for it is probable that pinfire guns were mostly made for sportsmen who wished to try them out before going all the way with them. This was just as well, for the centre-fire cartridge was soon to supplant the less adaptable pinfire cartridge.

CHAPTER FIVE

The Centre-fire Hammer Gun

WHEN in 1861 George Daw introduced into England the central-fire cartridge that was in all essentials the same cartridge that we use today, the breech-loaders, which had barely held their own against the muzzle-loaders, now took over the ascendancy. Within the space of a few years the centre-fire had become established as the cartridge of the future at the expense of the pinfire cartridge, and even the most solidly entrenched rearguard of the muzzle-loading supporters were soon won over.

This cartridge that Daw introduced was Schneider's version of that invented by M. Pottet of Paris, and Daw endeavoured to control the patent rights of it in England; however he was thwarted in this when defeated in the courts by Messrs Eley Bros, because the original patent rights had not been kept in force in France. This freedom from patent was a help to all those gunmakers who within a short time were bringing out a variety of efficient centre-fire guns aided by their earlier experience of the pinfire breech-loaders.

Before looking at the further development of guns to fire Daw's cartridge, it is interesting to look at one or two earlier centre-fire guns and their cartridges.

An ingenious central-fire cartridge and gun were introduced by Needham around 1850 (plate 42) in which the needle-like striker pierced the outer covering of the base of the cartridge to fire the per-cussion cap. In this gun the barrels were fixed to the stock and the breech opened to allow loading by the swinging out of a bolt-like breech block that was released by raising the bolt arm upwards rather in the manner of a bolt action rifle except that when released the movement was outwards and not backwards. The cartridge, which did not have a rim, was not extracted after being fired, but instead the remaining card base, stiffened with a zinc washer, was pushed forward by the next cartridge to act as a top wad. The gun had some success but the design of the cartridge limited its use.

The Lancaster central-fire gun and cartridge of 1852 was far ahead of its time, for in a number of respects the gun and cartridge have more in common with the early 1860s. The cartridge was similar to the later central-fire cartridge with the difference that the ignition was achieved by striking the base of the cartridge between which and a perforated disc inside was contained the detonating mixture. The perforated disc acted as the anvil and as the copper

Figure 11. Daw's Centre-fire cartridge case.

outside covering was not pierced there was no backward escape of gas. The cartridge had a rim and was extracted by the familiar extractors which move out as the barrels drop. The barrels were secured to the action by means of a projecting extension from the lump which slid under the breech face. In order to release this projection the barrels first moved forward on swinging the under lever outwards and then a slot in the fore-end of the lumps allowed them to move forward over the hinge bolt before dropping down. This gun cost 60 guineas and the cartridges were more expensive than the pinfire cartridges, so its distribution was limited; however it certainly anticipated future events in a remarkable way (plates 70, 71).

The centre-fire cartridge offered a number of obvious advantages over the pinfire, amongst which may be mentioned that they could be carried safely, they could be loaded any way round, unlike the pinfire that had to fit the pin to the top groove in the barrel end,

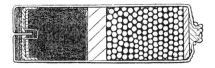

Figure 12. Section of cartridge for Needham's needle-fire gun.

and this groove, which could let in water, was no longer needed. There was also no escape of gas through the pin hole of the cartridge. In spite of all these advantages there were objectors principally on the grounds that it was no longer possible to see at a glance whether there was a cartridge in the breech, the pins sticking up making this obvious in the case of pinfires as the percussion caps had done in the case of muzzle-loaders. To meet this objection some

early centre-fire guns were fitted with little pin indicators which projected slightly above the top of the action when a cartridge was in
the breech. This arrangement was soon found in practice to be
unnecessary, because it was so easy to open and shut a snap action
and see the situation directly.

Although the under lever screw type action remained one of the
most popular of the means of fastening down the barrels, increasing
use was made of various types of snap action. Daw's first snap action
centre-fire gun was opened by means of an under lever that was
pressed forward from its position under the trigger guard. The
'Purdey' under lever snap action was continued, activated by a
thumb lever in the front opening of the trigger guard (plate 46)
and this was sometimes accompanied by an interesting safety device.
There must have been some fear at this time that in opening the
breech while the gun was loaded and cocked a trigger might be
accidentally pressed causing the cartridge to be struck when the
breech was slightly open and no longer bolted, with obviously unpleasant results. The safety device acted as a stop on the triggers and
prevented their being pulled except when the gun was completely
closed or completely open. It also acted as a safeguard in case the
lever which was out of sight under the gun had failed to spring back
completely and bolt the barrels securely.

Another curious feature of some early Purdey centre-fire guns

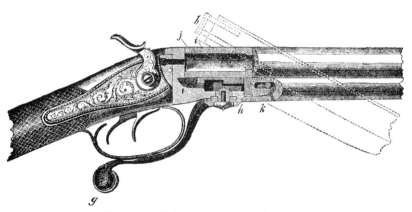

Figure 13. C. Lancaster's central fire gun.

Figure 14. C. Lancaster's cartridge showing perforated disc.

was that the hammers were made to look like pinfire hammers but with smaller heads, while the strikers, connected to the hammers, were struck by the breast of the hammer (plate 43). It is revealing to notice this reluctance to take a clean step forward, without dragging behind a past relic that no longer had any more purpose than to recall superficially what had gone before.

Early centre-fire guns still had hammers that had to be drawn back to half cock before the barrels would open, the pressure of the hammer keeping the striker pressed into the dent in the cap. The invention of the rebounding lock around 1866 (plate 49, centre), improved by Mr Stanton of Wolverhampton in 1869 (plate 49, bottom), was a great help, for the hammers rebounded automatically to half cock allowing the loose or sprung strikers to clear the breech face after being struck. These locks were also safer for when down they could not be knocked forward to fire a cartridge and when let down from full cock they went readily to half cock.

The great majority of pinfire guns had back action locks largely because the forward action lock or bar lock necessitated a larger amount of metal being cut away from the action. On the other hand less wood is cut in the case of bar locks so that the grip of the stock is stronger. With improved knowledge of the stresses involved, and better designed actions, the bar lock was again used for most best guns. The hammer heads had for the most part a look of modified percussion dolphin heads, the earliest ones even retaining a shallow version of the cup-shaped head, but also popular with a number of gunmakers was a short strong hammer with a tall rabbit ear spur or grip, rather in the style of those on Lancaster's early centre-fire gun (plate 70).

Most important in the development of the breech-loader was the introduction of the top lever operated Purdey bolt, the most widely adopted of all the mechanisms for holding down the barrels (plate 47). The convenience in operating the Westley Richards top lever had no doubt been duly noted and also the fact that being on top it could

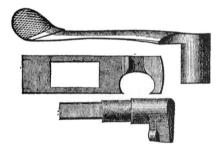

Figure 15. Purdey bolt and lever.

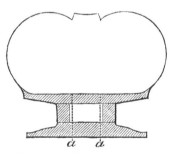

Figure 16. Section of Purdey bolt action of 1867.

be seen to be closed. On pressing the top lever to the right the sprung bolt was slid back to clear the lump slots and allow the barrels to fall open. On being returned, the curved lump pressed back the bolt until the slots were reached and the bolt sprung home.

The barrels, of various types of Damascus twist, tended to contain a higher percentage of steel; from six parts steel to four of iron to as high as eight parts steel to two and a half of iron in the case of silver steel Damascus. The breech ends of the barrels were generally strengthened at this time and the lumps in the better guns were dovetailed neatly into the breech ends.

With the aim of strengthening the action at a point at which it was found that there was a tendency for the breech ends of the barrels to gape away from the standing breech, various forms of doll's head extensions from the rib were tried out.

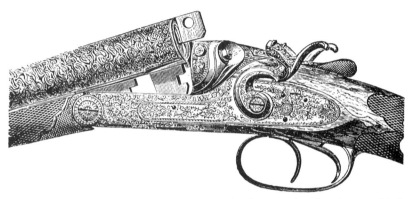

Figure 17. W. W. Greener's patent treble wedge-fast gun showing the round hole in the rib extension to receive the top cross bolt.

Westley Richards had first used an extension from the rib as the sole means of holding down the barrels (plate 44), but later he also used the doll's head grip in combination with the Purdey bolt snap action, making a treble grip. W. W. Greener brought out his much publicised treble wedge-fast breech mechanism in 1873, which in addition to the double grip snap action, had a round cross bolt that passed through a hole in an extension brazed to the top breech ends of the barrels. This cross bolt slid to the left to release the extension on moving the top lever across to open the gun. According to W. W. Greener this action may be said to have originated in his cross-bolt gun of 1865 but was not perfected until 1873. This extra bolt through the rib extension was, if carefully fitted, a powerful extra aid to holding the barrels up to the breech face, and was used with considerable advantage in large bore guns and rifles firing heavy charges, but it was found in practice to be an unnecessary addition to a soundly made gun firing normal charges. However it proved in its time to be a good selling point with the appeal of something extra in the way of a safeguard, and so it continued to be used in a variety of versions, notable among which was J. and W. Tolley's Giant grip cross bolt. In general it was the Birmingham gunmakers that used the extra bolt, for the London gunmakers contended that their best guns were quite strong enough without it and neater in the breech in consequence. Remembering how some of these best London hammer guns stood up to the firing of tens of thousands of cartridges in a season without getting the shakes, it can be fairly taken that their assumption was correct.

A neat type of third bite was later used on some Purdey guns designed for powerful charges; a small projection of about $\frac{3}{16}$ in. from the barrels just above the centre of the extractor was engaged by a bolt in the upper centre of the standing breech (plate 53). So far as is known this type of third bite was only used on guns fitted with Whitworth steel barrels around and after 1880.

In the 1870s the side-nail or bolt and escutcheon means of fastening the fore-end to the barrels was replaced by the lever grip or one of the sprung-on grips such as the Anson with the press catch at the top end or the Deeley fore-end with its recessed catch in the middle. This is a useful rough guide in dating a hammer gun, for a bolt and escutcheon fastening is likely to be before about 1875, while the other types are generally about or after that date.

Iron heel plates were mostly discontinued and instead the butts were finished in chequered wood, sometimes with the addition of small iron heel and toe plates, or with horn heel plates. The strikers were of two types, those that were cleared from the breech face by means of a small coil spring and those that were pushed back by the extractor on opening the gun, small grooves in the bottom of the extractor being filed in for this purpose. A broad-headed striker was sometimes used to reduce the tendency of the striker head to be dubbed up by repeated blows of the hammer.

The period during which the hammer gun flourished as a best gun was not much longer than about 1865 to 1885, it being remembered that both pinfires and percussion muzzle-loaders were still being made well into the 1860s and also that from the early 1870s the hammerless actions were beginning to focus attention on what was to become the gun of the future. Because of the relatively short period during which the best hammer guns were made, and because many went on to endure nearly one hundred years of use or unfortunately abuse or neglect, they are rarely to be found in anything approaching original condition. Most collectors had not become interested in these guns until recently, but happily this situation has now changed. The finest hammer guns have a grace and elegance combined with a fineness of finish and soundness of construction that places them in parity with the best in any age. For the most part those with bar-locks have more elegant lines than those with back action locks, while those with the stock carried forward past the locks and up to the hinge bolt, usually known as wood-bar or bar-in-wood, have a particular attraction that combines the style of the muzzle-loader with that of the breech-loader (plates 50, 51, 52). Such hammer guns at their best had the finest Damascus barrels, a boldly figured stock, perhaps of Circassian walnut with its dark blackish veins contrasting with the lighter wood, the fences of the action carved in sweeping curves around the striker nipples, well shaped lock plates and hammers graceful as a swan's neck. All was combined together with an elegance of proportion that made superfluous any ornament but the fine and unobtrusive engraving (plate 47).

The hammer guns of the later '70s had achieved a graceful efficiency, but in addition to this quality they now had the advantage that the increased shooting capabilities of choke boring could bestow. Choke boring was of tremendous importance, not only in advancing the effective range of the shot gun, but also it placed in the hands of the gunmakers a means by which the closeness of the pattern could be controlled.

Although there were prior claims to finding the secret of making a barrel shoot close, it is to William Pape of Newcastle that the honour goes for being the first to record a type of choked barrel. This plan for boring a gun barrel was provisionally protected in 1866 and in 1875 Pape was awarded a prize as the inventor of choke boring, there being no other claimant. W. W. Greener, as in other cases, was quick to appreciate the importance of the new idea and to him must be given full credit for developing it to the point of its general application, and to publicising energetically the shooting qualities of choke bored barrels. The original and normal means of choking a barrel was by boring the barrel to within a short distance of the muzzle leaving a constriction of up to 30 to 40 thousands of an inch; more constriction than this so deformed the shot as to defeat the purpose. Another method of boring involved recessing the barrel for two or three inches behind the muzzle constriction. R. M. Fairburn patented such a method in America in 1872. This method had the advantage of achieving a higher degree of choking with less constriction at the actual muzzle and because less pellets were deformed more consistent patterns could result. However, as any benefit was marginal and the process more involved it was not much used after the first few years of choke. Two other methods were used for improving the shooting of cylinders: one involved boring a recess two or three inches long behind the muzzle which was left the same diameter as the remainder of the barrel and the other method was to bore the barrel true cylinder and then constrict the muzzle end by means of outside pressure.

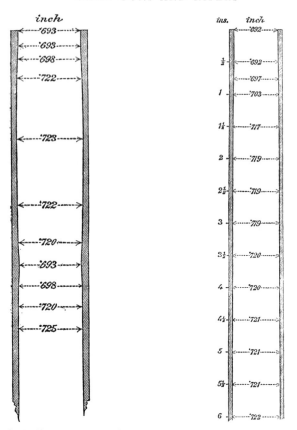

Figure 18. Tulip or recess boring.   Figure 19. The long choke—Greener's.

There had been some practice of a type of choke boring in America prior to the New York trial held in 1873. A Mr A. L. Johnson advertised a plan in 1872 by which the choking was achieved by screwing a nose cone, of smaller gauge than the barrel, into the muzzle, and later achieved a similar effect by swedging (or forcing in) the muzzle. These two methods were subsequently discontinued in favour of the normal method of choke boring. The New York trial of 1873 was won by Scott of Birmingham with Green of Cheltenham second. Both these used a type of choke boring, while W. W. Greener's guns being bored on the cylinder principle, were left well behind. W. W. Greener was obviously impressed with the new type of boring and a year later he had developed the principle to the extent that he guaranteed patterns far beyond any thought possible at this time.

When W. W. Greener in 1874 advertised choke bored guns capable of regularly throwing patterns quite beyond any normal expectation, letters of disbelief poured in to the sporting magazines, and as had happened in the case of the muzzle-loading versus breech-loading controversy, the editor of *The Field* magazine, Mr Walsh, again rose to the occasion and arranged for a series of public trials to take place.

The Field had printed the following on 5 December 1874: 'Mr W. W. Greener is now prepared to execute orders for 12 bores warranted to average 210 pellets of No 6 shot in a 30-inch circle (at 40 yards) with 3 drams of powder, the weight of the gun being 7¼ pounds. (The shot load was 1¼ oz or 338 pellets.)'

The great gun trial of 1875 was one of the most comprehensive public gun trials ever undertaken and it aroused widespread interest. There were classes for guns ranging from 8 to 20 bores, and in the trials superior patterns were thrown by the choke bores, with better penetration than was the case with the cylinders. There were in all 33 competitors who entered 114 guns and the silver cup presented by *The Field* was won by W. W. Greener with a gun of 12 bore throwing an average pattern of 214 in a 30-inch circle at 40 yards. (The No 6 shot load was 1⅛ oz.) It is interesting to note that two of the worst choke bores gave patterns less good than many of the cylinders, possibly through being over constricted at the muzzle.

Following the clear demonstration of the superiority of choke boring in the matter of closeness of pattern, the opponents of the system contended that the constriction at the muzzle must quickly wear. So, also in 1875, *The Field* arranged a 'Wear and Tear Trial' with the object of putting this contention to the test.

Three guns were chosen to go through a series of tests over six weeks. In these tests 200 shots were fired, the gun wiped out, and two hundred more fired the following morning. Twelve rounds were fired at a target after every 200 and after 400 shots had been fired the gun was cleaned and locked away until the following week; presumably the idea was to simulate normal usage. About 2,500 rounds were fired from each gun, the best average pattern was 185 (1⅛ oz No 6 in 30-inch circle at 40 yards), and it was clearly demonstrated that there was no falling off in the quality of the shooting. The gun giving the best average pattern and penetration was in fact made by W. W. Greener.

The choke bores having excelled at the expense of the cylinders in the preceding trials, the champions of the cylinder now held that, so far as practical shooting at game or at trap-pigeon was concerned, the cylinder barrel was the better. It is interesting to note here that the reason Pape gave for not proceeding with the full patenting of his choke boring method was that he considered that choke bored guns were not suitable for game or trap shooting because they shot too close. In this opinion he was supported to some extent when the first novelty of the choke had worn off.

In 1876 the first trial at pigeons was shot off at the Gun Club, Notting Hill, in which the cylinder guns, aided by the use of concentrators, won by 2 birds at 27 yards rise and 7 birds at 33 yards. Mr Walsh mentions however that the best shots were on the side of the cylinders, and their guns included those by Messrs Purdey, Lancaster, Grant and Boss.

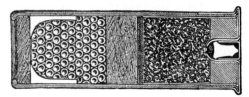

Figure 20. C. Lancaster's improved concentrator.

The concentrators referred to in the above pigeon match were cartridges loaded with the addition of cylinders of very hard paper, half an inch long, which were pushed into the top of the cartridge, round the shot. The system was invented by Charles Lancaster about 1865 and later improved by the addition of a domed paper cylinder in place of the former plain cylinder. When Mr Walsh tested these concentrators against ordinary cartridges in 1869, he found that the concentrators gave an average increase of pattern of 24% and an average increase of penetration of 28%. However Mr Walsh did say that the patterns were not as regular as with a good choke, and there was some chance of dangerous balling (that is a number of pellets being forced together to form a 'bullet' that could carry with deadly effect far beyond the range of normal shot).

In 1877 James Purdey offered a 50 guinea silver cup to be shot for at pigeons by the two types of boring, but this time the use of concentrators was excluded. The result showed clearly in favour of the choke bores and the cup itself was won by Mr Cholmondeley Pennell, who made the best score at 30 yards using Greener's gun, but at 40 yards he missed his first two birds, changed to a Dougall gun and killed his next three. He won the cup by one bird from Captain Aubrey Patton who used a Dougall gun throughout. The total score at 30 yards rise was chokes 26, cylinders 28; and at 40 yards, chokes 19 cylinders 13. The chokes won over the combined ranges by 4 birds, but what is most revealing is that the cylinders had the advantage at 30 yards while at 40 the closer pattern of the choke came into its own.

A further match was shot off in which 18 present fired at 3 birds each, first with cylinders and then with chokes. At 28 yards the chokes won by 2 birds but at 35 yards 36 birds were killed by the chokes against only 24 by the cylinders. W. W. Greener was successful in *The Field* trials of 1878 and 1879 and later in 1881 he won a 100-

guinea cup at Hendon against other choke bored guns, clearly establishing the fact that, though he had not invented choke, he had played a major part in perfecting it.

Choke bored guns had proved superior in pattern and penetration when aimed at 40 yard marks, and they had also proved superior when used over the longer rises at trap pigeon. In the first instance the mark was 40 yards and in the second the longer rises would involve shots at from about 40 yards upwards. In both cases the shooting was at a longer range than was average in general game shooting, and therefore it was questionable that success in these specialised types of shooting necessarily qualified the chokes to succeed cylinders as game guns.

Many sportsmen were so impressed with what chokes could do at long range, that it was not until they put them to practical use in the field that they discovered their limitations. Those who had gone all the way with double full choked barrels were to discover that moderately close shots which were fair game to a cylinder, were with a choke, either clean missed or so completely raked with shot as to be unfit for the table. Few birds should in fairness be fired on at ranges much beyond 40 yards, even with a choke, and as the majority of chances were to be had at 30 yards or less the case for the use of full choke in normal game shooting was certainly not a good one. Those who had maintained all along that the cylinder was best for game shooting were to find their point of view shared by some disillusioned users of choke, but in the course of a few years, the majority sought a compromise. Some used a modified choke (60–65 per cent of shot in 30-inch circle at 40 yards) in both but a popular compromise was a good cylinder or improved cylinder in the right barrel and some degree of choke in the left.

While on the subject of choke it is interesting to find that, of the two greatest game shots of the period, Lord Walsingham used only cylinder guns while Lord Ripon used some degree of choke. It is often mentioned that Lord Ripon used double full choked guns and it is indeed true; but this was for suitable occasions, such as the very high driven pheasants, when the shooters were placed in a valley.

Lord Ripon's obvious success with chokes on such occasions was taken by some as a recommendation for heavily choked guns for game shooting, but in fact at the same time (1894) James Purdey and Sons built him a pair of double full chokes, they also built for him a pair of guns which were bored true cylinder in the right and modified (about ½) choke in the left (plate 56). He obviously found this pair much to his liking for he had a third gun built to the same specification two years later.

Two points stand out clearly: first, that Lord Ripon was a good enough shot to perform well with full chokes at the longer ranges, and secondly he was sufficiently experienced to appreciate the value of more open boring for closer range work. It is significant that when Lord Ripon was asked whom he considered to be the best game shot he had seen, he said Lord Walsingham was, both in speed and accuracy in aiming. Both these great shots were very quick as well as accurate in their shooting, as they needed to be to take two driven birds in front and two behind, changing guns in between. The greater spread of open bores was an aid in shooting quickly and they had their second two birds down before they had got to full choke range.

This is a question like the size of shot that can be argued interminably; as indeed it was, and with some heat, in the last quarter of the 19th century, with such practical shooters as Lord Walsingham and R. Payne-Gallwey being as strongly in favour of open boring as W. W. Greener was that choke had every advantage. In a sport like wildfowling where the average distance of shots was likely to be longer, some degree of choke was certainly desirable, though a half choke would probably be more suitable for all but the very best shots. There could be few things more annoying than to miss a good chance at moderate range because the gun was too tightly choked. This was, and is, all too often the case.

Although the hammer gun as a best gun began to decline in the 1880s in favour of the hammerless gun, there were a number of sportsmen who preferred to continue shooting with their hammer guns with which they were familiar. Certainly the hammerless gun must have looked strange to those who had all their lives been familiar with percussion, pinfire, and centre-fire hammers; some likened the newcomers to the appearance of a spaniel without ears.

Amongst those who preferred to continue using hammer guns were some of the greatest game shots of all time including King George V, Lord Ripon and Lord Walsingham. Not only did these sportsmen continue to use the hammer guns they already had, but some had hammer guns specially built in the 1890s and early 1900s. As already mentioned James Purdey and Sons built five for the Marquess of Ripon and they also built sets of three of 12, 16 and 20 bore for King George V. A number of other sportsmen also followed in the footsteps of the great ones and had similar hammer guns built.

These hammer guns (plate 56) were strongly constructed but reasonably light, fitted with Sir Joseph Whitworth's fluid pressed steel barrels, back action locks and neat hammers. The action was gracefully rounded on the underside. Most of these guns were fitted with ejectors which were triggered off by an arm that extended from the tumbler and moved down as the hammer moved forward between the half cock position and contact with the striker. Some other leading gunmakers built guns as hammer ejectors and ejectors were

31 Double-barrelled 12 bore pinfire gun by Joseph Lang, No. 2686, of 1864, showing back-action locks, hammers at half cock and forward under lever in closed position.

32 Lang pinfire gun, No. 2686, showing action in open position. Note there are no extractors — cartridges were pulled out by the pins.

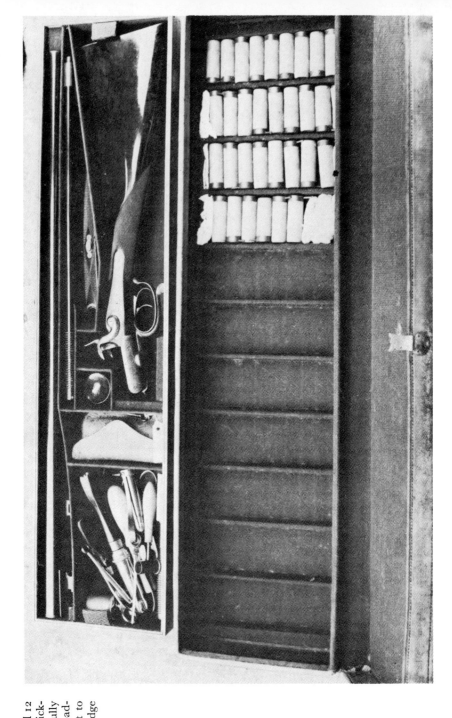

33 Fine example of a cased 12 bore pinfire gun by John Dickson, No. 2313, of 1863, fully equipped with cartridge reloading tools. Top tray lifts out to show neat and safe cartridge storage underneath.

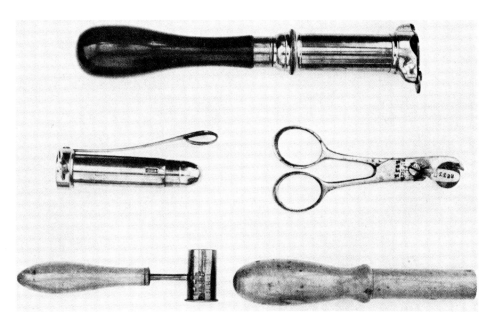

34 Tools for John Dickson pinfire gun No. 2313. *Top:* turnover tool. *Middle, left:* recapping tool. *Middle, right:* cartridge end trimmer. *Bottom, left:* adjustable measure. *Bottom, right:* wad rammer.

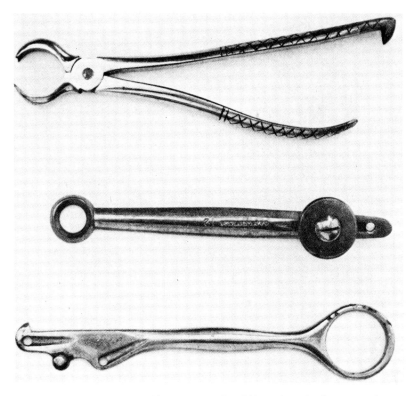

35 More pinfire tools. *Top:* pincers for lifting the pin for recapping. *Middle and bottom:* tools for hooking out cartridges by their pins.

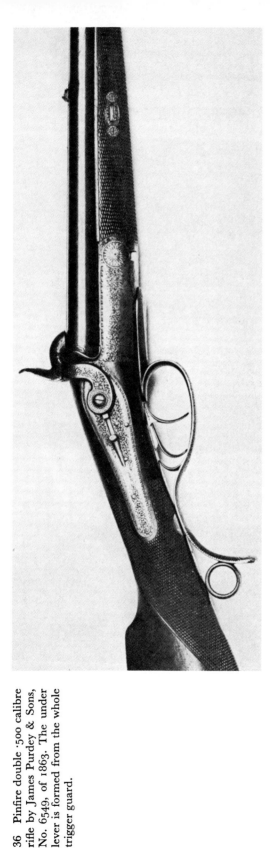

36 Pinfire double ·500 calibre rifle by James Purdey & Sons, No. 6549, of 1863. The under lever is formed from the whole trigger guard.

37 Double-barrelled 12 bore pinfire gun by Westley Richards, No. 10402, c.1862, showing early pull-back top lever which engages the doll's head extension.

38 Pinfire double 32 bore rifle with a sliding breech action of the Bastin Lepage type, built for Sir Edwin Landseer by James Purdey & Sons, No. 6254, in 1861.

39 Pinfire double ·500 calibre rifle by Joseph Lang, No. 2079, of 1857, showing back-action locks and forward under lever.

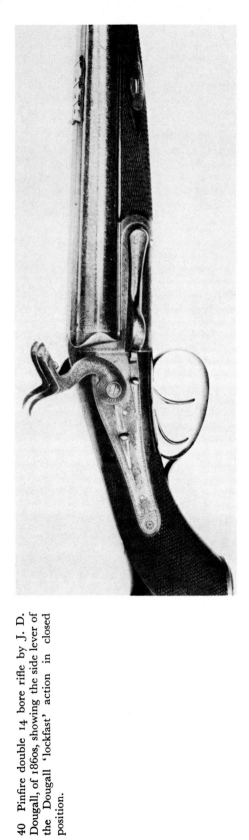

40 Pinfire double 14 bore rifle by J. D. Dougall, of 1860s, showing the side lever of the Dougall 'lockfast' action in closed position.

41 Dougall 'lockfast' rifle, No. 2404, showing action open after it has moved forward from the breech face to clear the bosses that fit into the breech ends when the gun is closed.

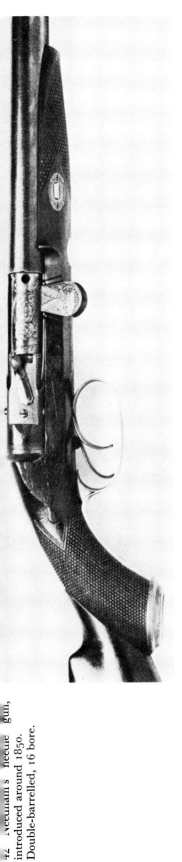

42 Needham's needle gun,
introduced around 1850.
Double-barrelled, 16 bore.

43 Double-barrelled 12 bore
centre fire gun by J. Purdey,
No. 7202, of 1866, showing the
pinfire-style hammer heads,
which are simply ornamental;
the breast of the hammer hits
the striking pin. Hammers still
retain the half-cock position
and must be drawn back to this
position to open the gun after
firing.

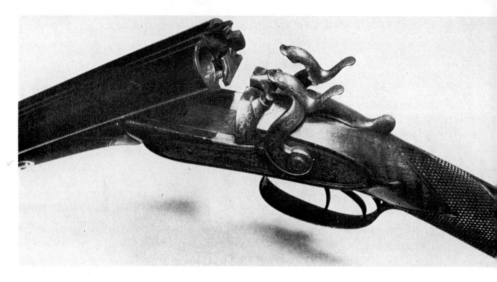

44 Double-barrelled 12 bore centre fire gun by Westley Richards, No. 12486, c.1871, showing bar-in-wood action curved to the shape of the barrels and pinfire-style hammer heads, which hit the curved striking pins. The side-moving top lever engages the notch in the doll's head extension on closure.

45 Double-barrelled 12 bore centre fire snap-action gun by J. Purdey, No. 7745, of 1868, with bar-in-wood carried forward to cover the hinge bolt, rebounding locks and sprung strikers. Bold Damascus barrels.

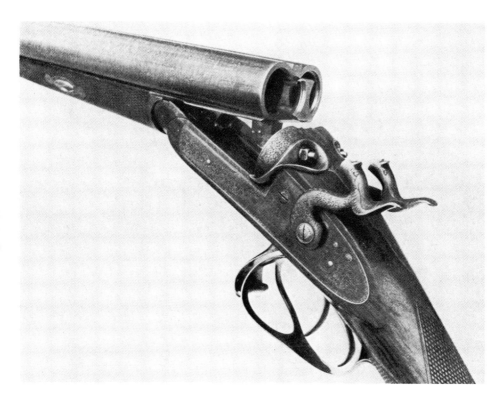

46 Purdey hammer gun, No. 7745, with action open, showing thumb-lever in front of divided trigger guard, early form of extractor and gracefully carved fences around the strikers.

47 One of an elegant pair of double-barrelled 12 bore bar-in-wood guns by J. Purdey, Nos. 10485 and 10486, of 1879, with top lever snap-action open, showing broader type of extractor, fine Damascus barrels, graceful fences and hammers and very fine floral style of engraving. The barrels are bored half-choke and throw wonderfully consistent patterns.

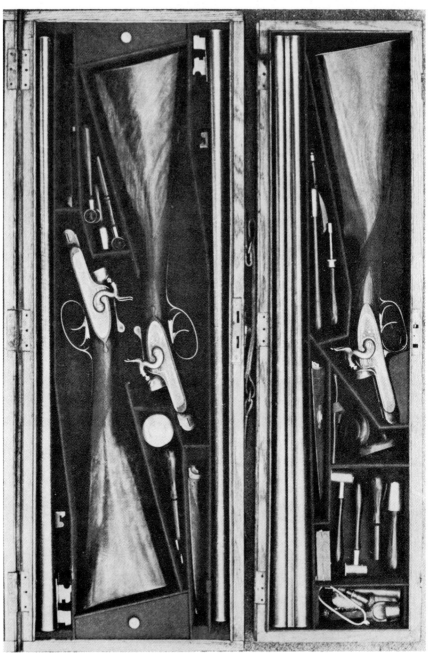

48 *Top:* The cased pair of bar-in-wood guns by J. Purdey, Nos. 10485 and 10486, of 1879, with some reloading equipment. Label on the inside lid of case gives charges for these guns: 3 drams powder, $1\frac{1}{16}$ oz shot; as a lighter load, $2\frac{7}{8}$ drams powder, 1 oz shot; spreading charge for covert shooting, 3 drams powder, $\frac{7}{8}$ oz No. 5 shot. Curtis & Harvey's Medium Basket grain.

Bottom: The Purdey gun, No. 7745, in its case with original fittings for reloading cartridges and cleaning. Leather wallet contains brushes for cleaning extractor holes, and small box contains spare lock pin. Label on inside of lid gives charges for this gun: light, $3\frac{1}{8}$ drams powder, $1\frac{1}{8}$ oz shot, or medium, $3\frac{1}{4}$ drams powder, $1\frac{1}{8}$ oz shot. Curtis & Harvey's No. 2 size powder.

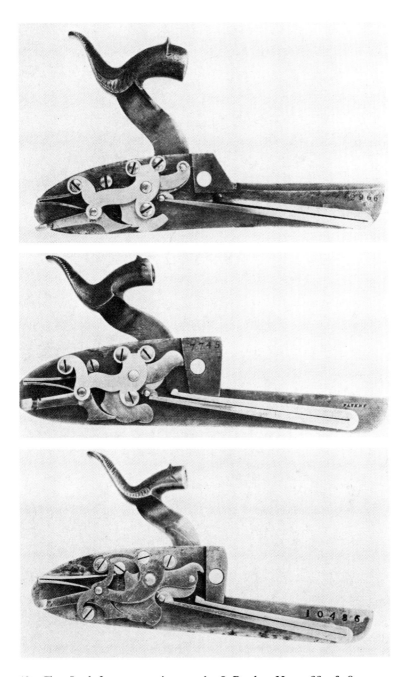

49   *Top:* Lock from percussion gun by J. Purdey, No. 2966, of 1837.

Centre: Rebounding lock from centre fire gun by J. Purdey, No. 7745, of 1868.

Bottom: Rebounding lock of later design from centre fire gun by J. Purdey, No. 10486, of 1879.

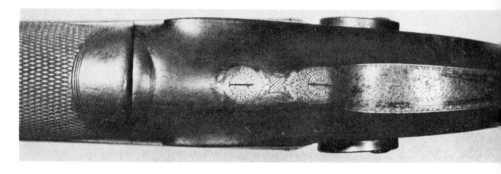

50 Bar-in-wood gun by Westley Richards, No. 12486, of 1871.

51 Bar-in-wood gun by J. Purdey, No. 7745, of 1868, showing the wood covering the hinge pin and thumb-lever in front of the trigger guard.

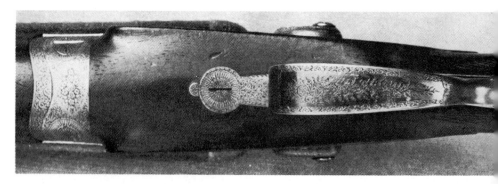

52 Bar-in-wood gun by J. Purdey, No. 10486, of 1879, showing the usual style of the Purdey bar-in-wood hammer guns.

53 Double-barrelled 12 bore pigeon gun with bar-in-wood action by J. Purdey, No. 11922, of 1884, showing third bite above the extractor, Whitworth steel barrels and broad file-cut rib. Hammers lay back out of sight when cocked.

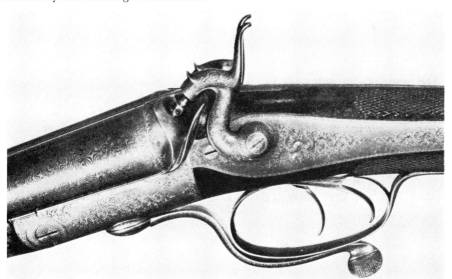

54 Double-barrelled 12 bore gun by J. Woodward, No. 3249, of 1873. Back-action locks, under lever, extended top strap on top of the grip and boldly patterned Damascus barrels.

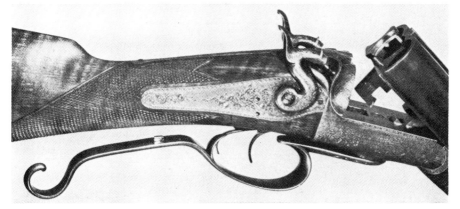

55 Double 34-in. Damascus-barrelled 8 bore gun by J. Purdey, No. 6727, of 1864. Back-action locks, combined trigger guard and under lever and extended top strap on top of the grip.

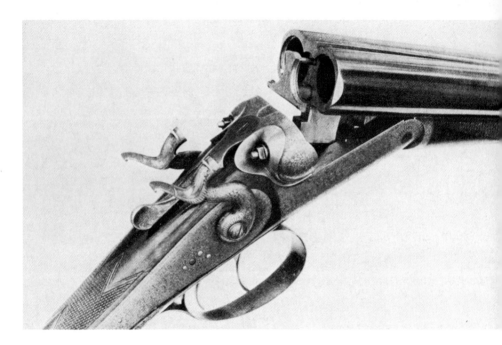

56 Double-barrelled 12 bore gun by J. Purdey, No. 14979, of 1894: one of the pair built for the Marquess of Ripon. This gun is fitted with ejectors and has Whitworth steel barrels, bored cylinder in the right and modified choke in the left. The gun has back-action locks and side clips. Weight is 6 lb 12 oz.

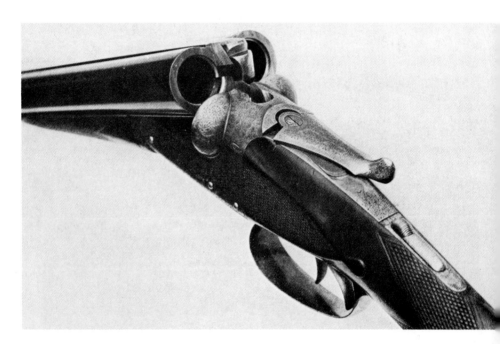

57 Double-barrelled, 12 bore, hammerless box-lock gun by Westley Richards, No. 14402, of 1889. An example of the Anson and Deeley action of 1875 with the fore-end ejectors patented in 1884. Clearly shown is the top lever and third bite in the doll's head extension.

58 Earl de Grey, born 1852, Marquess of Ripon from 1909, died 1923. Generally acknowledged to be the greatest game shot of his time, he is shown holding one of his Purdey hammer-ejector guns.

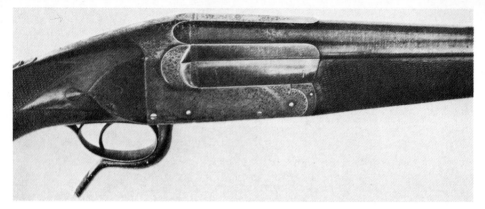

59 Single-barrelled 4 bore hammerless gun by H. Clarke & Sons, c.1885. Fine quality Damascus barrel. Weight of gun, 15 lb.

60 Double-barrelled 12 bore hammerless ejector pigeon gun by J. Woodward, built 1901. Whitworth steel barrels, third bite above extractors, finely carved fences and side clips. Weight, 7 lb.

61 Cartridge reloading tools. *Left to right:* screw measure for powder and shot, decapping and recapping tool, powder and shot measures, tool for guiding wad into cartridge, and turnover tool.

fitted to existing hammer guns; but in both cases there were not many of them.

As well as the comparatively few best hammer guns that were made for game shooting, there were also some made for such specialised sports as trap-pigeon shooting as late as the 1920s, because certain pigeon shooters felt happier with the simplicity of hammer locks. Also sportsmen going abroad to places where skilled attention to hammerless locks was lacking preferred to take hammer

Figure 21. Bland and Sons' 4 bore wildfowling gun.

guns and rifles. In rough country abroad, or at home on the salt marsh, where the guns were likely to suffer, the generally lower price of the hammer guns was a recommendation. The hammer gun in various grades below the best became the keeper's gun, farmer's gun and wildfowler's gun. Messrs Bland and Sons were pioneers in the provision of strong, reliable but reasonably priced hammer guns to fill this need, and major Birmingham gunmakers also brought out a variety of sturdy hammer guns, which after some eighty years and in a number of cases in spite of severe neglect, still manage to preserve their owners from injury.

In addition to earlier self half-cocking guns, several methods were later tried out for full-cocking the hammers. One of the best of these self-cocking actions was that used by both Joseph Lang and James Woodward around 1875. There was but slight difference between them: in both the lever under the trigger guard was pressed forward to open the gun and at the same time it bore internally on the tumblers, pressing the hammers back to full cock.

Messrs Holland brought out an under lever self-cocker in 1879 in which an arm, worked by the lever, projected through a channel behind the standing breech to push the hammer heads back to half or full cock. Messrs Holland claimed for this gun that: 'This gun is opened, and the locks placed to half-cock or full-cock at pleasure,

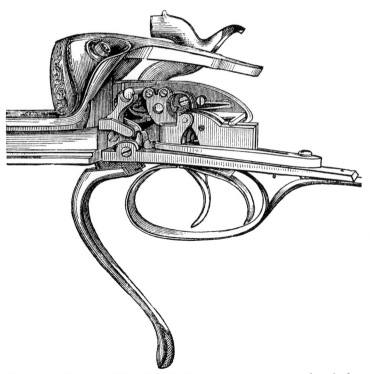

Figure 22. Section of Woodward's Automaton gun open and cocked.

with the minimum of force applied to the lever, which can be placed
either under the guard, or between the hammers as a top lever. The
great object obtained in this principle of action is its simplicity,
and the ease with which the bolts of grip are opened, and locks
placed at full or half cock. The first is obtained by applying the lifting
arm to the extreme end of the hammers. In all other self-cocking
actions as applied to double-barrelled guns, the lifter is nearer the
axle, consequently less leverage is obtained, and more force is re-
quisite to raise the hammers. Ordinary gun locks are used.'

Hammer guns in the late '70s and '80s tended to be lighter than the
earlier types which averaged 7 pounds and over. The reasons for
this were first that with better understanding of the stresses involved,
their design was improved, and second that by making use of choke
boring it was possible to use lighter loads more effectively. To illus-
trate the difference in loads we may take as typical examples two
cased guns, one of 1868 and the other of 1879, which conveniently
have the recommended load cards attached to the insides of the lids.

For the cylinder gun of 1868 (plate 48, lower) the recommended
load of Curtis and Harvey's No 2-28 size powder was, for a light
load $3\frac{1}{8}$ drams to $1\frac{1}{8}$ oz shot, and for a medium load $3\frac{1}{4}$ drams to

1⅛ oz shot. The original measures are for 3⅛, 3¼ and 3⅜ drams of powder and for 1⅛ and 1³⁄₁₆ oz shot. For the choked gun of 1879 (plate 48, upper) the recommended load of Curtis and Harvey's Basket medium grain powder was, as a light load 2⅞ drams to 1 oz shot, and for a medium load 3 drams and 1¹⁄₁₆ oz. But it is also interesting to notice that, to compensate for the close shooting of the chokes at shorter ranges, it was recommended that for covert shooting a spreading charge should be used of 3 drams powder to ⅞ oz of No 5 shot.

The 1868 gun case has all its original fittings including powder and shot measures, ebony rammer, a hand turnover tool and a rosewood base with a hole in the centre on which the cartridge rested to have its old cap knocked out. Also there is a rosewood block which fitted into the breech ends of the barrels to form a rest when using the cleaning rod from the muzzle end, with a Turk's head brass brush on it. A Turk's head, if pushed out of the muzzle from the breech end, cannot be pulled back without difficulty, hence the reverse or then traditional method and the need to guard the breech ends when they rested on the floor.

The hammer gun era was one of vastly increased interest in shooting, game rearing and driving on a grand scale. It was an age of great shots and prodigious bags and so it is fitting to close this chapter with Lord Walsingham's account of his day's shooting in 1888 on Blubberhouse Moor with his cylinder bored hammer guns and two loaders.

'On August 30, when I killed 1,070 grouse to my own gun in the day, I shot with four breechloaders. No 1, a gun made in 1866 by Purdey, subsequently converted from pin-fire to central principle, to which new barrels were made last year. Nos. 2 and 3, a pair of central fire breechloaders, made also by Purdey, about 1870, for which I have likewise had new barrels. No. 4, a new gun made by Purdey this year to match the two mentioned above, but with Whitworth steel instead of Damascus barrels. The guns are all 12 bore, with cylinder 30 in. barrels, not choked. My cartridges were loaded by Johnson, of Swaffham; those used in the downwind drives containing 3⅛ drs. Hall's Field B powder to 1⅛ ozs. No 5 Derby shot; those used in the up-wind drives (where birds, of course, came slower) had 3 drs. only of the same powder, with the same shot; not hardened shot in either case. I find I never go out shooting without learning something. If I had the day again, I should cut off the extra eighth of an ounce of shot, not on account of recoil or discomfort of any kind—from which I never suffer, although always using black powder—but because I failed to get as much penetration at long distances as I do with an ounce only. I distinctly remember firing three barrels at one bird, striking well in the body every time, but killing dead only with the last shot; the powder seemed to burn too slow. Another thing I learned was that Whitworth steel barrels are not desirable for a heavy day's shooting. The explosion in them makes quite a different sound from that given off by Damascus barrels: there is more ring about it, and I can imagine that this might prove a serious annoyance to anyone who minds the noise of shooting. I have no recollection myself of ever having had a headache from gun-firing. Moreover, the Whitworth barrels become hot much more rapidly than the Damascus; and this is a serious drawback, especially to a man who shoots without gloves. I can well imagine that they last much longer, and are in many ways suited for ordinary light work; but I am now replacing them with Damascus, as in all my other guns.'

There were twenty drives and forty drivers were employed. The bag was made between 5.15 a.m. and 7.30 p.m. and 1,510 cartridges were used.

James Purdey and Sons have kindly given their records of the shooting of the 12 bore hammer ejector guns built for the Marquess of Ripon in 1894 (plate 56). These records are of particular interest because they show the thoroughness with which guns were shot by Purdeys and also it was around this time that Lord Ripon took to using Schultze in preference to the regular and fast No 2 Black. Certainly the 40 grain Schultze charge with 1 oz of No 6 shot gave excellent results.

The Marquess of Ripon, Gun No 14979
Right: Plain (true cylinder)
Left: Modified (about $\frac{1}{2}$ to $\frac{3}{4}$ choke)

POWDER	SHOT	PATTERN		PENETRATION	
		Plain	Modi-fied	Plain	Modi-fied
$2\frac{7}{8}$ drams No 2 Black	1 oz No 6	134	173	33	34
$2\frac{7}{8}$ drams No 2 Black	$1\frac{1}{16}$ oz No 6	144	175	34	35
$2\frac{7}{8}$ drams No 2 Black	$1\frac{1}{16}$ oz No 5	118	156	36	37
40 grains Schultze	1 oz No 6	150	205	32	32
42 grains Schultze	$1\frac{1}{16}$ oz No 6	149	216	32	32

The black powder was Curtis and Harvey's Diamond No 2. The patterns shown for the Plain (true cylinder barrel) and the Modified (about $\frac{1}{2}$ choked barrel) were the number of shot in a 30-inch circle at 40 yards and the Penetration figures shown were the number of thick paper sheets penetrated at 40 yards. The figures would represent the average of a number of shots fired with each load.

The pair of full choked guns that were also built for Lord Ripon at this time were shot with black and Schultze powder and $1\frac{1}{16}$ oz of No 5 shot giving patterns ranging from 159 to 187.

CHAPTER SIX

Centre-fire Hammerless Guns, Ejectors and Single-triggers

I T was not until the 1870s that hammerless guns began to gain in popularity, and the 1880s before they finally replaced hammer guns as best guns. However they had been early upon the scene, for when, in 1861, George Daw introduced the centre-fire cartridge and hammer gun, he followed it within a year with a form of hammerless gun. Daw's hammerless gun was not a thing of much attraction either in external appearance or in its mechanical efficiency. Also the move from muzzle-loaders and pinfires to hammered centre-fires was a sufficient step for most shooters to take at one time, so that it is hardly surprising that Daw's hammerless gun evoked little interest.

In Daw's gun the long sprung strikers were set behind the breech and when cocked the rear ends of the strikers projected backwards externally. The cocking was achieved by pushing the under lever well forward, opening the breech at the same time. This gun had a very simple safety device in the form of a bar which slid through the standing breech. When pulled out to the side a short way it effectively blocked the strikers from the breech face.

Green's hammerless gun of 1866 was similar in principle to Daw's gun but better organised in several respects. The strikers no longer projected at the rear when cocked, and the strong lever served as part of the trigger guard, giving added leverage in a compact form, the more so because the axis used required less force. The strikers were bolted for safety by giving a quarter turn to a half round rod that fitted through the standing breech. Like Daw's gun before it, this gun did not achieve popularity.

The first hammerless gun to achieve a substantial degree of success was that patented by T. Murcott of the Haymarket, London in 1871. In this gun the under lever, on being pressed forward, served both

Figure 23. Murcott's hammerless gun (patented 1871).

Figure 24. Lock of Murcott's hammerless gun showing the cocking bar on the internal hammer.

to open the snap action and thrust back the tumblers to full cock. The cocking arm of the lever bore directly on cylindrical projections on the weighted top of the tumbler which acted as a hammer. Hinged strikers were attached to this tumbler head. Apart from the use of the tumbler as an internal hammer the locks used were normal side locks of the well tried and strongest type. In addition to the usual double grip action a further small bolt projected from the top of the breech face, and this entered the end of the rib on closure of the gun. A top safety bolt secured the gun against accidental discharge and the cocking arm prevented the strikers firing a cartridge should the gun not be completely closed and the under lever returned to its full extent.

This gun of Murcott's was mechanically efficient, strong and reliable, and it also had the advantage of the clean graceful lines and balance of a sidelock gun. It was hardly surprising that this gun had a considerable success and the distinction of being the first serious rival of the hammer gun.

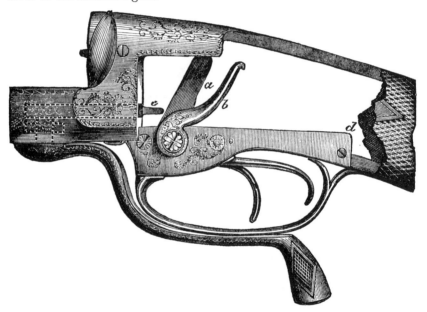

Figure 25. Gibbs and Pitt's original action and lock.

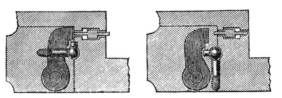

Figure 26. Gibbs and Pitt's safety bolt: left—fire, right—safe.

In 1874 Gibbs and Pitt of Bristol brought out a gun in which the cocking was achieved by an extension to the rear of the 'Purdey' bolt that thrust back the internal hammers, when the gun was opened, by means of either a top or an under lever. The hammer mechanism was attached to the trigger plate which curved down to occupy some of the space in front of the fore trigger; this was altered in later models. External levers acted as indicators as to when the hammers were cocked and these could also be used to let down the hammers to half-cock and to re-cock them at will. George Gibbs did not favour automatic safeties, but as he explained in his catalogue he replaced the earliest form with a neat lever on the lock plate which

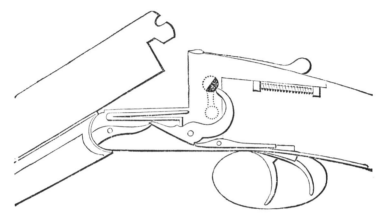

Figure 27. Westley Richard's Anson and Deeley box-lock action (patented 1875) showing gun open and at safe.

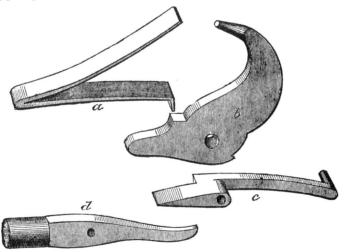

Figure 28. The limbs of the Anson and Deeley lock: *a.* mainspring, *b.* combined tumbler and striker, *c.* sear, and *d.* cocking lever.

on being pressed down placed a barrier in front of the hammer, effectively preventing contact with the striker. A danger was that the hammers could fall forward if the safety block was returned to the firing position after the sears had been jarred off.

A most important hammerless gun was that of Anson and Deeley (plate 57), patented in 1875, because it contained the basic mechanism of what was to become the universal box-lock hammerless gun. The work of cocking the locks was done by the fall of the barrels on opening the gun; the cocking lever pivoted on the same axis as the hinge bolt, and its projecting end engaged a slot in the fore-end. The tumbler, hammer and striker were combined in one sturdy limb and the main spring was simplified by eliminating the swivel and hook of ordinary locks. Westley Richards produced the first guns with the Anson and Deeley lockwork in 1875, and in them the barrels were secured to the action by Westley Richards' top lever connection to the 'doll's head' extension of the rib. A danger present in the hammerless guns was that they must at all times be carried at full cock. To ensure safety from the accidental pulling of the triggers, or the hammers being jarred off by a knock or fall, aided perhaps by a dirty or worn sear, it was essential that the triggers be bolted, and also that a block should prevent the accidental fall of the hammers. It was in respect of safety that the first version of the Anson and Deeley gun was deficient. The half round bar which passed through the standing breech, and was operated by an outside lever, certainly prevented the fall of the hammers when set in the safety position. However, until this bar was manually turned the gun was at full cock and ready for firing. The triggers were not bolted and when set at safe it was found that should the sear be jarred off or the triggers be pulled unknowingly the hammer could fall, firing the cartridge, on turning the safety bar from the safety to the firing position.

These early models were in fact recalled and the original safety

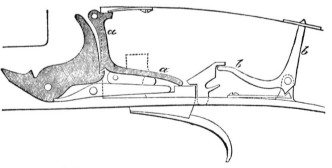

Figure 29. Anson and Deeley's safety bolt of 1882: triggers bolted and tumbler safe from being jarred off.

bar replaced with a bar that bolted the triggers. In 1882 Westley Richards introduced an automatic and very neat safety mechanism that both bolted the triggers and also effectively prevented an accidental fall of the tumbler striker by hooking into a projection on the rear of it.

W. W. Greener was quick to appreciate the possibilities of the Anson and Deeley action and in 1878 he brought out his own version, the 'Treble wedge-fast hammerless gun'. This gun was called by him the *Facile princeps* because of the greater ease of cocking, facilitated by a swivel hung from the lump, which caught the forward arm of the tumbler and gave increased leverage with less friction. This swivel was replaced in later models by a cocking rod, which was raised with the lumps to connect with and lift the cocking arm of the tumbler. This gun could be had with or without the top cross bolt, but Greener considered the extra top grip was essential to the security of the gun and its use was strongly recommended.

Mr Walsh designed a hammerless gun cocked by the leverage of the barrels, and in accordance with his strongly held conviction, this incorporated an automatic safety that bolted both triggers and tumblers. He prevailed upon Messrs Bland and Sons of Birmingham to manufacture these guns, which they undertook only after considerable modification of the original design. However as the action was more complicated and more expensive to produce than the best of those based on the Anson and Deeley action, and it had a rather ugly external appearance, it was not long kept in production. In 1878 W. & C. Scott of Birmingham brought out a hammerless gun which cocked by means of a connecting rod through the action body

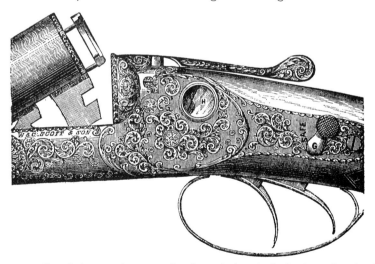

Figure 30. Scott's hammerless gun showing window in lock plate, for viewing position of tumbler to see if cocked or fired.

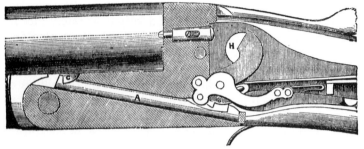

Figure 31. Plan of Scott's action showing cocking rod with gun closed.

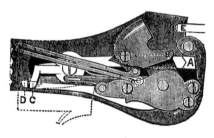

Figure 32. Scott's safety block at A preventing the fall of the tumbler until A is lowered when the lever at C is lifted as the trigger is pulled.

which, on the fall of the barrels, was pulled forward by a hook on the forward end of the lump, the rear end of the rod hooking onto the bottom of the tumbler bringing it to full cock. Unlike the Anson and Deeley mechanism the lockwork was contained in independent back action sidelocks and the striker was independent of the tumbler heads. A novel feature of these locks was the round glass window in the side, which enabled the shooter to view the position of the gold plated tumbler heads, to see in fact if they were cocked or fired. Scott's gun was also fitted with a most ingenious safety device. An arm was used that contained a block that prevented contact between the tumbler and the striker, the other end of which lay beside the part of the sear arm which was in contact with the trigger. When the safety catch was moved to the firing position both the sear and the arm were moved up together, and as the arm was pivoted, the other end with its block moved down to allow the tumbler head to hit the striker. Should the tumbler be jarred off at any time this system ensured that the block would always be in position to prevent contact with the striker.

The Scott gun was manufactured by some London gunmakers. Messrs Holland and Holland, then of New Bond Street, brought out, in 1879, their version, which they named the 'Climax safety hammerless'. The writer has used, with every satisfaction, a finely finished version of Scott's gun by J. Blanch.

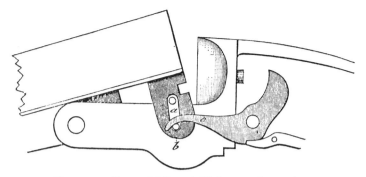

Figure 33. Gye and Moncrieff's hammerless action.

Messrs Gye and Moncrieff's hammerless gun patented about 1878 closely resembled the Anson and Deeley action, but simplified it. The forward extension arm of the tumbler hooked onto a swivel suspended from the rear lump, in such a way that as the barrels dropped the cocking arm of the tumbler was lifted until the sear rested in the cocked position. The striker was in this instance independent of the tumbler. Externally a bulge showed in front of the trigger guard where allowance was made for the extension to the rear lump; some considered this to be unsightly but there was no denying that the mechanism was simple and efficient.

The firm of Joseph Lang who had been the first in England to construct a gun on the Lefaucheux principle, also followed the trend towards hammerless guns. In 1877 Lang brought out a hammerless gun which in principle was much like the Anson and Deeley though

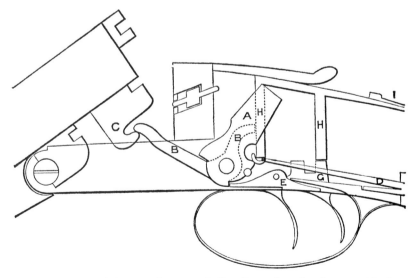

Figure 34. Lang's hammerless gun of 1877 (later altered to lever cocking).

differing in detail. The cocking was achieved by an arm extending from the tumbler which was lifted by a hook on the bottom of the rear lump. The main spring was set behind the tumbler and the striker was set independently in the breech face. The safety bolted the mainspring and the triggers. Possibly because of the actions brought by Anson and Deeley for the infringement of their patent, Lang soon adapted his hammerless gun to cocking by means of an under lever. This gun had sham bar lock plates, and indicators set on top of the break-off (the part of the action immediately behind the breech).

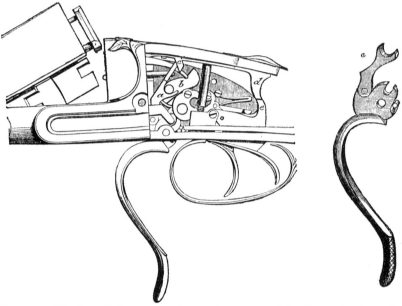

Figure 35. Woodward's Automaton hammerless gun: cocking done with the cocking lever shown detached.

James Woodward and Sons of St James's Street produced about 1877 a hammerless gun adapted from their earlier self-cocking hammer gun. The following is a description given by the inventors:

'One of the numerous advantages is that the same locks and action are used as in ordinary bar guns, with the exception that the hammers are inside instead of out, in other respects the outlines are precisely the same. The hand lever centred on the trigger plate has a lifting bar hinged to it, which bears on the arms projecting from the tumblers. It raises the locks, and at the same time moves a safety bolt over the ends of the triggers and one in front of each hammer, so that should the lock be jarred off by a fall, the safety bolt in front of the hammer would catch it in the throat immediately at starting, rendering it impossible for any accidental explosion to happen. The construction of the lifting bar, hinged on the hand lever, is so arranged that very little force is required to raise the locks, consequently the same weight mainspring can be used as in a gun with outside hammers, avoiding any chance of missfires so often complained of in hammerless guns.'

The writer also used one of these guns for general game shooting and found the cocking lever was easy to manage and the whole gun handled very well indeed.

In 1880 Tisdall of Birmingham produced a hammerless gun at the very low price of 12 guineas. This gun was soundly constructed, ingeniously designed, and led a trend towards good but moderately priced hammerless guns. The cocking was performed by the top lever, which moved the action bolt back by means of cogs. The action bolt as it moved back had an extension to the rear which cocked the tumblers. A safety bar was also automatically brought into action, which was turned to firing by a small lever on the right hand lock plate.

Also in 1880 Walker of Birmingham patented his 'Umpire' hammerless gun which apart from its top lever cocking resembled closely the Anson and Deeley gun. It had some claim to advantage in that little wood needed to be cut from the stock to fit the action.

Interesting were the hammerless actions of the Edinburgh gunmakers James MacNaughton & Sons and John Dickson & Son, which were patented about 1880. In these actions the lockwork was built on the trigger plate.

The Dickson action might be described as the more sophisticated version, and was to become well known as the Dickson 'Round Action' on account of the rounded external shape of the action body (plate 82). The main and sear springs were bow springs and were fixed to the trigger plate in positions behind the lockwork. Ejectors were added to the Dickson gun about 1886 and these were also unusual in that the coil spring, rod and ejector kickers were contained within the action body.

The MacNaughton ejector work was however contained in the fore-end as was usual.

Some Dickson Round Action guns were made with dummy side plates for clients who preferred the external appearance of a sidelock gun while wishing to have the lockwork of the 'Round Action'.

The ingenious mechanism of Messrs Purdey's hammerless gun of 1880 was the work of that remarkable inventor Frederick Beesley. The work of cocking and firing the tumblers depended on the alternate use of the arms of the mainspring. When the gun was opened this movement was assisted by the mainspring, the stronger upper arm of which raised the tumbler to full cock. On closing the gun a cam bore on the mainspring bringing into tension the lower and

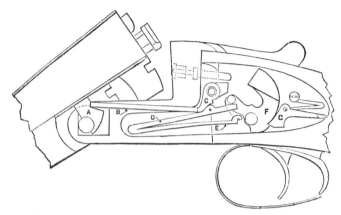

Figure 36. The Purdey hammerless action of 1880 showing breech open and tumbler cocked. The mainspring is put under tension as the action is closed.

less strong arm of the mainspring, which provided adequate force to drive the hammer head of the tumbler forward on to the striker when the trigger was pulled. When the gun was open or put away with the barrels removed the mainsprings were not in tension. The sear and bent were of great strength and because of this it was considered at first that only an automatic safety operating on the triggers was necessary; however intercepting blocks were added later for greater security. Gas escape from the caps of some cartridges was something of a problem then in hammerless guns because of the connection through the striker channel with the lock. The Purdey gun had an efficient vent to prevent such an escape of gas into the lockwork.

Sir Ralph Payne-Gallwey, writing in the 1887 edition of the Badminton Library *Shooting*, mentions that the demand for the above gun had rapidly increased, so that at that time (1887) no less than 65% of their guns were made on this principle. Gallwey adds: 'In the hands of sportsmen who shoot as heavily as do great numbers of Messrs Purdey's customers, guns are necessarily subjected to the most severe tests, and in face of this, the increasing demand is an indication of the gun's success.' A factor which no doubt assisted in making this gun popular was the neat and graceful external appearance of the locks and action. In this respect it certainly was in advance of most of its contemporaries. It is remarkable to reflect that this is almost precisely the design of a Purdey gun of today and that the clean functional lines seem as right to us today as they did to those who found them so more than eighty years ago.

In 1881 F. B. Woodward of Birmingham patented the 'Acme' hammerless gun which was sold in London by Beattie and Co. of Queen Victoria Street, E.C. The under lever released the action bolt and at the same time cocked the locks. The lock plates were false but served to hold the bolt and coil spring firing mechanism. Only the triggers were bolted by the safety.

In 1882 there appeared Rigby and Bissell's improved hammerless gun, this being a sound action of the under-lever cocking type with back-action side locks. It had an efficient safety device which blocked the 'hammers' as well as bolting the triggers. In addition to the Purdey bolt this gun had a top connection which was held by an upright bolt.

In 1882 also there appeared the hammerless gun of Stephen Grant of St James's. This was a box-lock gun, cocked by an under lever, which could also be made with the lever curved round to form a side lever operated on the right-hand side. The safety only bolted the triggers and the main springs were long coil springs set on rods which operated on the rear hammer heads of the tumblers.

In 1879 W. W. Greener brought out a hammerless gun with conventional side locks on a system of under lever cocking derived from Murcott's action. By rearrangement of the parts the cocking pressure was reduced and the hammer heads of the tumblers were tapered into strikers. This was quite a neat and serviceable gun made to be sold at the moderate price of 18 guineas but it lacked a safety block for the hammers.

About 1882 J. & W. Tolley of Birmingham brought out a hammerless gun cocked by means of an extension to the Purdey bolt operated by the top lever and using side locks. This gun had an automatic safety that bolted both 'hammers' and triggers. The gun was named 'The Perfection' by its makers; it was certainly a serviceable gun.

P. Webley and Son brought out a side lock hammerless gun around 1882, which used an under lever (sometimes brought round to the side) which opened both the Purdey bolt and the top connection, and at the same time cocked the tumblers. A neat and strong safety bar engaged a notch in the rear of the tumbler. The locks were the normal bar action type.

Messrs Cogswell and Harrison around 1882 brought out their 'Desideratum' cheap hammerless gun which was a combination of the Gibbs and Pitt action using the Purdey bolt plus a top connection with the addition of Scott's safety bolt to the bar action side locks. The small round window in the side of the lock was included to enable the shooter to see when the tumblers were cocked. This plainly finished but neat gun, with barrels of Damascus iron, was sold for 16 guineas.

A novel form of hammerless gun, having four barrels, was brought out by Charles Lancaster in 1882 (plates 67, 85). The idea of four-barrelled sporting guns and rifles had been tried out in muzzle-loading times. Lancaster's worked on the revolver principle except that the barrels remained static while the 'hammer' set on a rod revolved, hitting each striker in turn. The first model had a single ring trigger which on being pulled had first to turn and draw back the 'hammer' to full cock; it rebounded to half cock after each shot. The barrels were secured by means of either a snap bolt or a double (screw) grip using a side swinging under lever. In addition there was a top rib 'doll's head' extension. In the second version of this gun, brought out later in 1882, the trigger was formed in two parts, the rear one, on being pulled by the second finger, drew back the hammer cylinder from rebounding half cock, to full cock. When in this position the forward trigger was pulled with the same sort of pull as a normal gun. Should the shooter not fire, the second finger let its trigger fall back to half cock again. This gun constituted a considerable achievement in gunmaking, for all four barrels had to be skilfully soldered together to converge on the same mark; however it was considered rather unsporting, even by those who shot with pairs or more of guns. Even those accustomed to the slaughter of the battue seemed suddenly mindful that the annihilation of game was not the only object. The gun could be built as a 12 bore for wildfowl, especially flight shooting, and as a 16 or 20 bore for driven birds and battues. The 20 bore weighed 7 lb 5 oz and was regulated to 3 drams of powder and 1 oz of shot. Boss & Co. in 1898 brought out a 3-barrelled gun, the barrels set in a row and fired by a single trigger.

Holland and Holland's 'Royal' hammerless gun was well recommended in the Badminton Library *Shooting* of 1887 for the following reasons: 'Simplicity and strength of the action, and non-liability of the locks to get out of order. Regularity and delicacy of the pulls of the triggers. The ease with which the gun can be opened. Absolute safety of the lock mechanism.'

The locks of the 'Royal' were brought to full cock by the fall of the barrels acting on a lever which connected the forward lump with the tumblers. The independent side locks were strongly constructed and a sliding mainspring acting directly on the tumbler enabled the claws and swivel to be dispensed with. The mainspring was so arranged that it assisted the opening of the gun. There was an efficient automatic intercepting block safety in addition to the triggers being bolted. This could be built if desired with a third grip in the form of a doll's head extension.

It is interesting to see how contemporary sportsmen viewed hammerless guns. For instance Sir Ralph Payne-Gallwey writing in 'Letters to young shooters' (1890) expressed the following thoughts on them: 'Hammerless guns, before the advent of ejectors were considered the acme of perfection; and so they are now, if well made. A good hammerless of the present day is about as perfect an

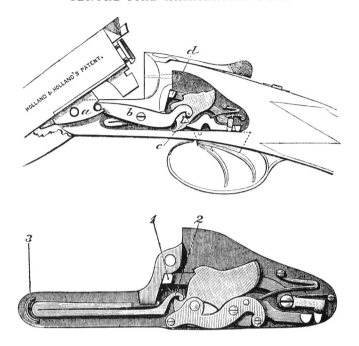

1. Intercepting safety block; 2. Front of sliding mainspring, dispensing with swivel and claw. 3 shows the space into which the mainspring slides as the lock is fired down.

Figure 37. Holland and Holland's 'Royal' hammerless gun and its lock.

article as a shooter could desire to possess; yet it is only within the past five or six years that these guns have generally become reliable. A few seasons ago the owner of a "hammerless" was always sent first over a stile or through a hedge, as these weapons not seldom exploded (fired) without warning, or failed in some less dangerous manner.

'Now, every gunmaker of note has his own particular "bantling" in the form of a special gun, christened with what he considers a taking name—which often suggests that his gun is alone, of all others, the safest and best; though their patents are nearly all modifications or downright imitations of the original invention of Messrs Anson & Deeley, to whom honour is due as the earliest to introduce good weapons of this description to the public. When first invented, hammerless guns were extremely complicated, and, from their numerous parts and dependent mechanism, often signally failed in use; but latterly gunmakers have greatly simplified the construction of these guns, and have reduced to a minimum the number of pieces their locks contain—of course, adding much to their success and safety thereby.

'A good hammerless gun may now be relied on to fire 5,000 shots a season for years without requiring repairs; and if it is capable of such a hard strain as this entails, I do not see much more need be required of it. The locks may run many years without repair, and with very slight supervision in the way of cleaning—and I have good proof of this in my own guns.

' "Hammerless" are as safe as guns can be, provided they are fitted with a reliable intercepting block that is always between the hammers and the cartridge—a safeguard that protects the gun from discharge by a fall or jar, and which is only removed by the shooter pulling the triggers. The first question a young shooter should satisfy himself upon is whether the gun he proposes to purchase, if it be a hammerless, has this block; and let him have nothing to do with it should it be without such a vitally important protection from accident.

'In purchasing a hammerless gun—even supposing it to be absolutely reliable and safe in every respect—there are other secondary qualities to be looked for. It should work evenly, and without any perceptible jerk, or undue exercise of leverage, in opening or shutting; else it will be found a slow gun to load in a hurry, and not so quick as a hammer gun in this respect. It should easily and smoothly do the work of compressing the mainsprings in cocking; and, on turning the opening lever, the barrels should drop down of themselves to receive the cartridges. They should do this almost as freely as those of a hammer gun, and without any noticeable pressure on them from the left hand of the shooter—a pressure which means waste of time in loading.

'The gun should open to the extent of at least an eighth of an inch between the top of the false breech and the lower edge of the extractors. A gun that opens like this always does its work best; for, from the barrels falling well down, it obtains plenty of leverage to divide the work of cocking over a considerable space, and the power then used to compress the springs is scarcely felt. When a gun opens but a slight distance it feels stiff and heavy in the act of cocking, as its mainsprings have to be compressed by a short and cramped movement, instead of by a long, easy one.

'Many hammerless guns are so constructed that their barrels only just drop clear of the breech. A shooter has then to notice carefully his gun every time he loads, to see if it is far enough open for him to insert a fresh cartridge. Some gunmakers leave this opening space so narrow that, unless the barrels are held perfectly level, and at their lowest angle, the rim of the cartridge-case will catch against the top edge of the breech, either in loading or unloading. Of course, a gun on these lines is faulty; for it is difficult to load and fire it as fast as a few quick shots may at any time necessitate. A hammerless gun should open well clear of the breech; there is then no difficulty in placing the fingers, however cold, well round the cartridges to pull them out, or, if necessary, to enable an extractor to be applied with full force. At the same time, the shooter should be careful to chose a gun that cocks before it can be reloaded, or else the locks might not be fully cocked when he wishes to fire.

'In all hammerless guns the springs are compressed when the gun is shut and ready for use; and, as gunmakers cannot well alter this state of things, they tell us compressed springs are of no consequence. That this is not the case stands to reason; therefore, at the end of the day, invariably insert dummy cartridges fitted with springs in their centres, and pull the triggers. Empty cases should never be used for this purpose, as the strikers drive into the caps after a few blows, and the points of the former are then liable to wear and tear from the force required to free them on opening the gun.

'The sliding stud that moves the trigger-safety of a hammerless gun should be fairly large; it is then convenient to the touch. It is often made too small, and safety and utility are sacrified to unnecessary neatness. This safety stud should be large enough to be felt and manipulated easily with the thickest gloves or the most benumbed fingers; and, for my part, I should prefer one that required a downward as well as a sliding pressure, as a precaution against accidental movement.'

J. H. Walsh in his capacity as Editor of *The Field* became the arbiter of what qualities hammerless guns should possess in order that they could be recommended to sportsmen. He was adamant regarding the need for automatic safeties that bolted the triggers and also placed an intercepting block in front of or otherwise bolted the hammers. Also Walsh considered that bar locks so weakened the action as to make a top rib connection essential, he therefore recommended back-action locks if the top connection was not used. As a recommendation by *The Field* was a considerable selling point, many gunmakers, particularly the less established ones, were obliged to conform to Mr Walsh's views. With regard to safety bolts, these views were certainly justified and soon no good quality gun was to be built without them, but his fears regarding the need for a top connection with bar locks has not been borne out in practice. Numerous best quality guns endured the hardest shooting, season after season, without the aid of a top connection.

By the 1890s the development of the hammerless gun divided into two main channels. For the most part the best grade of gun had some form of side lock, while in the moderately priced gun some form of the Anson-Deeley box-lock was used. Shooters had now been relieved of most of the manual tasks associated with the use of their guns, and compared with the muzzle-loaders of but a few years ago, the best hammerless guns must have seemed perfect. However as early as 1874 Mr J. Needham had brought out an ejector gun and, although many sportsmen considered them unnecessary at first, such is the love of mechanical ingenuity that it was not long before the demand grew and gunmakers experimented with similar automatic ejectors. Although these experimental ejectors developed side by side with the various hammerless actions they are for convenience being considered separately.

EJECTOR MECHANISMS

J. Needham of Birmingham was the first, in 1874, to apply the principle of self-extraction of the fired cartridges to double sporting guns. In his gun the extractor was divided into two halves, one for each barrel, and the force required for throwing out the empty cartridge cases was provided by the mainspring. The ejecting was achieved by an arm, projecting forward from one side of each tumbler, which was lifted by a hook on the rear lump, and before the tumbler was cocked, it slipped down on to a lower hook, hitting a small lever smartly on the way. The top end of this lever flicked out the ejector arm, causing the cartridge to be flung clear. The cocking was then completed as the cocking lever was pressed forward to its full extent.

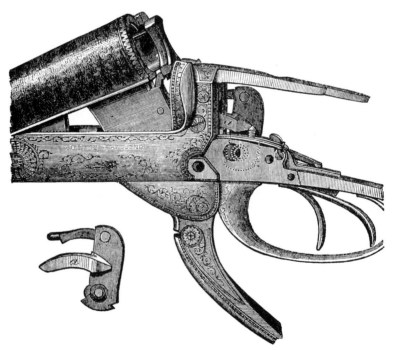

Figure 38. Needham's ejector gun.

If the cartridge was not fired the tumbler remained at full cock, so the arm that projected forward from it was out of contact with the lump as it raised, so only a fired cartridge was ejected. This was certainly a most ingenious invention, not least for its simplicity and economy of parts.

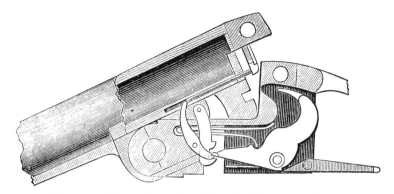

Figure 39. Greener's version of the Needham type ejector.

About 1881 W. W. Greener utilised the principle of Needham's ejector, when he combined it with his version of the Anson and Deeley action. This gun, with a top lever, had cleaner lines externally, and even further simplified and refined the parts involved, the extra arm on the tumbler being eliminated. On opening the gun the cocking arms of the tumblers were caught by the top hook of the swivel that hung from the forward lump. On the barrels being opened wider the tumbler arms slipped from the top hook on to the ejector lever, flipping out the cartridges, which had already been partially extracted in the normal way by the lever in the fore-end. The cocking arm was then caught by the lower hook on the swivel and raised to full cock by completing the opening of the gun. The rib extension provided a convenient slide for the top of the ejector arms.

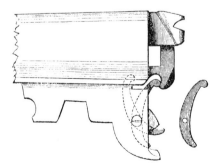

Figure 40. Action of the ejector in C. Lancaster's version of the Needham type ejector of 1879.

Charles Lancaster in 1879 also brought out an ejector gun which utilised Needham's ejector principle. In his version a top lever was used, and the work of cocking was done by the barrels. The ejectors worked by the slipping of the cocking arms onto the ejector levers. It differed from Greener's version in that the ejector levers were fitted into the rear lump and bore on the breech end of the extractor arms. As a safety measure this gun could not be closed until it had been fully opened and the tumblers cocked. This avoided the possibility of an accidental discharge should the barrels be snapped up before the tumblers were fully cocked, allowing them to fall with sufficient force to fire a cartridge. This gun did not have an automatic blocking safety and also had a rather unsightly projection in front of the trigger guard caused by the cocking hook extension to the rear lump.

The Holland and Holland 'Climax' gun was, about this time, also fitted with ejectors of the Needham type.

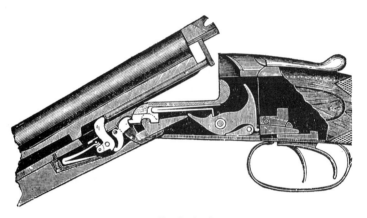

Figure 41. Deeley's ejector gun.

In the preceding ejectors the force was supplied by the mainspring fulfilling a dual function. However, the type of ejector mechanism set independently in the fore-end was eventually to be the most widely adopted. The first of this type was patented in 1878 by Mr Perkes, a London gunmaker, whose rather crude mechanism had little to commend it. The extractor was in one piece unlike a normal ejector, so that in order to prevent the ejection of an unfired cartridge, stops were provided which projected above the standing breech. If the tumbler had fallen this was automatically withdrawn and the cartridge thrown clear. If on the other hand the tumbler had not fallen the stop remained up and prevented the unfired cartridge from being ejected.

The Deeley ejector mechanism patented in 1886 was altogether a more satisfactory form of fore-end ejector. In this ejector, unlike Perkes', the mechanism was duplicated so that the ejector only functioned when a cartridge had been fired. The actual mechanism contained in the fore-end was basically similar, though smaller in scale, to that concerned with firing the cartridge. It also had a tumbler, the head of which acted as a hammer on the rear of the ejector arm, a mainspring, a sear and a sear spring. When the firing tumbler had fallen its mainspring moved forward, and this movement was utilised to move forward the ejector 'trigger' to the point where it engaged the ejector sear. On the gun being opened to the point where the cartridge cleared the standing breech, the tumbler was freed from its sear and fell sharply upon its ejector arm. The ejector tumbler was cocked again by the ejector arm bearing against the standing breech as the gun closed.

There were a number of variations of the separate mechanism type of ejector in which some sort of rod conveyed the fall of the main tumbler to the ejector. Truelock's ejector mechanism patented in 1890 had such a rod which was pushed forward by the fall of the tumbler until it engaged the sear of the ejector lock.

Baker of Birmingham used this rod connection to move forward with the tumbler and trigger off the ejector but also, by an alternative arrangement, the rod was pressed forward by the raising of the tumbler, on opening the gun. The actual ejector mechanism, which had spiral springs, was set in the fore-end in such a way that it pivoted up and down. On the gun being opened, the rod which had been thrust forward by the tumbler, engaged the ejector mechanism and raised it upwards on the pivot to the point where the ejector tumblers were put out of their bents, and performed the task of ejection.

In Ross's ejector mechanism of 1891 the connecting rod between the tumbler of the side lock and fore-end served both as an ejector trigger and also to cock the tumbler.

Maleham's ejector mechanism of 1891 was arranged to avoid the cocking of the ejectors by the normal method of forcing them home by pressure against the standing breech on closing the gun. In Maleham's system the ejectors were cocked as the gun was opened just prior to being triggered off as the opening was continued.

In Harrison's ejector the extractor arms were directly acted upon by spiral springs. On opening the fired gun an arm first engaged a slot in the cocked ejector arm, and held it until the right moment, when it tilted down, slipped out of the slot and allowed the ejector arm to do its work.

The mechanism produced by Perkes in 1892 was much more complex than his earlier system. The ejector springs were compressed as the gun opened by the novel means of raising the spring at its bend. When opened sufficiently, the continued movement upwards displaced a sear from its notch in the extractor arm allowing the tumbler to act on the end of the extractor arm and eject the cartridge. This arrangement had the advantage that the ejector spring was only compressed when required to do its work.

In Holland's ejector patented in 1893 the cocking arm was utilised to operate the ejector mechanism, reducing the working parts of the ejector to two. F. Beesley patented an ejector using only two parts, a spring and a striker.

The Purdey ejector mechanism of the early 1890s was triggered by rods that had a sideways action on the ejector sears. The ejector tumblers which were set close to the hinge bolt were operated by powerful V springs which were cocked by the ejector arms bearing against the standing breech when the gun was closed. A particular feature of the Purdey gun was the wide opening and the fact that the unfired cartridge was drawn well out by the extractor; this enabled unfired cartridges to be taken out with ease. A constant necessity in the interests of safety during a day's shooting, this need for withdrawing unfired cartridges by hand was not appreciated by some of the early designers of ejectors. This type of ejector was also fitted to the hammer ejector guns built by Purdey in the 1890s, a difference being that the mechanism was larger and stronger when put into the hammer guns, there being more space available than was the case with the hammerless guns with their lock cocking mechanism.

By about 1895 ejectors were reliable and in general use, and the major gunmakers had by this time developed from the above pioneer mechanisms, ejectors which have for the most part, changed little in all essentials since that time. It is interesting to hear a contemporary view on ejectors given by Payne-Gallwey in his book, *Letters to Young Shooters*, 1890:

'EJECTOR GUNS

'These are hammerless guns fitted with extractors, which, by means of springs, jerk out the exploded cartridges. Here we have the last improvement in guns, and one that is not yet perfected.

'Every gunmaker has, of course, his own simply infallible ejector, and, according to him, the only one in the trade that really works properly. It is not, however what a picked gun in a shop will do in the hands of its inventor; it will there jerk out the cartridges with force enough to put your eye out or break the windows. What one requires to know is, what the gun will do in the field with hard usage. I write 'hard usage' advisedly, for a gun must stand that or nothing, as we do not want guns that require extra care or moderate use.

They must all be—to use a school phrase—as 'hard as nails', and fit for anything. There are only a few really reliable ejectors in the market at present, and which do their work in a manner that defies criticism; and I consider the best are those of Mr Purdey, Mr Holland, Mr Greener, Messrs Westley-Richards (Deeley's patent), Mr Lancaster, Mr Woodward, Mr Grant, Mr Boss, Messrs Cogswell & Harrison, Messrs Rigby, and last, certainly not least in its excellence, Mr Maleham's.

'That ejectors are the guns of the future there is not the slightest doubt; for a shooter is quite as ready to appreciate and patronise a decided convenience as anyone else. If a shooter can afford £40 to £45, by all means let him purchase an ejector, as for this price he should be able to get a good one. I do not believe a less sum could purchase one such as I should care to recommend; for 'ejectors' are still in their infancy, as far as the trade of gunmaking generally is concerned, or they would be sold at a more moderate sum than is now the case.

'A well-made ejector—one that works smoothly, and does not require more leverage to cock it than an ordinary hammerless— can, without doubt, be loaded and fired with great rapidity; so fast, indeed, that a dozen shots in quick succession out of each barrel would make the gun too hot to hold.

'The great advantage of an ejector is, that a man who uses but one gun can, if occasion demand, shoot nearly as fast as if he had two guns and a loader. This, of course, means bagging more game. And it is no very difficult feat for a shooter armed with an ejector to drop three partridges, one by one, out of a covey rising near him—so quickly can he reload.

'But an ejector needs be very perfect in every detail; and it is no advantage that it can be used as an ordinary gun should its ejecting mechanism fail—an alternative sometimes described by its inventor as a recommendation. If we give an extra price for an ejector, we expect it to act as one, and not as an ordinary hammerless; and a statement of this kind implies a want of faith on the part of the maker of the gun, in regard to its reliability.

'Most ejectors, however well they eject, have one decided dis- advantage; and that is, they do not withdraw unfired cases far enough for the shooter conveniently to unload with cold fingers, or to enable him to extract a case which is at all tight. Many ejectors do not draw back a loaded case more than a sixteenth to an eighth of an inch, which gives a very small edge for the fingers to grasp, particularly if the barrels have dolls'-heads, or other unsightly pro- jections to take up space, and shut out the base of the cartridge from the fingers when it is wished to withdraw the former. The extractors of an ejector should project, when the gun is opened in an unfired state, a full quarter of an inch. Messrs Purdey's ejectors are particularly good in this respect.

'When about to purchase an ejector, be careful to ascertain that, if the barrels compress the mainsprings on opening, the locks are cocked before the cartridges are ejected. Open the gun very slowly, and you will hear the locks cock by the clicking sound they give, either before or after the cartridges are jerked out, as the case may be. This is important in an ejector, as the fact of the cartridges being ejected gives, especially to an assistant, the idea that the gun may be closed, and is ready for use.

'For this reason I prefer an ejector that cocks as the barrels are closed, after the cases are ejected; there can then be no possible doubt about the gun being ready for firing. Perhaps the best ejector of all is the one that half-cocks its locks on opening the breech, and full-cocks them on closing it. The gun that does this divides its work very evenly, and is pleasant in use, as no particular exercise of strength is required to charge it; and it can certainly be fired and reloaded faster than can a gun that compresses its springs in the one motion of either opening or closing.'

SINGLE-TRIGGER MECHANISMS

It might be thought that with the hammerless ejector actions for the most part perfected, both gunmakers and sportsmen would rest content. However the restless energy which had achieved so much in so few years was again harnessed to finding an ideal single-trigger mechanism. As with ejectors there were those who thought single-triggers an unnecessary further complication, but when once a demand had been created, all the leading gunmakers found it necessary to have their own solution to offer.

The idea of a single-trigger to serve two locks was not a new one, but when applied to shot guns it was necessary to preserve the directness and ease of pull of double triggers, and at the same time to guard against the sort of involuntary pull that could result in a double discharge. One of the difficulties facing the designer of a single-trigger mechanism was the considerable variation in the ways sportsmen had of pulling the trigger.

One of the most successful of the early single-trigger mechanisms was that designed by John Robertson, the proprietor of Boss & Co. He discovered that the double discharge which tended to take place with single-trigger mechanisms was due to the involuntary contraction of the muscles of the hand including the trigger finger when the grip was shifted by the recoil of the first barrel. First the trigger was released, and then a second pressure was applied to the trigger as the hand quickly re-gripped the recoiling gun. It was necessary, to prevent any chance of a double discharge, to delay the connection with the sear of the second barrel until after the second and involuntary pull had taken place. Robertson's single-trigger mechanism was designed to prevent the accidental discharge of the second barrel. The means used was that of a vertical drum containing a coil spring. On the first pull of the trigger a stop on the drum arrested the trigger blade until it was released by the second, involuntary pull. On this second pull the trigger blade lifted over the stop and moved across to engage the other sear. A similar sort of single-trigger mechanism was applied to Boss's three barrelled gun. Also Boss later brought out a selective single-trigger mechanism in which the right-left, or left-right sequence was governed by a slide set on the right hand lock plate just above the trigger.

A number of other mechanisms were brought out in the 1890s designed to allow for the second or involuntary pull. That of Frederick Beesley had a fan-shaped piece with two recesses with serrations between, which was designed to spring forward as the first pull released a key from the front recess. The fan piece engaged the involuntary second pull, and then moved forward to the second recess, placing the trigger blade in position under the sear ready for the second true pull of the trigger. This mechanism depended on a careful balance between the speed of the explosion and the strength of the spring which operated the fan-shaped piece.

The Jones-Baker system worked on the same principle of an intermediate stop to account for the involuntary pull but the mechanism was more complicated.

In the Lancaster mechanism patented by H. A. A. Thorn, the proprietor of that firm, the trigger blade switched from right to left but was arrested half way by a stop to the rear. The sprung trigger blade was released to swing under this stop, by the involuntary pull following the first discharge, and then moved under the second sear (plate 63).

The single-trigger of Boss and also Purdey relied upon the involuntary pull, to place the trigger blade in position for the second barrel; but the Holland and

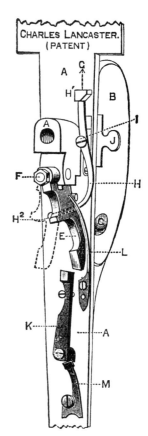

Figure 42. Charles Lancaster's single trigger mechanism.

Holland system depended upon a time lag caused by the moving forward of a slide by means of a spring to the second sear position. On the first pull of the trigger this slide was carefully timed to move forward slowly enough to take in the involuntary pull, and fast enough to cause no apparent delay in firing the second barrel.

After the appearance of the first of these new single-trigger mechanisms around 1894, some thirty or more were patented within a few years. From these evolved, through practical usage in the field, the few reliable mechanisms which have stood the test of time and are still used.

The main advantages of the single-trigger were that the shooter need not move his grip between the first and second barrels, thereby enabling aimed shots to be taken slightly more quickly on average. There was less likelihood of bruised fingers on the fore trigger or rear of the guard, and there was a larger space in the trigger guard for large or gloved fingers. It was thought that a novice could more readily shoot with a single-trigger than adapt to the use of a double.

The single-trigger was at its best in a game gun bored equally in both barrels or in a trap pigeon shooting gun firing the more open barrel first as a matter of course. In a general game gun with one barrel open and one choked to some degree it was no particular advantage to have a single-trigger if the selector must be moved to left first or vice versa before the shot could be aimed. When only the shortest time was available to select the appropriate barrel the normal double trigger was the more direct.

CONCLUDING REMARKS

By 1900 the guns built were in all essentials modern game guns. Only in minor respects, such as in a fashion for rather shorter barrels, has there been any change. It is certainly remarkable that, in spite of all the technological changes that have taken place since, a man may take the field today with a gun built in 1900, and know that his gun is neither inferior to nor easily distinguishable from guns built recently.

The first fifty years of the development of the breech-loader had been marked by a surge of extraordinary inventiveness and industry. Numerous gunmakers of the highest calibre were ever on hand to tackle and overcome a succession of problems, and there can be no higher tribute to their skill and ingenuity than the fact that much of their work stands unbettered today.

CHAPTER SEVEN

Shooting 1860 to 1900

The breech-loading era up to 1900 was a tremendous time for quantity, quality and variety of shooting. When the early breech loaders appeared there was a considerable period of trial and experiment before they were generally adopted. However in the 1860s reliable centre-fire hammer guns became available and, because of the ease and safety with which they could be loaded, large scale shooting became both more practical and pleasant.

The provision of a suitable gun for the job coincided with a time when the trend towards the extensive rearing and preserving of game was well under way and when driving as a means of putting the birds to the 'guns' was increasingly the popular method. On their return from the Crimean War sportsmen set to work with renewed energy to improve their estates by increased rearing, particularly of pheasants, improving or planting coverts, stricter vermin control and generally better game conservation. In addition to providing the birds, much greater thought and organisation was directed towards the best methods of driving the birds to the guns, to give the most sporting shots. On large estates drives were carefully planned with the precision of a military exercise. Large numbers of beaters in white smocks and carrying white flags were marshalled into orderly ranks by the keepers, stops were stationed in position and the 'guns' were carefully placed, sometimes in depth, to receive the birds. The 'guns' themselves were supported by loaders, retrievers and pickers-up. The general plans were designed to work the birds round an estate, making use of the natural features to show the birds well.

In the earlier years of the century by far the largest bag was made up of partridges, but by the 1860s pheasants formed the largest part. It is revealing to compare the bags of Colonel Hawker, Lord Malmesbury on whose estates more than average numbers of pheasants were raised for that time, and the Marquess of Ripon

Figure 43. Driven grouse: the approaching direct shot. From *The Art of Shooting* by C. Lancaster.

(then known as Lord de Grey). The numbers bagged are not comparable because Lord Ripon shot over many of the greatest estates in this country and the continent while Hawker and Lord Malmsbury shot only over their own estates and perhaps one or two of their neighbours'. The proportion however of partridges to pheasants clearly shows the trend towards the vastly increased rearing of pheasants. Colonel Hawker, between 1802 and 1853, shot 7,035 partridge to 575 pheasants, Lord Malmesbury, between 1798 and 1840, shot 10,744 partridges to 6,320 pheasants, while Lord Ripon, between 1867 and 1895, shot 89,401 partridges and 111,190 pheasants. So far as grouse were concerned the contrast is dramatic, for Lord Malmesbury shot none, Colonel Hawker shot 16 and Lord Ripon had shot 47,468 by 1895. The increase in the numbers of grouse shot was due partly to better management of the grouse moors both in Yorkshire and Scotland, helped by a more thorough knowledge of the birds' habits, burning the heather to provide new growth for food and more keepers to keep down predators and poaching. On the more important grouse moors well organised driving largely took the place of walking up with pointers and setters, but the old method still had a place where birds were scattered in very rough terrain.

Sportsmen of the old school had, as an ideal, prided themselves on killing a bird with every shot or at least keeping the average within reasonable proportions. When shooters were able to have large numbers of grouse, partridges and pheasants driven towards them, the emphasis was placed on the size of bag that could be amassed, and to this end speed of shooting and the taking of all possible chances was a necessity. The average suffered but the bag was vastly increased.

The speed and variety of shots taken, and not least the stamina and concentration required, brought forth exponents of the art who, from the grouse in August to the cocks in January, were invited to shoot on the finest estates throughout the length and breadth of the land. Such was the obsession of some land owners to acquire the status of record bags, that these 'star' performers were preferred to the locals who had previously had the pleasure of the shooting. Those who were invited to shoot on continental estates, where enormous bags were made, felt it incumbent upon themselves to provide similar sport in return. Where foreign royalty and nobility were to be entertained, Britain at the summit of her power and influence, was obliged to put on shooting parties in the grand manner. Those sportsmen who enjoyed shooting for its own sake, the field craft, the intimate knowledge of the game, the pleasure of working their dogs and the vigorous exercise which was all part of the day's sport, regretted the fashionable trend towards large-scale shooting parties. The splendour of fashionable shooting parties at great houses increased as the reign of Queen Victoria drew towards its end. These parties were usually of three to four days' duration and the ability to overcome the temptations of high living and start the morning with a clear head, was most necessary if a hammering by the gun-fire was to be avoided.

The following was the sort of routine at shooting parties attended by The Prince (later Edward VII) and Princess of Wales. Breakfast was served at 9.30 in the dining-room, the ladies wearing elegant costumes of silk or velvet to see the men off. The ladies changed into tweeds to join the men for luncheon in a tent or suitable lodge, the food being carried out in containers and served by a full retinue of servants. After luncheon the ladies would usually watch a few drives and then return to change into an afternoon gown in time for tea. Then the returning sportsmen and the ladies dressed for dinner, the women in brocade or satin with a full complement of jewels. As it was not the done thing to appear in the same costume twice in one visit, the expense was considerable and no doubt tempered the pleasure of some fashionable sportsman at being invited; however, the enjoyment of so many new costumes must have helped to keep their wives happy.

This going off to see the men shoot after lunch was not without its hazards, for it is recorded that a certain lady received a shot pheasant that came plummeting down, square upon the head, completely stunning her, and she did not in fact fully recover for some weeks. King Edward had a narrow escape, when shooting from a Bath chair because of some leg injury. Lord Ripon killed a high pheasant which seemed destined for the royal head, but just missing, burst on impact upon the arm of the chair.

There were many first-class and widely experienced shots who attended such shooting parties, but of course there were also those who shot because it was the fashionable thing to do, and some young men coming directly to shooting driven birds tended to think only in terms of marksmanship and the size of bag. This new generation, who had grown up with driving, had not worked for their game in the old style, like Lord Malmesbury for instance, who walked a mile for every head of game he bagged. Lord Ripon reflecting years later upon the changes in shooting wrote:

'With these improvements came an increase of luxury in the conditions of shooting, and sometimes when I am sitting in a tent taking part in a lengthy luncheon of many courses, served by a host of retainers, my memory carries back to a time many years ago when we worked harder for our sport, and when seated under a hedge, our mid-day meal consisted of a sandwich, cut by ourselves at the breakfast table in the morning, which we washed down by a pull from a flask; and I am inclined to think those were better and healthier days. Certainly the young men were keener sportsmen.'

There was a great deal of correspondence in the sporting press on the subject of driving game versus the traditional methods, and good arguments were put forward, often with some heat, by the supporters of one or the other. There was however a place for well-managed and sporting driving for the sort of shots who could cope with it, and there was a place for the traditional methods for those who preferred them. But where bad driving produced a slaughter of unsporting birds, or unskilled shooters plastered or wounded birds in all directions, or greedy or dangerous shots spoiled the day for others, then there was little to justify such shooting. Traditional methods of shooting could be as unsporting if birds, especially immature birds early in the season, were found by dogs and then plastered at close range. Most sportsmen are to some extent bag conscious, though within widely differing limits; but the stimulus of breech-loading guns combined with large numbers of birds certainly caused some to take the pursuit of record bags to extraordinary lengths. Particularly in the last quarter of the 19th century, deliberate attempts were made to achieve record bags of a magnitude such as is not likely to be equalled again. This is just as well, for deliberate attempts at records usually result in circumstances and attitudes that are not in the best interest of the sport. In the period under discussion picked shots and conditions were necessary to many of these shooting marathons, and while we can admire the skill and endurance of the performers it can be appreciated that too much concentration on numbers of game killed could lead to a wrong emphasis.

These record bags are a part of shooting history and a selection will serve to show what was done. Lord de Grey's personal bag 1867–95 totalled 316,699, of this total 47,468 were grouse, 89,401 partridges and 111,190 pheasants. The best year was 1893 with a total of 19,135 head. Lord de Grey killed 240 partridges in one drive in 1893 on Baron de Hirsch's estate in Hungary. Lord Walsingham on 30 August 1888 shooting alone killed 1,070 grouse with 1,510 cartridges. The Maharajah Dhuleep Singh shot 780 partridges at

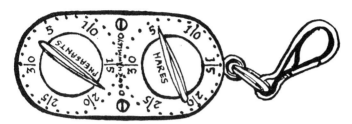

Figure 44. Game counter in various metals, iron for pheasants, nickel for hares, brass for rabbits and copper for partridges, on brass and nickel plates, by G. & J. W. Hawksley (c.1880).

Elvedon on 8 September 1876. Sir Frederick Milbank killed 728 grouse in 8 drives at Wemmergill in 1872, killing 190 in one drive. Mr Rimington Wilson's party of nine killed 2,648 grouse on the Broomhead moors on 20th August 1893. Lord Ashburton's party of six guns killed 1,458 partridges at The Grange, Hampshire, on 4 November 1897. On the St Johan estate in Hungary, between 6 October and 7 November 1893 26,605 partridges were brought in. The best day was 2,983, killed on 11 October by a picked team of seven guns: Earl de Grey, Lord Ashburton, Lord Chelsea, B. H. Vane-Tempest, Henry Chaplin, Seymour Finch and their host Baron de Hirsch.

Contemporary opinion is pretty unanimous regarding the great shots of the period. Earl de Grey, later the Marquess of Ripon (plate 58) is generally placed at the top of the list. Certainly he kept up a consistently high standard of performance over many years. His total bag from 1867 to 1923, when he dropped dead in the heather when out grouse shooting, was 556,000 head. He was particularly well known for the stylish way he dealt with the highest of high pheasants, for his continued use of 30-in. barrelled hammer guns, and for sticking to his favourite No 2 Black powder as late as 1894 when he was finally persuaded to use the improved Schultze powder. Lord Ripon had his hammer guns handed to him at full cock and this aided him in getting off his shots with extreme rapidity.

Lord Walsingham, 1843–1919, who before he succeeded was The Hon. Thomas de Grey, was considered by Lord Ripon to be the quickest and most accurate shot he had seen. Lord Walsingham not only favoured hammer guns, and continued to use them after hammerless guns came in, but he also preferred Damascus barrels and cylinder ones at that. The bags obtained by him speak well for the game shooting qualities of good cylinder barrels. Lord Walsingham contributed quite a lot of writing about shooting, especially notable being his contributions to the Badminton Library *Shooting*, 1887.

Sir Harry Stonor was a very fine game shot notable for his graceful style of shooting; Lord Huntingfield of Heveringham in Norfolk was a great performer at partridges; the Maharajah Duleep Singh was a fine shot and his estate at Elveden in Suffolk saw many picked shooting parties.

Others frequently referred to as excellent shots by their contemporaries are Lord Lovat, Lord Rendlesham, Mr Rimington-Wilson, Mr Heatley Noble, Sir Frederick Milbank, and the sporting artist A. J. Stuart-Wortley who illustrated several shooting books and painted the striking portrait of James Purdey the younger that hangs in Purdey's Long Room. The Duke of York, later King George V, was considered to be one of the finest of game shots; he also used Purdey hammer ejector guns and had a particular liking for high pheasants.

WILDFOWLING

Wildfowling was followed as a sport with enthusiasm by many who had perhaps read the great Colonel Hawker's book. More study was made of the habits of wildfowl and a great deal of knowledge added. There were guns for every type of wildfowling from 12 bore guns designed for heavy loads to double 8 bores and single 4 bores. For those who wished to try the big gun of the professional wildfowler there were single and double breech-loading punt guns; some fine ones were built by Holland & Holland.

In his concluding remarks on wildfowl shooting in the Badminton Library series, Sir R. Payne-Gallwey gives a summary of the situation in the 1880s in the British Isles:

'The estuaries on the coast of the British Islands where punting is chiefly carried on are as follows:

'In Scotland, Dornoch Firth, and Beauly Firth are about the best, and in hard winters fowl are killed by punters on the Tay and Firth of Forth, but the latter are never such good places as the former. In Scotland punting is not nearly so systematically undertaken by amateurs as it is in England and Ireland, yet a few gunners of our acquaintance do extremely well with their big guns on both the east and west coasts of Scotland.

'In England punting is in vogue on all parts of the coast, from

Berwick round to Carlisle. In the Humber punting is always going on. On the shores of the Wash punt gunners abound, and, what is more, venture afloat in the narrowest and most unsteady of all the crafts used in the pursuit of fowl, whether at home or abroad. The Lynn punts are, however, very fast, and in safe waters most successful. They are from 17 to 18 ft long, and only 20 to 23 in. broad across

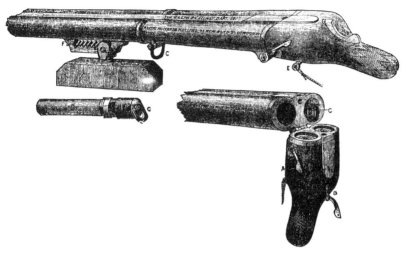

Figure 45. Double swivel punt gun by Holland & Holland showing breech end and action: bore 1½ in., weight 200 lbs, length 9 ft. 6 in.; to fire about 1 lb of shot in each barrel. Both barrels could be shot together to give broad pattern.

the floor; across the deck they are from about 2 ft 6 in. to 2 ft 8 in. The Lynn gunners declare that no other punts can compare with these narrow and dangerous floating planks of theirs. But that is always the way—our own things are always superior to those of others. Anyhow, they kill fowl in them well enough when they get the chance, which is the main point. Yarmouth is the next abode of big gunners, who are always on the watch for birds at sea as well as for rare specimens on the adjacent Norfolk Broads.

'Then we have Lowestoft and Harwich, and so on to the Essex coast, and that very home of punters, the Blackwater estuary.

'There is but little shooting at the mouth of the Thames or on the north coast of Kent, nor is there any gunning to speak of till Southampton Water is reached. But the Solent is full of punters, especially about Lymington and other parts of the Hampshire coast that lie opposite the Isle of Wight.

'There are no finer feeding grounds in our islands than the flats that fringe for miles the north bank of the Solent, but gunners are numerous, and the fowl have but few chances of feeding and resting in peace. Yet in severe winters, when ice and snow prevail and east winds are in force, the Solent is full of fowl, though they soon become so wary from constant persecution by sailing-boats, steamboats, and every other kind of craft, that the fowlers have not a fair chance of making good bags. It is not as if the use of sailing-boats and steamers brought sport to their owners, for they never did and never will. They are merely 'bird frighteners' of the most unsportsman-like and selfish kind, and their owners may be seen reclining at ease in the bow or stern, firing bullets at the geese or ducks, shooting shot at impossible ranges, and bringing aboard nothing in the shape of feather. Meanwhile the poor fowlers, whose living in the winter depends upon their being able to shoot a few fowl now and then, are woefully disappointed; for the birds, getting no rest from these idle, useless, sport-spoiling persons, leave the locality soon after their arrival for less persecuted spots. If a fowler be a rich amateur and desire to shoot fowl, he should set about it in a proper way. If he only wants to frighten the birds for the sake of obtaining two or three a day, he had better remain at home, and keep away his puffing, sport-destroying steam launch, which all honest fowlers would wish to occupy a berth at the bottom of the sea.

'Poole Harbour is the next gunning station west of the Solent (as Christchurch Bay is given over to shore shooters). This fine estuary is from six to seven miles square, and was formerly one of the best grounds for wildfowl in the kingdom. Now it is overrun with professional punt gunners; a glance at the rows of punts to be seen there on the beach about Christmas easily accounts for the wildness and scarcity of the birds, and the lack of sport now compared to what it was in days gone by.

'After Poole, and continuing our tour round the coast towards the west, we reach Weymouth, which is not a good punting neigh-bourhood, as the fowl take shelter in the famous decoy close at hand.

'The Exe is also unfavourable for gunning, the birds being very wild and scarce.

'Falmouth Harbour is too noisy, from the amount of shipping, to hold fowl, and all round the coast of Cornwall and the north of Devon and Somerset the shores are rocky and unsheltered, and there are no good feeding grounds to attract and keep birds.

'In the Bristol Channel we have seen large numbers of widgeon, but this may be called the open sea, and it is useless for wildfowl shooting.

'In Milford Haven we have also seen good numbers of widgeon, and there are a couple of fowlers there who now and then do well.

'We have tried Holyhead for gunning, and though we have seen fine shots thereabouts, for a swivel-gun, they were invariably in open and dangerous waters. There are two or three punters who shoot round Holyhead Island and off the west coast of Anglesea.

'The estuary of the Dee, though apparently a first-rate ground for punting, abounds in sandbanks and lacks the green weed necessary to attract wildfowl. It is natural that where food is not to be had birds are not to be found. Punters, therefore, are not partial to the Dee—at least, we know of only a couple who shoot there.

'The Mersey is still less adapted for fowling, being wide, unsheltered, and crowded with shipping. We have seen a few fowl round the coast from the mouth of the Mersey to Whitehaven, in Cumberland, but only in hard winters are they ever fairly numerous. Twenty-five years ago a friend of ours killed forty widgeon at a shot at the mouth of the Ribble; ten would be considered good now. This coast, however, could never have boasted one-tenth of the fowl that were to be seen on the eastern shore of England. It is not suited to them, as it is chiefly hard sand; there is but poor feeding for the birds, and it is the wrong side of England for migratory fowl to drop in.

'The chief punting stations in Ireland are Belfast Lough, Strangford Lough, Dublin Bay, Wexford Harbour, Cork Harbour, Dingle and Tralee Bays, the Shannon (on which there are about a dozen double-handed punters), Galway Bay, Killala and Sligo Bays, as well as Lough Swilly and Lough Foyle.

'We have shot (with one or two exceptions) on all the waters we have named, and had grand sport on some of them; but, alas! fowl are getting scarcer and gunners more numerous every year, and we fear that a bag of over 1,500 duck and geese, besides plover, etc., in a season will not be our lot again in the British Islands, as it was in the hard winter of 1880–81.

'A heavy shot at fowl is becoming a rare chance now on our shores, and is only achieved in very severe weather. Some ten years ago, off the mouth of the Blackwater, in Essex, a wonderful shot was made at brent geese. A vast herd of these birds had collected on the ooze to feed. All the local punt gunners, to the number of a dozen, were attracted by the sight, and setting together to the geese just as they were densely packed on the last bit of feeding ground left by the rising tide, aimed and fired by signal. The result was that the gunners picked up close on 300 fowl. This incident was recorded in various sporting papers at the time, and was related to us by a gentleman who had actually seen the occurrence.

'Within the past ten years we have known of several shots that realised from forty to fifty widgeon on the east coast of Scotland, but such luck has not been had on any part of the English coast as far as we can learn for many years. A gunner of our acquaintance in 1881 killed thirty-seven widgeon at a shot in the Solent by night, and two or three times from fifteen to twenty brent at a shot by day the same year.

'In Ireland we have many times killed fifty to sixty widgeon at a shot, and now and then from sixty to seventy. Our friend Mr Vincent has on several occasions bagged eighty widgeon at a shot—once ninety-six—and, again, 105 teal (the latter a flying shot) off the coast of Ireland. We have known of forty-seven grey geese to be bagged at one shot in Ireland, and several times between thirty-five and forty-five brent. Colonel Hawker speaks of having once obtained nearly a hundred brent at a shot from his double swivel-gun in the Solent, after one discharge of both barrels at the same time, and we have several times quite lately, both at home and abroad, set up in our punt to packs of widgeon and brent geese of which, could we have got in fair range of them, we should have bagged fully a hundred at a single shot.

'Daniel, in his "Rural Sports" (written at the beginning of this century), mentions that he knew a punter of the name of Bowles, who cleared £100 in a season's shooting. The birds were sold to the dealers at 2s a couple, one with another, which, allowing £30 for current expenses, would represent 2,600 wildfowl brought to bag in some five months' shooting.

'The heaviest shot which we can personally vouch for at widgeon brought down 127, which was the number picked up with a gun firing only twenty ounces of shot.'

From Peter Hawker onwards a number of keen amateurs had written with much eloquence of the delights of wildfowling, but the regular enthusiasts and the professionals grumbled with some reason at the rush to the marshes of the 'bang at everything boys' whenever some new wildfowling extravaganza appeared in print. Perhaps the effect of these literary sallies would have been less if, instead of describing the few 'big days', more had been made of the usual blank days of bitter cold or wet, when wearied from slogging through the gripping ooze, the wildfowler returned with no bag happily heavy with duck or goose to lighten his tread, and only the clinging slime to weigh him down. If he was a true wildfowler, however, the hopeful vision soon returned and when the 'big day' did come at last, the knowing ones did not boast about it—certainly not in print.

PIGEON SHOOTING

Towards the end of the 19th century there was an increased awareness of the potentiality of the wild pigeon as a sporting bird worthy of the attention of the finest game shots. So far as the rock pigeon was concerned the method used was the sometimes perilous procedure of picking them off from a bobbing boat as they darted from the sea cliffs.

It was the widely spread woodpigeon with which they were mainly concerned. In the ordinary way the pigeon rarely offered a shot at moderate range, and when it did it was liable to swerve as the gun was raised. Perhaps for these reasons, it was either often missed when fired at, or neglected for more manageable targets.

Lord Walsingham records bags of from about 70 to about 120 in the 1870s and 80s, obtained mostly in woods, and sometimes aided by wind or snow, but also in the harvest fields. It was however to Lord Walsingham's cousin, Sir Ralph Payne-Gallwey that much credit is due for his painstaking study of various guileful means of bringing the wily woodpigeon to the gun, and for publicising his methods in *Instructions to Young Shooters*. It was the skilful use of decoys that really swung the balance in favour of the shooter. The decoys were either stuffed or imitation birds and were used on the ground, or very effectively on the tops of trees, pushed up on the end of long rods. Though using decoys was a great help, good shooting at pigeons was also a matter of waiting for suitable conditions aided by an intimate knowledge of the birds' habits. With all the aids and conditions apparently right woodpigeon shooting was notoriously uncertain, but when all came off at last there was such shooting as could hardly be bettered.

PIGEON SHOOTING FROM TRAPS

Pigeon shooting, which had reached its height of popularity in the second half of the 19th century, had already begun to decline by the end of that century. The early days at such gun clubs as the 'Old Hats', the 'Red House' and Hornsey Wood House had given place to regular and well run meetings at such clubs in the London area as 'The Gun Club', Notting Hill and the Hurlingham Gun Club. At these clubs the highest standards were enforced as to treatment of pigeons and rigid enforcement of the rules to ensure fair play.

These pigeon shooting clubs fulfilled something of the same function with regard to guns as Grand Prix motor racing does today where cars are concerned. Here the enthusiasts met to try their skill and also on hand were the leading gunmakers, and powder, shot and cartridge makers, to put their products to the test before potential customers and enjoy the wider publicity given to announcements of results in the sporting press. Notable amongst the gunmakers who were in constant attendance and considered by contemporary sportsmen to be especially knowledgeable on pigeon shooting were Boss, Grant and Purdey and towards the end of the century Churchill was very much to the fore. James Purdey was however one of the earliest in attendance, and one of the last to retire when pigeon shooting declined as a fashionable sport at the end of the century.

Figure 46. The Gun Club, Notting Hill.

This decline was in part because the Princess of Wales made it known that she no longer wished to be present at the meetings.

Pigeon shooters had been slow to adopt breech-loaders and it was not until centre-fire hammer guns and their cartridges became thoroughly reliable that they used these in preference to the muzzle-loaders. With the limitation of the size of bore to 12 and the shot load to 1¼ oz a fairly standard type of pigeon gun was developed. This gun was heavier than a game gun (later limited to 8 lb) and was stocked and ribbed to throw the centre of the shot pattern high of the point of aim. The greatest care was taken to ensure regularity and evenness of pattern and of course with the advent of choke boring in the '70s, the use of concentrators gave way to choke regulated barrels.

This was a time when smokeless powders were replacing the good old standard black powders, and the manufacturers of these new powders made full use of the publicity potential provided by the pigeon clubs. They did in fact go as far as commissioning 'crack' shots to use their powders, and saw to it that any favourable results were duly 'puffed' in the press or their advertisements.

A list of some of the best shots at the Hurlingham Club and the Gun Club was given by A. J. Stuart-Wortley, himself an excellent pigeon shot, in the Badminton Library *Shooting*. These shots were named as Lord Hill (plate 7), Lord de Grey, Captain Shelley, Mr Berkeley Lucy, Mr Dudley Ward, Mr Aubrey Patton, Mr H. J. Roberts and Lord de Clifford.

In the 1880s two professional pigeon shooters arrived from America each claiming to be champion of the world. The first of these, Captain Bogardus, brought a new type of dedicated professionalism to this 'sport' and at first swept all before him; however he was eventually held to a tie by Mr Dudley Ward, each killing 84 out of 100, and the shoot off was won easily by Mr Ward.

Dr Carver, who incidentally beat Bogardus in matches in America, also fairly swept all before him, but on 8 December 1882, when shooting at Hendon, for a stake of £500 a side, he was held to a tie by Mr Stuart-Wortley, each killing 83 out of 100.

In America the shooting of clay pigeons had attained considerable popularity, and there were reports of clays being broken in straight runs of up to 150 while 95 per cent of clays broken was not unusual.

In Britain the clay bird was mostly thought of as a practice target, and as such was destined to play a vital role in the shooting schools of the '80s and '90s. However, there were some early clubs formed, mention being made of the establishment of the Botley Clay Pigeon Club at Botley, Hampshire in 1884. This club used the then popular Ligowsky clay pigeon, which was a saucer-shaped target of baked clay thrown from a spring loaded trap. These were the first practical 'clays' and took the place of the numerous other targets, the most popular of which were glass balls filled with feathers. The true clay targets soon gave way to the 'Blue Rock', a target very similar to that now used, composed of tar and ash. These new targets thrown by English-made traps such as the 'Taunton' and the 'Swiftsure' were adopted by the Inanimate Bird Shooting Association. W. W. Greener wrote of the new sport: 'It seems probable that the sport will increase in popularity and become world wide.'

SHOOTING SCHOOLS

There are those who seem to leave their cradles with such an instinctive feeling for the handling of guns, that they would be hard put to recall any time when a gun did not seem a natural part of them. For those denied this good fortune by nature there was yet a chance, and indeed a hope of salvation, held out to them by the new shooting schools.

A number of leading gunmakers already had their own shooting grounds where they could test guns and let their customers try the fit of their new guns, but in the 1880s some began to offer courses of instruction to novices, and help to more experienced shots in simulating the birds that they found most difficult. The new 'clays' or tar 'Blue Rocks' made such a simulation of the flight of various game birds more feasible, and very much in demand at this time were 'high pheasants' thrown from a tower.

Mr W. P. Jones opened one of the first of the shooting schools within easy distance of the Birmingham gunmakers to whom it was also open for gun fitting purposes. Mr Watts supplied the answer to many shooters' problems at the London Sporting Park, while Mr Holland opened an extensive ground as a shooting school, named 'The Badminton' by permission of the Duke of Beaufort. This school provided amongst other novelties the flighting of clays over and through trees to simulate pheasants driven from a wood.

H. A. A. Thorn, proprietor of the firm of Charles Lancaster, claimed to be one of the first in the London area to use his shooting ground for instructional purposes. The celebrated Annie Oakley (Little Sure Shot) took instruction from Thorn when she visited England in 1887 with Buffalo Bill's Wild West Show. She was obviously pleased with the instruction she received at the clays, for she wrote:

'Since using your guns, and receiving a few lessons from you at your splendid private shooting grounds, my shooting in the field has so much improved that I now always make a good score, even at fast and difficult birds. With many thanks for the pains you have taken in making me such perfect fitting and fine shooting guns.'

Thorn early claimed to be able to see the shot and was thereby aided in his instruction. The idea of such a thing was quite novel then, although common enough now. An added claim to fame worthy of mention was his treatise on *The Art of Shooting* published in 1889. This book, illustrated with line drawings both pleasant and instructional, was, and still remains, one of the best of its kind. The period costume and the delightful advertisements now add to its charm but its shooting wisdom is as pertinent as ever.

Though most sportsmen agreed that shooting schools and clay birds were not the same as game shooting, there were few who sought instruction who did not benefit in some measure. Perhaps this benefit is best measured by the fact that shooting schools are still flourishing today.

CHARLES LANCASTER'S
IMPROVED
"EXPERT" TRAPS AND
"CLAY" PIGEONS

(Cheapest and Best).

SMOKELESS POWDER CARTRIDGES.

Specially adapted for "Clay" Bird Shooting, at greatly reduced prices.

1,000 sent CARRIAGE PAID in one consignment, by GOODS TRAIN, to any Station in Great Britain.

PRICE, **32/6** NET.

Complete with Pegs, Cord, Stand, etc., in Box.

"CLAY" PIGEONS.

Prices:

In Barrels of 500, **17/6** Net;

In Boxes of 100, **4/6** Net.

Carriage on Traps and Birds not prepaid.

Figure 47.

CHAPTER EIGHT

Breech-loading Game Rifles

THE breech-loading principle was not applied to game rifles as quickly as might have been expected considering the numerous advantages to be gained thereby. In fact they lagged considerably behind the adoption of breech-loading in shot guns. It should perhaps be noted at this point that the advantage of loading a bullet at the breech end had been appreciated early in the history of firearms, for it ensured a tight-fitting bullet undamaged by ramming from the muzzle. Examples of breech-loading matchlocks, wheellocks and flintlocks exist, and of these the 17th-century rifles with screw-off barrels and the 18th-century Ferguson rifles achieved considerable success.

In the pursuit of dangerous big game the advantage of a rifle that could be swiftly reloaded in the heat of the moment was such that life itself could depend on it. Also, as Lieutenant Rice reminds us in *Tiger Shooting in India* (1857), it was necessary then to carry, with the aid of bearers, a battery of at least three double rifles. These were thrown down when fired as the next loaded rifle was handed forward by the gun bearer. This situation had many disadvantages: it increased the number of men a sportsman had to engage and rely upon to be up with him when needed, there were three times as many rifles to be cleaned at the end of a hard day or unloaded and re-charged if caught in a tropical downpour, and as Lieutenant Rice found to his cost on one occasion the chance of locally employed gunbearers going off with expensive rifles. When shooting from horseback the breech-loading rifles were much easier to re-load and enabled some control of the horse to be exercised while doing so.

To explain delay in adopting breech-loading for game rifles it must be appreciated that in the 1850s some pinfire shot guns had breech actions which were scarcely able to stand up to the relatively small charges required, and as the tendency in big game rifles was

Figure 48. Single barrel 4 bore elephant gun of the type used in South Africa. This has the thin skin from the inside of the elephant's ear shrunk on round the lock, breech and grip to bind the gun together.

towards very powerful charges, it was considered that the muzzle-loader was best suited to such charges.

The famous hunter Frederick Courtney Selous, when he landed in South Africa in 1871, did in fact bring with him a double breech-loading deer rifle, which was unfortunately soon stolen from him, but he was to do his early elephant shooting with 4 bore muzzle-loaders. He bought two of these guns in South Africa for £6 each when he was some 600 miles north of the Cape, describing them as being smooth-bore duck guns of the commonest description weighing 12½ lb and taking a ball of 4 oz. They were made by Isaac Hollis of Birmingham. These guns were charged with a handful of common trade powder, about 20 drams, and he said that although he had since shot with very expensive large bore breech-loaders, charged with the best Curtis and Harvey powder, he had never used a rifle that drove better than did these common old muzzle-loaders. However he goes on to say that they kicked most frightfully and the punishment he received from these guns affected his nerves to such an extent that it had materially influenced his shooting since, and he was heartily sorry that he had had anything to do with them. However this may be, the fact remains that even such crude muzzle-loaders were still, in the 1870s, considered superior in striking energy to most of the breech-loaders then available. Selous in three seasons killed some 78 elephants with them, shooting on foot, often running after the herd loading as he ran. The harsh recoil of these elephant guns can be understood when it is realised that the weight of the charge was at least four times that of a 12 bore gun but the weight of the gun was only double. These 4 bore guns would have needed to weigh about 20 lb to absorb a reasonable proportion of the recoil.

For deer stalking, and for the shooting of moderate and large game where the accuracy of the rifle was needed, the two groove muzzle-loader was still popular, being made in the 1860s (plate 16) and used well into the 1870s. However a few pinfire rifles were made, mostly in the smaller bores, but when made in the larger bores moderate powder loads were generally used. The actions used included almost every variety already described in the case of shot guns.

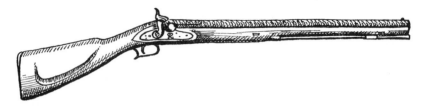

Figure 49. Single barrel 4 bore elephant rifle, showing cheek piece for left handed shot. Usually these were smooth bore. The lock is an old Tower musket lock.

A small number of sporting rifles were constructed on the percussion cap breech-loading principle, such as those of Prince, Calisher and Terry, Leetch and Westley Richards. Charles Lancaster produced double sporting rifles on the principle of his early centre-fire gun with drop-down barrels, previously described. The rifling was of his oval bore type, a popular size being ·498, with the twist 1 in 32 inches, the length of the barrels (plate 70).

Revolving rifles by Colt, Tranter (plate 23), Adams, Harding and Daw were tried out for sporting purposes but were found to lack both the power and accuracy of the muzzle-loaders; the gas escape was unpleasant so close to the face and they were not suitable for large bores. Lieutenant Rice, author of *Tiger Shooting* (1857) tried one out on a dead tiger and found that the penetration was such as would only enrage the beast, without doing more than superficial damage.

Mr Walsh writing in his book *The Shot-Gun and Sporting Rifle* (1859) gives his opinion that the two groove rifle fitted with the conical winged bullet was still the most satisfactory form of all-round sporting rifle. He adds however that for a double breech-loading rifle, he had seen nothing superior to the drop-down principle as applied to shot guns, and he considered that if well constructed very good shooting could be obtained with such rifles.

In the 1870s and 1880s centre-fire double barrelled sporting rifles were being constructed with small, medium and large bores, the barrels held down by the powerful under lever screw grip. As the bullet was now entered from the breech it could be made large enough to fill the bore completely. The deep two, three or four groove rifling of muzzle-loaders was no longer necessary or desirable, the tendency was therefore towards broad but shallow grooves and lands of approximately equal width. Big bore rifles designed for ball, or short conical lead bullets, needed rifling of greater depth and of a type that gave more grip.

For large and dangerous game in both India and Africa the most popular weapon was the double-barrelled 8 bore rifle, weighing about 15 lb, and firing the spherical ball or short conical bullet, propelled by 10 or 12 drams of powder (plate 68). A few 4 bore double-barrelled ball guns and rifles were made weighing about 20 lb (plate 69) and also some single-barrelled 4 bore ball guns and rifles (plates 72, 82). In some cases the 4 bore barrels were reduced in length to make these heavy rifles more manageable. They were mostly carried by a gunbearer as reserve armament, to be handed forward to stop the charge of a wounded elephant, rhino or buffalo at close range. Also when following up such a wounded beast in thick bush or tall grass the charge was often sudden and very close; there was no time for aiming at vital places and therefore it was essential to have a weapon that would deliver a tremendous shock, wherever it hit, sufficient to stop the most savage onslaught. In such circumstances a smaller bullet, except by a lucky chance, would fail to stop and could further enrage the beast. Lord de Grey once bagged two rhinos with a right and left from a 4 bore double rifle, when shooting from the back of an elephant in India, 1883.

So far as medium game was concerned the double 'Express' rifles in the larger bores were most popular. Such calibres as ·577, ·500 and ·450 were commonly used (plates 78, 79), while ·400 and ·360 were suited to buck and deer (plates 64, 65). Rifles of the same calibre could vary considerably in their power and effectiveness according to the weight and type of bullet and the black powder charge. Express rifles were designed to give a low trajectory so that between 50 and 150 yards there was little drop and a single sight could be taken for most shots. The rifles used cartridges with brass cases of varying degrees of length, taper or bottle shape and a variety of bullets, short or long, hard or soft lead, solid or hollow nosed. Sometimes the paper patch was retained on bullets intended for sporting use. It was of the greatest importance that the correct bullet with the appropriate powder charge be chosen for the type of animal hunted. Such bullets as were ideal for a stag would break up and fail to penetrate sufficiently the tough muscle and bone of a tiger, and completely fail on hard skinned animals.

The graceful lines, style and actions of these double rifles followed much the same pattern as the shot guns of the period. The rifles however, because of the need for extra strength, used for a longer period the powerful under lever screw grip in preference to snap actions, and the grip of the stock was usually finished in the form of a pistol grip. Sling mounts were fitted to the under side of the barrels and to the butt to take a sling if required. Back action locks were generally preferred as they did not require metal to be taken from the action body. Sometimes side clips were used; these were small projections on either side of the standing breech which bore on the bevelled sides of the breech ends of the barrels; the object being to reduce any tendency to side to side looseness. Black powder double rifles, at their finest, have the same attractive elegance as their contemporary hammer guns, representing in their day the best in sporting rifles that could be built.

In the early 1880s Damascus barrels began to give way to steel, which was better for rifling than the metal of alternate iron and steel. Steel also stood up much better to the heat and corrosion of some of the early nitro and cordite loads. Although nitro powders were increasingly used for rifles in the 1880s and 90s, black powder remained the most stable and reliable, especially in conditions where extremes of temperature were likely to be met with, from sub-zero lows to tropical highs.

Hammerless locks were introduced into double rifles from the 1880s, though sportsmen had mixed feelings about them. The main advantage for hammerless locks cited by some sportsmen was that they were safer when being carried behind by a native bearer. On the other hand the simplicity of hammerlocks enabled them to be maintained or repaired in distant parts of the world, they could be drawn back noiselessly when stalking game, while some safety catches could click; but perhaps most important, heavy load rifles had been known to double discharge, the recoil of the first barrel jarring off the second. In a hammer rifle the second hammer could be left uncocked until the first barrel was fired thus avoiding any possibility of a double discharge. Such a double discharge from a powerful rifle could be most unpleasant and the fear that it could happen again did not assist in taking a steady aim.

Apart from the double rifles of this period there were single shot rifles that were used for sporting purposes. The most popular and celebrated of these was built with the Farquharson falling block mechanism (patented in 1872) operated by the downward movement of an under lever. Notably these rifles were built by the celebrated Bristol gunmaker George Gibbs and were adapted from his famous match rifles. Linked with the name of George Gibbs was that of the man who has been described as 'the father of modern rifling', William Ellis Metford. The combination of the talents of these two men led to the production of rifles of unsurpassed excellence.

Writing to George Gibbs in the '90s, F. C. Selous gave his full permission to have his name used in advertising what he refers to as excellent rifles. He goes on to say that the Gibbs-Metford ·461 rifle was the only one used by him during his last twelve years of African travel.

Of the other single shot mechanisms, the Martini action operated by an under lever was the most popular. It had the disadvantage that, unlike the Farquharson, it could not be cleaned from the breech end.

Of the bolt action, magazine rifles used for sporting purposes, the Mauser was perhaps the most popular but also used were the Lee-Metford, Mannlicher and Mannlicher-Schönauer.

A class of rifle popular for use in Britain at this time, was that termed a 'Rook and Rabbit' rifle. Some very attractive rifles of this type were made with various actions including the screw breech needlefire (plate 75), the Martini, the top lever Purdey bolt with hammer side lock, and also they were made with hammerless actions (plate 83). A requirement of this rifle was great accuracy up to about 100 yards, and striking energy that was just sufficient for its needs, so that the bullet spent itself before doing unintentional damage a long way off. Calibres in general use included ·380, ·360, ·300, ·320 and ·250. Messrs Holland and Holland and Rigby were particularly noted for fine rook rifles and they were among the first to introduce a top lever hammerless type.

The ball gun that had done much useful work for big game hunters was now largely replaced by the ball and shot gun invented by Colonel Fosbery, V.C. Adopted and built by Messrs Holland and Holland, who named it the Paradox, this gun was similar to a shot gun except that it carried sights and was rifled for the last few inches in each barrel. The spherical ball or conical channelured bullet was shot with considerable accuracy at 100 yards. These ball and shot guns were commonly made in 8, 10, 12 and 20 bores. In the bigger sizes, and especially those designed for heavy loads, it was possible to deal effectively with most types of animal. As their weight was not much more than that of a normal shot gun and as they could also fire shot with reasonable patterns, they were ideal where mixed game was to be had. This might vary from quail, the local type of 'partridge' and bustard, to small and large buck, and possibly an unexpected encounter with something bigger and more dangerous. They were, in short, ideal pot fillers and jungle guns.

Some side by side breech-loading combined gun and rifles were made (plate 86), and also particularly on the continent double-barrelled guns with a medium or small bore rifle barrel underneath were popular.

As rifles moved towards smaller bores and higher velocities, the difference in the shape and weight of the rifle barrel became such as made it difficult to lay them together with a shot barrel. Such a combination as a 12 bore shot barrel with a ·303 rifle for example was an awkward one.

The arrival on the scene of the Fosberry ball and shot gun which fulfilled the role of gun and rifle more adequately, hastened the departure of all but a lingering few of the side by side rifle–gun combinations.

There was at this time hardly a wild place anywhere in the world that was not penetrated by hunters or hunter-explorers; from the Arctic and the Rocky mountains, to the plains, mountains and jungles of Africa and Asia. Each place had its particular requirement for rifles and equipment. The Badminton Library *Big Game Shooting* (1894) covered shooting in almost every part of the world, with recommended batteries for India and Africa, where the majority of the shooting was done. The following guns were recommended for shooting in East Africa: a single 4 bore rifle with one sight for 100 yards, weight 21 lb, shooting 12 drams and spherical bullet. A double 8 bore sighted for 100 and 200 yards, weight 15 lb, shooting 12 drams and a spherical bullet. A double ·500 rifle sighted for 100 and 200 yards, bored for long bottle shaped cases, 'Magnum' shooting 6 drams of powder and long bullets of three kinds—solid, small hole and copper tube. A 12 bore shot gun or a 20 bore Paradox. Perhaps a single ·450 express with a telescopic sight up to 300 yards for long shots when game was wild, and a ·295 rook rifle.

Hammerless rifles and guns were recommended for their greater safety in the hands of native gun-bearers, as well as other advantages. Some hunters preferred the double ·577 Express to the double 8 bore rifle for African sport.

For shooting in a country so varied as India there was no such thing as a rifle or battery that was suitable for all places and occasions. For specific types of animal the following were recommended: for most soft skinned animals including tiger a double ·500 express with a charge of at least 5¾ drams. For elephant, rhinoceros, buffalo and sambur at least a 12 bore double rifle firing 6 drams or more or an 8 bore double rifle firing at least 8 drams. For antelope and gazelles a light single ·400 Express. The 12 bore shot gun was recommended as a necessity everywhere and as one of the best pot-filling guns; indeed, this was the chief use of a shot gun when after big game. For this purpose the shot and rifle gun with two 16 bore barrels over a ·450 rifle barrel was also favoured.

Some sportsmen preferred the 8 bore Paradox for heavy Indian game or a double ·577 Express.

In the muzzle-loading days, bullets of the bore required could be cast as the need arose. The sportsman setting out on a hunting expedition with breech-loaders was obliged to carry with him a good supply of cartridges for all his rifles as well as cartridges with different types of bullet. To run out of a particular cartridge meant a very long wait for new supplies and even then, unless great care was taken in ordering, a cartridge case with the wrong chamber length for a particular calibre could cause great frustration when supplies eventually arrived. This sort of difficulty being foreseen, some of the black powder rifles were furnished with bullet moulds and cartridge re-loading equipment so that some re-loading could be done if needed, wherever supplies of lead and black powder could be obtained. With cordite or other nitro loaded cases it was essential to bring sufficient supplies of ready loaded cartridges from the United Kingdom, packed in sealed tin boxes.

By 1900 the tendency towards smaller bores of high velocity was clearly established. The ·303 cordite rifle in single- and double-barrelled versions was widely recommended and used for deer stalking (plate 80). J. Rigby & Co. advertised their new ·450 special, designed for big game: its muzzle velocity was 2,050 feet per second and the weight of the bullet 480 grains. The striking energy at 100 yards was stated to be considerably greater than that given by an 8 bore with 10 drams of black powder. The rifle weighed 11 lb and had the accuracy of a ·303.

Even for the biggest game high velocity rifles using cordite or other nitro powders were tending to take the place of the big 8 and 4 bores. Some sportsmen went too far in placing undue reliance upon high velocity in the smaller bores. They found to their cost that although these could kill well if there was the time and opportunity to place a shot precisely, things could turn out very differently in unfavourable circumstances. Even if the hunter did not suffer for being under-gunned it is probable that a number of wounded animals did.

The character of the old black powder rifles, and their association with the great days of big game hunting make them most attractive collectors' items. Especially attractive are fine quality double rifles whether of big or small bore, Damascus or steel barrelled; they are particularly desirable when complete in their cases with their bullet moulds and all the equipment for re-loading cartridges. Of the single-barrelled rifles, those using a variety of the falling block are probably most to be desired but some of the rook rifles are well worthy of consideration besides of course the single-barrelled 4 bores.

CHAPTER NINE

Gunmaking in the Breech-loading Era up to 1900

I T was hardly surprising that the transition from percussion cap muzzle-loader to breech-loading hammerless ejector brought about considerable changes in gunmaking techniques and materials. The greatly increased numbers of guns with complicated actions, coupled with keen competition to reduce the price of the ready-made gun, inevitably had its effects.

In Great Britain the craft tradition was strongly entrenched, and there was a ready supply of skilled craftsmen in every branch of gunmaking.

Few gunmakers however had all these branches under their direct control; the majority were dependent upon a variety of specialists and out-workers in the trade, who supplied their needs: from barrel tubes to locks, and from screws to gun furniture.

In America there was a shortage of skilled craftsmen, a big demand for guns and need for rapidly increased production. This situation led to a development which anticipated future industrial developments. The American government called for a musket in which all the parts were interchangeable. This involved the making of each part to a precise pattern with a sufficiently close tolerance to allow any broken part to be replaced in the field by an unskilled man. In this way some good muskets could, if necessary, be made up from a number of defective ones.

Because of the shortage of skilled craftsmen various machines were constructed, which were able to bring the parts very close to their correct shape, so that only a small amount of finishing was required to make them conform exactly to the master pattern. The stocks too were turned on a special machine that reproduced the shape of an iron master pattern. Because each part was made to a standard specification, the assembly could be done without the aid of skilled craftsmen.

Robbins and Lawrence of America produced a rifle in 1841 in which all the parts were interchangeable, and examples of this rifle were exhibited in London at the Great Exhibition of 1851. The British government wished to equip their factory at Enfield for the large-scale production of the Enfield rifle. They were advised, by a committee they had set up to study the matter, to purchase rifle-making machines from America for this purpose, and this was done in 1854.

The considerable use of machinery in the production of military arms was not at first reflected in the building of sporting weapons, in the production of which in Great Britain, the craft tradition prevailed as strongly as ever.

However as gun actions and mechanisms became more complicated the advantages of machines to do some of the basic work was increasingly appreciated, but all the finishing and fitting was still carried out by skilled specialist craftsmen. When the moderately priced ready-made gun began to be produced in large numbers, especially the cheaper box-locks, standardisation and the use of machinery were of such benefit in reducing costs that enterprising gunmakers who specialised in this class of work were quick to see its advantages. There was nevertheless, even in these guns, still a fair amount of hand fitting and finishing.

Having looked at the general scene, we will now proceed to a more detailed study, starting with the barrels. When the early pinfire breech-loaders were being made, gunmakers used the available barrels which had been designed for use as muzzle-loaders. The breech ends of these had to be reduced in thickness by the boring of cartridge chambers and the resilience of the metal was lessened by the brazing on of the lumps. The fitting of extractors could further weaken the barrels at this vital point. Incidentally, the writer was made well aware of the above weakness when in his youthful ignorance he was so unwise as to reload a pinfire cartridge with the contents of a modern nitro one. The result was that four inches of the offside breech were blown clean away, fortunately without more damage to the shooter than singing ears and some scratched finger tips.

When barrels were forged specially for breech-loading guns, an extra thickness of metal was used for the coils at the breech ends, and a greater proportion of steel was generally used in the best quality Damascus. This allowed for loss of metal in chambering and the extractor holes and for any weakening when the metal was raised to brazing temperature. Though the lumps were at first brazed directly on to the flats of the barrels, or on to a V incision in the flats, they were soon in the best guns neatly dovetailed into the barrels, this being considered the strongest method.

Around the 1870s and 1880s the single iron Damascus contained iron and steel in almost equal proportions, English steel Damascus was composed of six parts steel to four of iron and silver steel Damascus had nearly eight parts steel to two or two and a half of iron. Laminated steel was normally composed of six parts steel to four of iron. Best barrels were normally composed of three or four twisted rods forged together into the ribbon, in various thicknesses depending on the part of the barrel for which they were intended; from about $\frac{1}{4}$ inch at the breech to about $\frac{1}{8}$ inch at the muzzle end. The forging methods remained basically the same as those described as applying to muzzle-loading barrels.

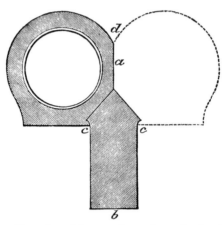

Figure 50. Section of barrels and lump as brazed together by the dovetail method.

In the 1870s, Marshall of Birmingham supplied the majority of Damascus shotgun barrels to the gun trade and although these were generally of sound quality they did contain rather a lot of 'greys'. These greys were caused by small pieces of scale, which became imbedded in the metal during the fire welding. They did not materially effect the strength of the barrel, but they did leave small marks when the barrels were polished, which rendered them unfit to be sold as the barrels of best guns. Prior to breech-loading, sportsmen had not been able to look down their barrels so as to notice such marks, but with breech-loaders they could find the slightest mark with ease. As these defects often only became apparent in the finishing stages of a gun, the annoyance and loss caused can be imagined. It was because of the greys that considerable supplies of Damascus barrels were imported from Liège in Belgium and St Etienne in France, particularly the former. These Belgian barrels were much clearer of greys but they were also softer.

Mr Thomas Webley and Mr Smith Casson (manager of the Round Oak Ironworks) joined forces to try to produce English Damascus of improved quality. P. Webley and Sons' report of the venture, and the visit made to Liège, to look into the forging methods of the Belgian barrel makers was most revealing and is given in full as it was printed in *The Modern Sportsman's Gun and Rifle* by J. H. Walsh (1882).

'A large quantity of Belgian tubes, called "Pointille", similar in figure to our iron Damascus (often called laminated steel), have been used in cheap guns for the last three years, and these are especially wanting in toughness and density of metal. These tubes are cheaper than iron Damascus made at Birmingham, are more regular in figure, and have fewer greys, but the result is obtained at the entire sacrifice of density and toughness of metal; for it is a fact that, though these tubes may stand proof, the iron is so soft and rotten that they will not wear or stand any extra or repeated strain. These remarks apply, but in a smaller degree, to all Belgian tubes, whether iron Damascus (Pointille), or Damascus (Damas turc). As one proof of this, when you see a choke-bored barrel bulge at the choke, it is almost sure to be a Belgian tube. We were, in common with our competitors, excepting for first and second quality, using a large proportion of these tubes; in fact, we think that quite three-fourths of the tubes used in Birmingham are Belgian make, and nearly all the London trade use them, with this difference, that they use the best quality, which are no doubt harder than the cheaper kinds, but are still softer and less durable than those of English make, and cost as much. Now we have for a long time felt very dissatisfied with this state of things, and determined to step out of our province as gun-makers and turn our attention to iron making, believing that the first fault lay there. For many years we have been almost entirely dependent upon one maker for Damascus, stub Damascus, and laminated steel iron; he, having a monopoly, has not cared to trouble himself to keep his iron up to its original good standard, notwith-standing the fact that, in consequence of its high price and want of clearness (freeness from greys), his trade has been gradually leaving him and going to Belgium. As you probably are aware, the mode of making gun-barrel iron, so as to give the various kinds of figure, is kept a close secret by the iron makers; we therefore had to begin with a very indistinct notion of what we were about to do. For-tunately, we made the acquaintance of Mr Smith Casson, the manager of the Earl of Dudley's Round Oak Ironworks—these works are of the most advanced type in the kingdom—and he kindly placed at our disposal all the resources of the establishment that we required, and gave us the benefit of his great experience. The first batch of iron that we made, although not just the figure we expected, turned out very well, was very clean, and of first rate quality, as well as much cheaper. After making several other lots, our Mr Thomas Webley, accompanied by Mr Smith Casson, paid a visit to the barrel-making districts of Liège, where they were singularly fortunate in getting to the bottom of the Liège system of making their various kinds of iron. They found that each barrel maker piled his iron and steel (very little of the latter, and that of the softest kind, so as to weld easily) into a faggot; it was then sent to the ironworks, put into a furnace, and, when heated sufficiently, rolled off into a billet, and then sent to the smaller mill, reheated, and rolled off into square rods; if intended for barrels, the rods had to be twisted, varying, of course, in size, as to whether they were intended for one, two, three, four, or six striped barrels; but if for what we call skelp twist (they call them "ruban") it is at once rolled off into flat rods of one width, varying in thickness for the breech and muzzle ends (though the additional thickness at breech ends is often obtained by first wrapping a piece of plain iron round the mandril). You will perceive that up to this stage the iron has not had one blow from a hammer, consequenly it is not at all hardened or toughened; but the piles lie more evenly than they would have done if the faggot had been put under a steam or tilt hammer, and hammered into a billet, as we do here, instead of being rolled right off. Now comes the next stage of welding proper. In consequence of the Belgians welding all their barrels on a chemise—which is a strip of common sheet iron of the necessary length and width, bent round a mandril, so that it forms a complete tube, round which the rods of iron are then wound—they are enabled to make a pair of ordinary breech-loading tubes out of about 12 lb of iron, without lining, instead of 17 lb, which it takes us. The result is that they work iron much nearer the finished size than we do, and but for the support of the chemise, they would not be able to carry the barrels when hot from the fire to the anvil. It thus necessarily only receives just sufficient hammering to weld the joints together, and is not hammered and reduced in thickness along its entire length, as we do here, which hammering greatly adds to the density and strength of the metal. Of course the amount of up-jumping and hammering that a barrel receives here (independently of the original quality of the iron) depends upon the quality of barrel it is desired to make, as more hammering and up-jumping means more iron, fuel, and the labour of three men.

'On remarking to some of the Liège makers that their barrels were sure to be soft made on their principle, and that that was the great objection we had to Liège tubes; their reply was that they only studied three things: First, to get the greatest possible distinction in colour (black and white when browned) between their iron and steel; secondly, regularity of figure; thirdly, clearness of iron; and that whether they were hard or soft was of no consequence to them.'

P. Webley and Sons.

There were some barrels of fine quality forged in Belgium and France but the tendency was to put figure before toughness.

One reason for the cleaner forging done by the Belgian smiths was that they used a smaller forge fire composed of a mixture of powdered clay and small coke that kept the work cleaner than the big coke fires of Birmingham.

When the facts about the use of Belgian barrels became widely known through the medium of the sporting press there were demands by sportsmen for true English Damascus barrels to be fitted to their new guns; formerly some Belgian barrels had been described as English Damascus and accepted as such.

At the very time that some excellent barrels were being made to meet this demand, leading gunmakers were quick to appreciate that Sir Joseph Whitworth's fluid compressed steel solved many of their problems. From the early 1880s Whitworth steel barrels were increasingly fitted to best guns and rifles. Because of the greater strength of this steel in proportion to its substance barrels could be made a few ounces lighter and of course the question of greys did not arise. The boring of rifle barrels was certainly made easier by having an evenly grained metal to work; also it stood up better to wear and the effects of some early nitro powders, particularly cordite in rifles.

Whitworth's fluid compressed steel got its name from the compression given to the ingot mould while the metal was still in a fluid or molten state. The object of this compression was to prevent the formation of a 'pipe' or central hole due to the contraction of the metal on cooling. It was of course essential that there were no flaws in steel used for gun barrels because the barrel length was forged from a shorter ingot piece. This meant that a flaw was stretched out lengthwise along the barrel and this was most dangerous; far more dangerous than a flaw in a twist barrel where it went round the barrel. Also because the grain of the steel was forged out along the length of the barrel, it was essential that it was of sufficient quality to resist the lateral stresses adequately.

The adoption of Whitworth steel for shot and rifle barrels was soon followed by the use of Siemens's and other makes of steel. Early steel barrels were put together by dovetailing and brazing the lump into the breech ends. Soon however it was appreciated that with steel barrels it was possible to forge out the blank tube with sufficient metal projecting from the breech end to form half the lump; the so-called "chopper" lump. The advantages of this arrangement lay in the greater strength and in the simplicity of having only the two barrels to braze together instead of the two barrels plus the steel lump. Good barrel steels used in the above manner had also to be hard enough to stand up to the sort of wear required of lumps. When a top extension to the rib was used this was usually brazed on between the barrels, for about two inches. The type of third bite which projected from the breech ends of the barrels just above the extractors, was formed from the same piece as the barrels, divided down the centre as were the lumps.

The idea of 'chopper' lumps had been tried out with Damascus barrels by forging on the extra piece, but as this metal was not so hard as the steel lump that was normally brazed on, it was found that it did not stand up to the work required of it.

The breech ends were brazed together for about three inches, the barrels being wired together while this was done. Next the ribs were fitted and laid with soft solder. If on shooting it was discovered that the barrels did not converge to throw their pattern on the same spot at forty yards, or if one barrel shot slightly up or down, then a few inches of the muzzle ends were heated sufficiently to loosen the solder; the adjustment made and the barrels resoldered.

Whitworth steel barrels were considerably more expensive than the other barrels used at that time. For comparison a few of the prices per pair of tubes follow:

	shillings
Whitworth's fluid compressed steel	90
English Steel, Siemens-Martin process	24
Foreign Steel, Siemens-Martin process	24
English machine-forged best Damascus in four rods	31
English hand-forged best laminated steel in 3 rods	31
English hand-forged best Damascus in 3 rods	31
English machine-forged chequered Damascus in 2 rods	25
Foreign Damascus in 3 rods	20
English machine-forged iron Damascus in single rod	13
English machine-forged fine skelp twist	13

The above are but a small selection of the English and foreign barrels that were available in the late 1880s. It is interesting to note that by far the greatest number of twist or coiled barrels were, by this time, being machine-forged by steam-powered hammers. In well-equipped workshops, machines used for boring the barrels were steam powered. After they had been bored, and if necessary tapped straight, they were turned to approximate length and shape on a lathe; at a later stage the chambering was also done on a lathe. Machines were also used for shaping the action forging, cutting the slots to receive the lump and bolt and also drilling the hole to receive the hinge pin. The use of machines for these purposes left more time for the highly skilled finishing and fitting of the various parts, and also ensured that the basic work was true.

Where a precise fit was required, the craftsman was assisted by blackening the parts with an oil burner; the points of contact were revealed by the bright patches where the lamp black had rubbed off. These bright patches were carefully filed away and the process repeated until a perfect fit was achieved. It was most important that the case hardening of the action was carried out skilfully to enable it to stand the strain at the angle between the horizontal action body and the upright 'break-off' (so named because in muzzle-loaders the barrels broke away, or unhooked from the stock at this point). The best breech actions were of stub iron, but on many cheap guns the commonest scrap iron was used or even cast malleable iron, so it will readily be appreciated that important as the case hardening was to the best iron, it was even more so to actions made from the poorer qualities of iron.

According to Mr Walsh, the Birmingham makers were using steam-powered machines in the early 1880s but in London the action filers still generally used the foot lathe. However, this situation changed rapidly, and by 1900 all the more enterprising London makers were equipped with powered machines to do the preliminary cutting.

In best quality guns there was still of course a great deal of hand finishing in each stage of the construction of the gun. Also a great deal of time was spent in shooting and regulating the barrels. This period coincided with the growth of shooting schools, and more care and time was taken over fitting the stock. In the muzzle-loading guns and the early breech-loaders, by far the greatest number are straight stocked, but around the 1880s and after, some degree of cast off or on, and varying degrees of bend, were usual on guns built to order. Although notable gunmakers had their own particular style by which their guns and rifles can be recognised, it is rare to find two guns precisely alike, except of course pairs. Best guns were built to the particular requirements of the sportsman and also there was a certain amount of variation according to which crafts-man was responsible for the individual parts and the final finish.

Towards the end of the century there was considerable contro-versy regarding the relative merits of machine-made and hand-built guns or rather it would be better to say between ready-made, or 'reach-me-down' guns, as they were sometimes termed, and guns built to individual requirements. The degree to which machines were used, provided they were skilfully used, was not the only factor. Obviously it was easier to set up machines to produce a standard design in large numbers, cutting the finishing and fitting of parts to a minimum, and in doing so cutting the cost of production. A number of gunmaking firms did specialise in such guns and good sound guns they were in many cases. The question was often asked why the so-called hand-made gun was so much more expensive. As already stated, most guns were to some extent machine made, but the individually built gun necessarily took very much longer as each of the main parts had to be shaped and fitted as an original item, unlike a ready-made gun in which the breech actions, for instance, could be produced in hundreds to a single specification by machines set for this purpose.

In the individually built gun only the best materials were used, the most expensive barrels, locks, a choice of the finest selected stocks and, most important and expensive, the additional time of the best of skilled craftsmen.

In 1896 W. W. Greener expressed the opinion that by adopting steam machinery and the division of labour, it was possible to reduce costs, and also the work was better done when a man specialised on one part of the work instead of doing three or four. Greener maintained that although he had the largest stock of ready-made sporting guns in England, running into thousands, no two guns (with the exception of pairs) were precisely alike. This assertion suggests that although organised for large scale production, the craft tradition was still strong enough to maintain some individual character in the work. Greener was of the opinion that in order to maintain a correct balance and proportion it was not possible to fit barrels of various lengths and weight to the same breech action and that the machine-made gun in which all parts were alike, was at best a mediocre production. It is understandable that gunmakers, who had been brought up in a tradition where pride in the skill of the individual craftsman played so great a part, were reluctant to see such human qualities overridden by machine production of guns which were all alike and gave no scope for the individualist craftsman.

Most gunmakers and their workers neither wanted nor were ready for any abrupt change but Mr Edgar Harrison of Cogswell and Harrison in London was an exception. He was so impressed with the machine-made rifles and revolvers from America and the price at which they could be produced that in the 1890s he set up a workshop equipped with the best machine tools from America. Some 400 different operations necessary to the making of a gun were carried out on machines set to work with great accuracy and yet with such simplicity that they were operated by girls. The skilled craftsmen then only needed to gauge, check, and give slight final touches to the work, before fitting them. Their judgement and skill was therefore spread to cover ten times the number they could deal with under the old craft system. The new method of manufacture enabled Cogswell and Harrison to produce a sound London made hammerless ejector gun for 15 guineas; this compared with their best gun at 59 guineas. Every part of their cheaper gun, with the exception of the tubes, was manufactured in Gillingham Street, near Victoria Station. These guns filled a demand for a good sound gun at a moderate price. They were designed to be manufactured by machinery unlike other moderately priced guns at this time in which the traditional craft methods were assisted by the use of some machinery.

Mr Walsh, in 1882, wrote that thousands of guns sold in London were altogether finished in Birmingham, while others were sent to London 'in the soft' and after the locks and action have been carefully adjusted they were sent back to Birmingham to be case-hardened and the barrels browned.

NITRO POWDERS AND CARTRIDGES

For centuries, black powder or gunpowder had provided the propellant force for guns and rifles. Sportsmen and gunmakers were accustomed to its qualities and the relationship between grain size and speed of burning. For the average game gun No 2 grain was a very fast burning powder suited to the lighter loads, while No 4 grain was suited to medium or fairly heavy loads. No 6 grain was the standard size for rifles and 8 bore wildfowl guns. No 8 grain was used for heavy loads in long-barrelled 4 bore wildfowl guns. Black powder was a very accommodating propellant; it ignited easily, so almost any reasonably good cartridge cap sufficed to give regular results, and the degree of resistance in the turnover of the cartridge made little difference. Also black powder was stable under most extremes of heat and cold. The qualities objected to in black powder were its smoke and dirty residue which spoiled the accuracy in rifles after a number of shots. The hard fouling left in both guns and rifles was a nuisance but it was not unduly corrosive and could be successfully cleaned out with water and brushes.

The challenge to black powder came from the nitro powders; the most successful of the early ones being the nitro-wood powder named Schultze, after its inventor Capt. E. Schultze, a Prussian artillery officer. Basically this powder was a regularly grained 'sawdust' which had been steeped in nitric acid. When first introduced it was rather too slow to give the necessary velocity but by the late 1870s it had been sufficiently improved to give some results comparable with black powder. The reason why only some results were as good, was accounted for by the tendency to treat the new powder as if it possessed the same properties as the old.

It was discovered after a great deal of trial and error that to obtain regular shooting the cap must have a hotter flame to ensure the best ignition of all the grains, but it must not be powerful enough to undo the turnover and loosen the grains before ignition had taken place. Also the wad must be of good quality and a tight fit in cartridge and barrel. Quite small variations of the above factors, which would have little effect on black powder, caused considerable variations in the shooting of Schultze and most of the other nitro powders that were to follow. So even when the problems were known it was essential that all the factors such as cap, wads, turnovers and compression of the powder, should be constant if regular results were to be obtained. The rule of thumb methods which were good enough for black powder were of necessity replaced by a more accurate and scientific approach.

For the first time in the long history of the gun the shooter was finding it necessary to delegate responsibility for his loading to specialists. Of course there were still some sportsmen who liked to load their own and experiment.

Following Schultze powder were a number of other nitro powders, namely E.C., Amberite, Normal, Sporting ballistite, Cannonite, Kynoch, S.S., Shot-gun rifleite and others.

Because of a number of serious explosions in guns, some of which involved the blowing out of the breech portion of the barrels, experiments were conducted and research undertaken into all the factors concerned with the use of these new powders. In some cases the danger was in the character of the particular powder but more often the danger lay in the lack of sufficient understanding of the nature of nitro powders. Bulk powders such as Schultze in which the dram measures were roughly equal to those of black powder were certainly less likely to be overloaded than the condensed powders where the use of dram measures would give loads that would exert extremely high pressure.

Another important area of research lay in finding out what pressures were exerted on the various parts of the barrel, both to see that the greatest strength of the barrel walls lay in the right places and also to ensure that the pressures of the powders used coincided with the ability of the barrels to contain them.

The barrel walls of the average 12 bore diminished in thickness from about ·194 of an inch at the breech to ·092 inch at 6 inches from the breech, ·048 at 12 inches and ·035 at 21 inches. The muzzle was about ·048 in a cylinder, but when choked, more according to the amount of choke. Where a 12 bore barrel was oversize, that was it had been reproofed at ·740 instead of ·729, the thinner part of the barrel could be reduced to as little as ·025 of an inch, or less in places where there were old rust pits. It can be readily seen that it was essential for powder makers and cartridge loaders to ensure that the highest pressures were concentrated where there was most metal. It was also necessary that the shot should achieve the maximum velocity as it left the barrel. It was hardly surprising that cartridge making and loading was increasingly left to specialist firms who were able to undertake the necessary research. Although a number of gunmakers continued to load their own, many found it more convenient to have them done for them but with their names on them.

62 Westley Richards gun, No. 14402, of 1889, in its case with cleaning and reloading fittings. On the inside of the lid are instructions for use and reference to the award of the Grand Prize at the Paris Exhibition. The additional pair of barrels are of Whitworth steel, No. 14740, with a flat top rib, probably for trap pigeon shooting; they weigh half a pound more than the Damascus game barrels.

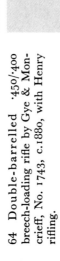

63 Double-barrelled 20 bore hammerless gun by Charles Lancaster, No. 7795, of 1896, with Damascus barrels and extra quality deep scroll engraving. Typical Lancaster backaction side locks; and this gun is fitted with his selective single trigger.

64 Double-barrelled ·450/·400 breech-loading rifle by Gye & Moncrieff, No. 1743, c.1880, with Henry rifling.

65 Under view of the Gye & Moncrieff, No. 1743, showing the unusual and very fine engravings of deer, and the complete absence of scroll engraving.

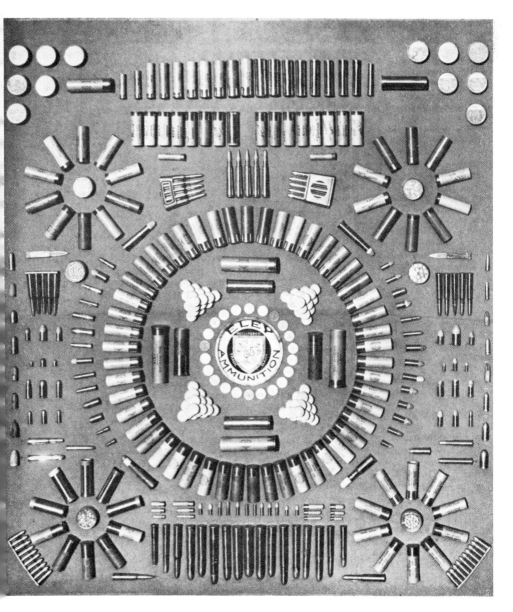

66   Display of Eley ammunition c.1890–1900, showing various types of sporting and other cartridges.

67 Four-barrelled 16 bore hammerless gun by Charles Lancaster, No. 5087, of 1882.

68 Double-barrelled 8 bore breech-loading rifle by Perrins of Worcester, c.1885.

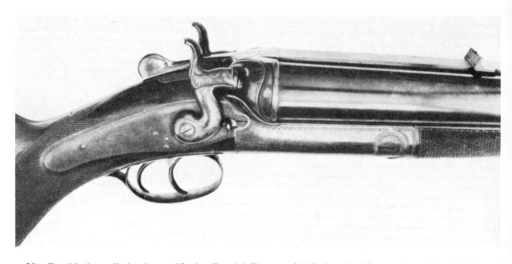

69 Double-barrelled 4 bore rifle by Daniel Frazer of Edinburgh, No. 2008, c.1885. Weight of rifle 22½ lb; designed to shoot spherical ball.

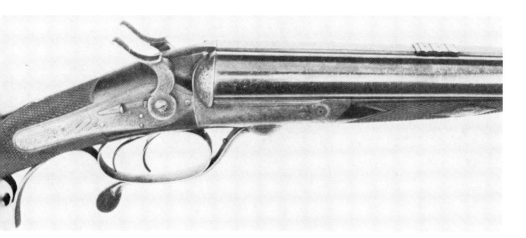

70   Double-barrelled oval-bore centre fire rifle by Charles Lancaster, No. 3991, of 1865.

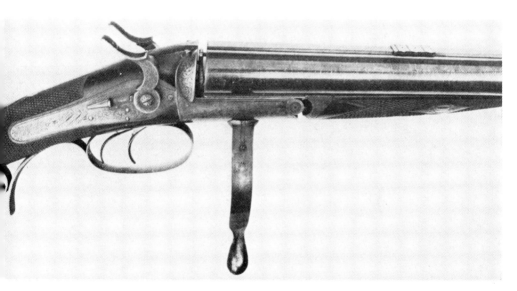

71   Charles Lancaster rifle, No. 3991, showing the way the barrels move forward before dropping down when the under lever is swung out.

72 Single-barrelled 4 bore rifle by J. D. Dougall, converted to centre fire from pinfire. This was the favourite rifle of G. P. Sanderson, author of *Thirteen Years Among the Wild Beasts of India*.

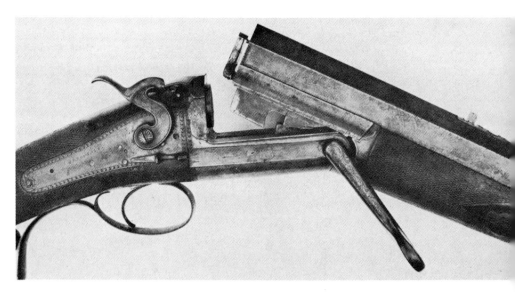

73 Dougall 4 bore rifle, built c.1860, showing the 'Lockfast' action open. Weight of rifle 17 lb.

74   Double-barrelled ·577 calibre centre fire rifle with strikers attached to hammers by Alfred
Lancaster, c.1870.

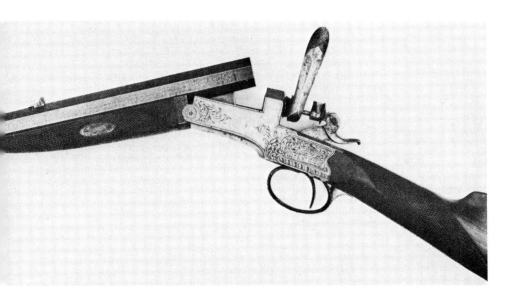

75   Single-barrelled screw-breech 80 bore needle fire rook and rabbit rifle by William and
John Rigby, No. 12168, of 1864. These rifles were very popular at this period. Note typical
Rigby etched Damascus barrel.

76   Single-barrelled falling block ·577 calibre rifle by Alexander Henry, No. 1437, c.1870.

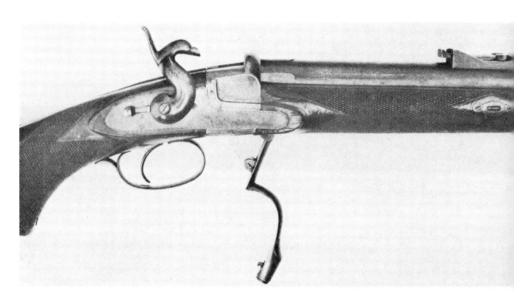

77   Alexander Henry rifle, No. 1437, showing action open.

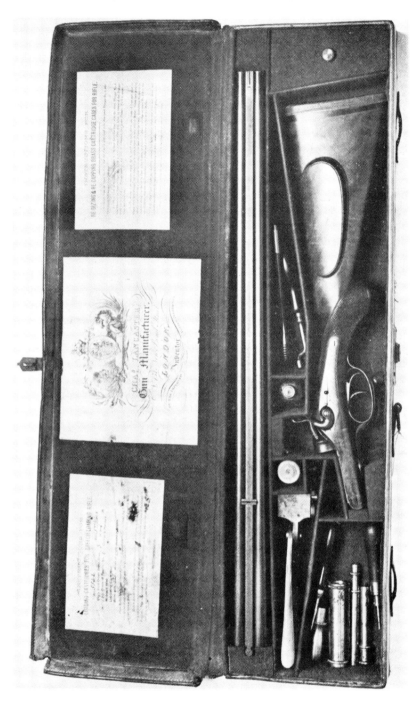

78 Double-barrelled breech-loading ·577 calibre rifle by Charles Lancaster, No. 5522, of 1885, in its case with bullet mould, cartridge reloading tools and instructions on the lid. Label states: 'Eley's solid drawn brass case 3 in. long, 160 grains No. 6 powder, millboard wad, lubricating cloth wad, and bullet with two wraps of paper dipped in grease. Hollow fronted Express bullets can either be filled with pure wax or with explosive composition.'

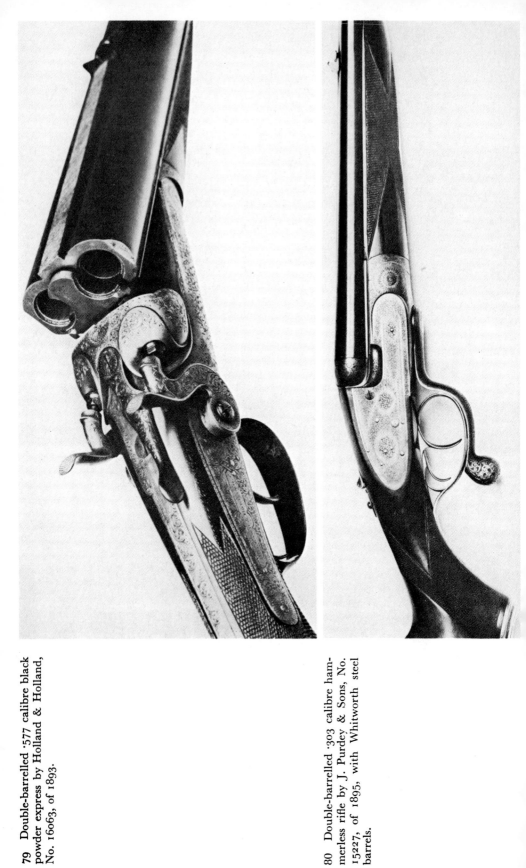

79 Double-barrelled ·577 calibre black powder express by Holland & Holland, No. 16063, of 1893.

80 Double-barrelled ·303 calibre hammerless rifle by J. Purdey & Sons, No. 15227, of 1895, with Whitworth steel barrels.

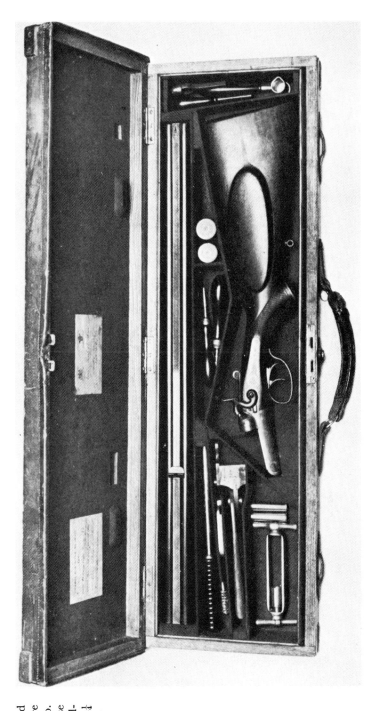

81 Double-barrelled breech-loading ·450 calibre rifle by J. Purdey, No. 11588, of 1883, in its case with all its cartridge reloading accessories. Load: 4¼ drams No. 6 black powder.

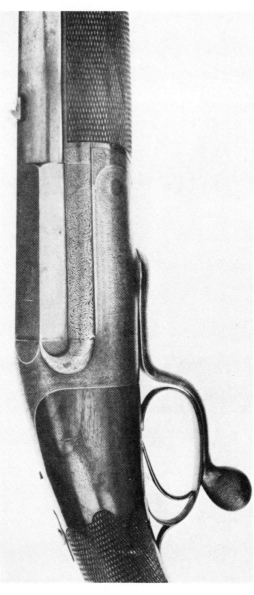

82 Single-barrelled 4 bore 'round action' rifle by John Dickson of Edinburgh, No. 4007, of 1886. Weight, 18¼ lb.

83 Single-barrelled ·250 calibre hammerless rook and rabbit rifle by J. Rigby, c.1885.

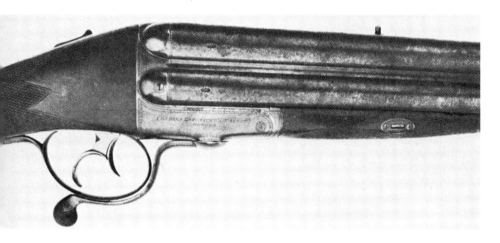

84 Four-barrelled 16 gauge oval-bore rifle by Charles Lancaster, No. 5146, of 1882. Improved model.

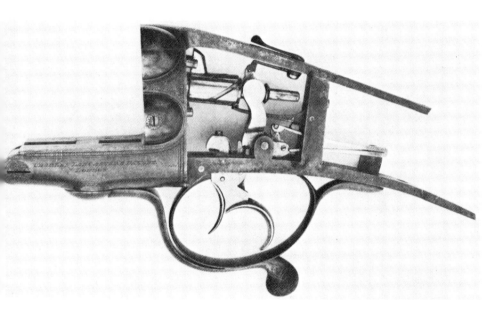

85 The action of four-barrelled Lancaster rifle, No. 5146, showing the lock work.

86 Combination gun and rifle, right barrel 16 bore shot and left barrel ·450 No. 1 black powder express, by I. Hollis & Sons, c.1885.

87 Westley Richards double ·458 calibre rifle, showing the famous W. R. patent detachable locks first introduced in 1898; this recently built rifle will, however, be one of the last to be fitted with this type of lock.

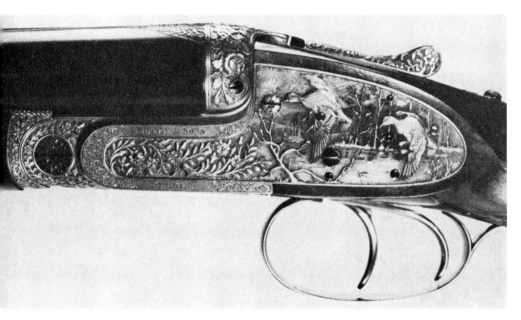

88 Recently completed double-barrelled, 12 bore gun by J. Purdey & Sons, deeply carved with game scenes.

89 THE GUNMAKERS' ASSOCIATION, 1929

1 H. W. Holland; 2 C. E. Greener; 3 Athol S. Purdey; 4 C. T. Lloyd; 5 Clifford J. Hellis; 6 Lt.-Col. C. Playfair; 7 Jenkyn Griffiths, B.Sc., F.C.S.; 8 C. S. Rosson; 9 E. G. Daw; 10 G. V. Powell; 11 H. W. R. Tarrant; 12 T. Page-Wood; 13 Leslie Taylor; 14 J. E. Martin; 15 Charles Hellis; 16 Alan H. Thorn; 17 W. Corrie; 18 S. Skimin; 19 Robert F. G. Churchill; 20 S. Robertson; 21 J. Robertson; 22 T. D. S. Purdey; 23 Theo Rigby; 24 W. Darlow; 25 H. Greener; 26 C. H. Greener; 27 T. G. Naughton; 28 W. W. Wallis; 29 W. Robson; 30 T. H. Turner; 31 Capt. James Purdey; 32 Alexander Robertson; 33 R. D. Robertson; 34 D. V. Johnstone; 35 C. Wallis; 36 C. O. Ellis; 37 Charles Riggs; 38 Rowland Watson; 39 H. Leonard; 40 W. J. Ford; 41 F. Ward; 42 A. Griffiths; 43 Charles Jeffery; 44 W. B. Chilton; 45 C. Stopp; 46 Frank Clarke; 47 John MacPherson; 48 T. Field Wilson; 49 James Watson; 50 W. Richards; 51 J. H. Fraser; 52 W. R. Milburn; 53 C. L. Woodward; 54 J. F. Smythe; 55 S. R. Jeffery; 56 R. Harmer; 57 C. Fletcher; 58 A. Lagden; 59 B. E. Webster; 60 F. Hadfield; 61 F. H. Green; 62 Edward Gale; 63 A. Thornton Woulfe; 64 Lionel G. Clough; 65 H. W. Barford; 66 H. J. Blanch; 67 H. J. Godwin; 68 E. Anson; 69 T. A. Appleton; 70 G. P. Holloway; 71 L. F. Hodges; 72 L. R. Tippins; 73 A. J. Rudd; 74 John Harper; 75 W. Baker; 76 G. E. Lewis; 77 A. B. Ward; 78 J. R. Redgrave; 79 A. G. Rickarby; 80 George Clarke; 81 S. P. J. Janes; 82 W. Bourne; 83 A. T. Bates; 84 A. B. Williams; 85 H. E. Akrill; 86 A. Howell; 87 Arthur Hill; 88 A. T. Saunders; 89 S. Wright; 90 W. Jones; 91 A. H. Watson; 92 O. Pidwell; 93 S. V. Hawkes; 94 Frank O. West; 95 C. W. Lightwood; 96 R. Blanton; 97 A. Cashmore; 98 C. Ingram Annan; 99 F. R. Furlong; 100 L. Keegan; 101 A. F. Ford; 102 S. H. Mackie.

Around the 1880s there was a movement towards the using of thin brass cased shotgun cartridges. The thin brass case enabled the chamber and cone to be almost or completely eliminated, to the extent that a 10 bore barrel was served by a brass cartridge case of the external dimensions of a 12 bore cartridge case. It was the custom to refer to these guns by the size of the cartridge, thus a gun that was bored as a 10 bore was called a 12 bore designed for the thin brass case. This was a very misleading description since by all precedence it was by the bore of the barrel that the gun was described. So a gun with a 10 bore barrel (·775 of an inch) should have been described as a 10 bore gun designed for thin brass cased cartridges.

Guns built for the thin brass case were developed by Dr C. J. Heath, then President of the Wildfowlers' Association. The object was to enable a very heavy load of shot (up to 2 oz) to be fired from a relatively light gun (about 8½ lb). In order to keep down the recoil from such a heavy shot load low powder charges were used; however, striking energy was maintained by the use of large shot (BB) which maintained velocity better than smaller shot. A reasonable pattern resulted in spite of the use of large shot, because of the heavy load.

An advantage claimed for these guns was that, by eliminating the chamber cone, damage to shot did not occur at this point and better patterns resulted. There was also the point that in 10 bore wildfowl guns, barrels need be no wider at the breech than for normal 12 bore barrels chambered for the paper case, and they could be made a little lighter than in a normal 10 bore gun for paper cartridges. Not only were new barrels constructed to take the thin brass cases but some others were altered by boring out the cone and fitting a steel bush or liner into the chamber, screwed in for about an inch at the breech. This was then bored to give the very slight chamber corresponding with the thickness of the thin brass, the end of the chamber being ·791 of an inch to take a thin brass cartridge in a 10 bore barrel of ·775 of an inch. Doubts were expressed about the soundness of this bushing method especially as it appeared to be contrary to the rules governing the proof of gun barrels. They should certainly have been submitted for re-proof after such work had been carried out; this in fact was insisted upon in 1882. The brass cases themselves were, on account of their thinness, liable to dent or damage and it was suggested that they be carried in a protective cartridge belt rather than loose in a bag or pocket.

Cartridge cases were generally improved and efforts made to standardise their size. A best 'gastight' long brass case was developed and when ejectors became general, an ejector case, having a long brass sheath over the paper as far as the turnover, was brought out to overcome some difficulty that had been experienced from paper cartridges sticking and failing to eject.

ALTERATIONS TO RULES OF PROOF

Alterations in the rules governing the proof of guns and rifles had of necessity to be made to take into account breech-loading guns and rifles and also to remove certain differences in the proof requirements of the London and Birmingham Proof Houses.

The Gun Barrel Proof Act of 1868 was most important and, although amended since, it still forms the basis of the present rules of proof.

Barrels for arms of the second and fourth classes, which covered rifles and shot guns, were normally sent for provisional proof:

'If of plain metal, shall be bored and ground having plugs attached, with touch-holes drilled in the plugs of a diameter not exceeding one sixteenth of an inch. Notches in the plugs, instead of drilled touch-holes, shall disqualify for proof. If of twisted metal, they shall be fine-bored, and struck up with proving plugs attached, and touch-holes drilled, as in the case of plain metal barrels.'

and later for definitive proof:

'The barrels, whether of plain or twisted metal, shall be smoothed in the finished state with the breeches in the percussioned state, huts filed up, bars of barrels intended for bar locks properly filed up on the top and bottom sides, the top and bottom ribs of double barrels shall be rough struck up, pipes, loops, and stoppers on, the proper breeches and nipples in, the thread of the screws sound and full, and all rifle barrels shall be rifled.

'Barrels for breech-loading arms, all of which are subject to provisional proof and to definite proof, shall receive the latter proof after the breech-loading action is attached and complete.'

The object of provisional proof was to bring to light any flaw in the barrels before gunmakers spent a great deal of time on them.

The provisional proof could be set aside by a request in writing to the Proof Master but in this instance the definitive proof was according to the heavier scale of powder charges laid down for provisional proof.

The marks denoting provisional proof were:

Figures 51a, b, c, d. Marks of proof.

For the Gunmakers' Company (London):
The letters GP interlaced in a cypher surmounted by a lion rampant.
For the Guardians (Birmingham):
The letters BP interlaced in a cypher surmounted by a crown.

The marks denoting definitive proof were:

[Fig. 51b

For the Gunmakers' Company:
The letters GP interlaced in a cypher surmounted by a crown and
the view mark, being the letter V surmounted by a crown.
For the Guardians:
Two sceptres crossed, a crown in the top angle formed by the cros-
sing of the sceptres, the letters BCP in the other angles. The view
mark: two crossed sceptres, a crown in the top angle and a V in the
lower angle.

*The marks denoting provisional proof of barrels proved in the state for definite
proof were:*

[Fig. 51c

For the Gunmakers' Company:
The letters VGP interlaced in a cypher surmounted by a lion
rampant.
For the Guardians:
The letters VBP interlaced in a cypher surmounted by a crown.

On all arms of the second and fourth classes (which included sporting rifles and shot guns) the marks were affixed as follows:

On arms provisionally and definitively proved, the provisional proof mark was impressed at the breech end of the barrel and the definitive proof mark and view mark were impressed upon the barrel above the provisional proof mark, and if the barrel was constructed with a patent breech, or a breech-loading action, or with breech blocks or chambers, the view mark was impressed upon them.

On arms proved provisionally in the state for definitive proof the mark denoting this was also impressed on the barrel and breech as above.

On all barrels the gauge size of the barrel was struck at the definitive proof.

The introduction of chokeboring in the 1870s caused the issue of new regulations in 1875. For definitive proof No 6 soft shot was used instead of a bullet, to the same weight as the appropriate bullet. Guns with one or more choke barrels came under regulations governing the Sixth Class.

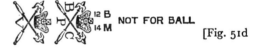

[Fig. 51d

In addition to the definitive proof marks, choke bored barrels were marked with the gauge size of the widest part of the barrel excluding the chamber, followed by the letter B, and the gauge size at the muzzle followed by the letter M. Added were the words 'NOT FOR BALL'. For example a 12 bore choke barrel might have been marked '12B' over '14M' followed by the words 'NOT FOR BALL'.

Where the recess method of choke boring was used and the muzzle and barrel were of the same gauge, the word 'CHOKE' was substituted for the words 'NOT FOR BALL'.

As a result of doubts expressed regarding the efficiency of the proof test for certain new types of arm and because of the introduction of nitro powders, a committee was appointed by the Gunmakers' Company and the Guardians who in 1887 drew up an amended scale of proof, and provision was made for an additional test with any nitro powder with which it was intended the gun should be used.

Attention having been drawn to the supplementary proof being little used, new rules were substituted in 1896, by which all guns intended to be used with nitro powders were to be proved with fine grain gunpowder, T.S.2, in addition to the ordinary test with the regulation powder. The words 'Nitro Proof' were first used for this supplementary proof and were changed to NP in 1904. The nitro proof test remained optional until 1925 but most guns were being submitted to this test long before it became compulsory.

In the classification of Small Arms under the 1896 rules, of special interest as sporting arms are those in classes Six, Seven and Eight detailed below:

The Sixth Class comprising all arms except of the Eighth Class, having one or more barrels choke bored, i.e. barrels whereof the diameter of the bore at the muzzle was less than the diameter of the bore at some point behind the muzzle other than the chamber or recess which contained the charge.

The Seventh Class comprising express rifles, i.e. rifles intended to be fired with a larger charge of powder than ordinary rifles, and which must be so declared in writing when sent for definitive proof.

The Eighth Class comprising choke bored barrels having all or a portion of the smaller diameter of their bore rifled. (For example the Paradox ball and shot gun.)

By the new rules of proof, arms in any class were, at the request in writing of any person sending them for definite proof, proved with Schultze, E.C. or any other powder specified, after and in addition to the ordinary definitive proof. The service load of the powder it was intended to use was impressed on the flat of the barrel, for example, 'Maxm Sch. 45 grs. Shot $1\frac{1}{4}$ oz.'

The gauge for barrels from 4 to 10 gauge was divided into three parts, for example 8, $\frac{8}{1}$, $\frac{8}{2}$, and from 11 to 17 gauge it was divided into two, for example 12 and $\frac{12}{1}$ (12 being ·729 and $\frac{12}{1}$ being ·740 of an inch).

The gauge size of the chamber or cartridge case with the letter C under, enclosed in a diamond shape, was impressed at definitive proof. Where the chamber was more than three inches long the letters L.C. were enclosed in a diamond shape under the gauge of the cartridge case.

The word 'CHOKE' was added to choke bored barrels and 'R. CHOKE' to rifled choke barrels.

Express rifles had the letters 'EX' following the gauge for example, '·577 EX'.

Barrels proved with T.S. 2 fine grain black powder as a supplementary test were marked, for example, 'Nitro Proof $1\frac{1}{2}$ oz. Maximum' or whatever the particular maximum weight of shot was to be used.

The above notes concerning the proof and marking of barrels are given both for their historic interest and for their usefulness in helping to date sporting arms of the period covered.

CHAPTER TEN

Gunmakers of the Period

THE following short histories of some of the notable gunmakers of the period covered by this book are given both for their historic interest and as an aid to collectors in finding the date when a gun was built.

In compiling these histories the writer is most grateful for the kind help given by many gunmakers and the generous way in which Mr W. R. H. Robson (for many years Managing Director of Atkin, Grant and Lang, Ltd) has made his notes on gunmakers available. Some of these notes have been used to bring the longer histories up to the present and the others are given in the chronological note form in which he compiled them. Although it was originally the intention that these histories should be given up to 1900 only, Mr Robson and the writer agreed that it was desirable that as much of the information as possible should be permanently recorded before some of the memories and records become lost as sources of information. Some records were destroyed during the last war and others have gone for a variety of reasons. While every endeavour has been made to check the information some sources conflict; for instance Boss and Co.'s version of their early history has been preferred though it conflicts with the version in Teasdale-Buckell's book *Experts On Guns and Shooting* (1900).

With regard to gun numbers and dates it should be understood that while some gunmakers had a single series of numbers, others used several series for different types or qualities of weapons. It can be taken that the numbers given will cover best quality guns and rifles. In the case of Purdey the series may include some pistols built by them, while Rigby on the other hand used a separate series for pistols and carbines. Where Lancaster, for instance, bought in various complicated breech-loading actions or guns, such as would obviously not be manufactured by him, to fill an occasional order he used a series prefixed by O. This would cover such items as Winchester

Repeating rifles or the few Spencer repeating shotgun actions which he imported, even though in this instance he fitted his own Damascus barrels and stocked them.

However even without the numbers, the date can be arrived at by the date of a particular type of action and the address of the gun-maker is often a useful indication especially where a gunmaker moved about, as indeed many did.

Where a muzzle-loading gun was converted to a pinfire or a centre-fire gun the barrel and trigger guard will normally bear the original number and the barrels the original address.

Towards 1900 and after it was the practice of some gunmakers to keep a proportion of best guns and rifles in stock partially finished and the date recorded in the book is usually the date of the sale, which may be some years after the gun was made. Where therefore an exact date for each number cannot be arrived at, the general average has been taken. In earlier years or when a gunmaker con-tinued to build guns to order only, the date of the number indicates the date of the order, the gun may not have been finished until the following year, certainly this would be so if ordered late in the year.

The addresses given in the following pages are in London unless otherwise indicated.

HENRY ATKIN

Henry Atkin served his apprenticeship with his father, also Henry Atkin, who was the first craftsman to be employed by James Purdey, with whom he remained for fifty years.

Having served his apprenticeship Henry Atkin junior left Purdey's to go to Moore and Grey, where he remained for twelve years. In 1877 he opened a small shop in Oxenden Street and in 1890 he moved to No 2 Jermyn Street.

Henry Atkin soon achieved a considerable reputation for finely balanced and highly finished game and pigeon guns, around 1900 his price for a pair of guns was £120.

In 1904 the firm became Henry Atkin Ltd and in 1905 moved to 41 Jermyn Street.

Henry Atkin died in 1907. The business moved to 88 Jermyn Street in 1918, then to 27 St James's Street in 1952, and in 1960 to 7 Bury Street on being amalgamated with Stephen Grant and Joseph Lang to form Atkin, Grant and Lang Ltd.

The following dates and gun numbers relating to Henry Atkin have been kindly given by Atkin, Grant and Lang Ltd:

In 1890 the gun numbers were about 100 and in 1900 they were about 1,400.

FREDERICK BEESLEY

Frederick Beesley is a name that will ever be remembered for his remarkable contribution towards the perfecting of hammerless and ejector guns. He started as an apprentice to W. Moore and Grey of Old Bond Street and subsequently worked for several London gun-makers, finishing with James Purdey and Son.

After inventing the outstanding Purdey hammerless action he left in 1880 to start business on his own in the Edgware Road and in 1891 at 2 St James's Street.

A remarkable series of inventions followed, some of which he sold to other gunmakers and others he used himself. Some are listed below:

DATE	SUBJECT	USED BY
3 Jan. 1880	Hammerless gun	James Purdey
14 Feb. 1883	,, ,,	F. Beesley
14 April 1883	,, ,,	Cogswell and Harrison
6 June 1883	,, ,,	James Woodward
2 Jan. 1884	,, ,,	F. Beesley
18 Feb. 1884	Block safety	Cogswell and Harrison
18 Aug. 1884	,, ,,	F. Beesley
2 July 1886	Hammerless gun	F. Beesley
24 Jan. 1887	Ejector gun	F. Beesley
31 Dec. 1889	,, ,,	F. Beesley
31 Dec. 1889	,, ,,	F. Beesley

He also invented two single trigger mechanisms, keeping the number of parts to a minimum. His ejector mechanism was reduced to two working parts only.

The firm has since 1939 been incorporated in the firm of Atkin, Grant and Lang at 7 Bury Street, St James's.

Atkin, Grant and Lang Ltd have kindly given the gun numbers and dates for F. Beesley, which are available from 1891:

YEAR	GUN NUMBER	YEAR	GUN NUMBER
1891: about 1100		1900: about 1650	
1895: ,, 1300			

THOMAS BLAND & SONS

The firm of Thomas Bland & Sons was founded in Birmingham in 1840 by Thomas Bland, and during the next thirty years the foundations were laid for the high tradition which has always been associated with the name. In 1872, Thomas Bland, Junior, eldest son of the founder, established the business in London at 106, Strand, where the business was carried on for 14 years, and in 1886 new premises were opened at 430, West Strand. Upon the death of the founder in 1887, Thomas Bland, Junior, succeeded to the headship of the firm. From that time until his death in 1928, his enterprise and inventions made the name famous in the world of sportsmen and big game hunters, and the firm made guns and rifles for nearly all the rulers of Europe and many Princes of India. Mary, Duchess to the Tenth Duke of Bedford and noted for her shooting and flying activities, bought numerous guns and rifles from the firm in the early years of the century.

Advertised in 1882 was the 'Keeper's Gun' at 6 guineas and the 'Wildfowler's Gun', a single-barrel 4 bore, at 21 guineas. The Birmingham address at this time was 41–43 Whittall Street and there was a Liverpool branch at 62 South Castle Street.

T. Clifford Bland, only son of Thomas Bland, Junior, joined the firm on leaving Harrow in 1906, and was a well-known expert on wildfowling, which branch of the business he took special pride and interest in developing. In 1900, owing to the expiration of lease, the firm removed to 2 William IV Street, and in 1919 to the present premises. Since the death of T. Clifford Bland in 1943, the business has been carried on by the Managing Director, Mr W. Caseley, who has had a long connection with the firm and whose enterprise and experience will carry into the future the high tradition of the past.

BOSS & CO.

The firm of Boss and Co. was founded in 1812 by Thomas Boss who set up business at 73 St James's Street. Thomas Boss is said to have served his apprenticeship with his father, one of Joe Manton's best workmen. He soon earned a reputation for the building of fine quality guns.

On the death of Thomas Boss, Mrs Boss took Stephen Grant into partnership as general manager about 1860. On the expiration of the partnership Stephen Grant set up business on his own, and a nephew of Thomas Boss carried on the firm until in 1891 he took into partnership John Robertson from Haddington, whose father had carried on a gunmaking business there for half a century.

At the age of nineteen John Robertson had left Haddington to work for Sir Joseph Whitworth at Manchester and there learned much of the latest techniques of rifle making. After some time with Westley Richards in Birmingham he left to spend the next ten years in the employment of James Purdey and Sons.

Having so thoroughly mastered the various branches of gun and rifle making he commenced to manufacture for certain London gunmakers, mostly for Messrs Grant, Lang and Holland. One important invention of his involved the solution of a problem that had baffled the gun trade for some time, namely the construction in 1894, of a reliable single trigger mechanism.

Under the leadership of Mr Robertson, Boss and Co. became well known for the building of guns that were second to none. While the sales department was left to the management of Mr Embleton, Mr Robertson was to be found in the workshop all day and every day, unpretentiously at his bench in his shirt sleeves.

In 1909 the firm moved to 13 Dover Street and Robertson brought out his over and under gun. After his death the business was carried on by his sons Jack, Sam and Bob. Jack was in charge of the shop, Sam managed the factory, first at Lexington Street, then at Osnaburgh Street, and Bob was the firm's shooting instructor at The Regent Shooting Ground, Hendon. Later they were joined by John Robertson's grandson Alex and the fourth generation.

In 1930 the firm moved to 41 Albemarle Street and in 1961 to 13–14 Cork Street, W.1, where they carry on past traditions. The factory is now near Southwark bridge.

The following details of gun numbers and dates have been kindly given by Boss and Co. Ltd.

YEAR	GUN NUMBER	YEAR	GUN NUMBER
1830 . . . 680		1857 . . . 1600	
1850 . . . 1400		1900 . . . 4700	

CHURCHILL LTD

Mr E. J. Churchill learned his business at the old establishment of Jeffrey & Sons in Dorchester. He then worked for fourteen years as an assistant to Mr Baker in Fleet Street and later in Cockspur Street.

E. J. Churchill started in business on his own at 8 Agar Street, Strand in 1891 where he was still in business in 1900, assisted by his son, H. E. J. Churchill, who died aged twenty.

The rise to prominence of Churchill in the 1890s was largely due to the notable success of his guns at Trap Pigeon. The high average of wins achieved by the users of his guns brought new custom and helped to establish a reputation for well-built guns skilfully fitted.

Churchill attributed some of the success of pigeon shooters to his cartridges; it seems that he favoured the fast lighter loads, which were not only very effective, but had the advantage that the second shot could be got off more quickly as the recovery was more rapid than that after a heavily loaded cartridge.

Around 1900, Churchill's nephew Robert (born 1886) joined the firm and when E. J. C. Churchill died in 1910 Robert took over the business.

The firm was then on the verge of bankruptcy, in part because latterly 'Uncle Ted', as he was known, was drinking harder than he was working as a gunmaker. Most of the London gunmakers thought that Robert Churchill and E. J. Churchill would soon go the same way many of their contemporaries were going. More so as Robert Churchill was not a practical man like his uncle, who thought he would be a better administrator than gunmaker.

Robert himself, however, was determined to become a famous gunmaker and gun expert in the ballistics field. In 1911 he persuaded one of his uncle's ex-shooting and gambling acquaintances to buy the business as a going concern for £2,000. One condition was that he would be kept on as the manager, at a salary of £4 per week, plus commission on the profits, for a period of ten years.

At first he carried on catering for the live pigeon shooters but he had already decided that the game shooters would be better customers than the pigeon shooters. With this in mind he started to experiment with a short barrelled lightweight game gun. He had already come to the conclusion that the new smokeless powders did not require barrels more than 25 inches in length and so he went ahead with his 'XXV' game gun.

In 1925 came the move to Leicester Square and the opening of his famous shooting school at Crayford, Kent. In 1934 the site was taken over for the Leicester Square Cinema and the firm moved to 32 Orange Street. In 1958 Robert Churchill died and the business was taken over in 1959 by Interarmco (U.K.) Ltd and carried on under the name of Churchill (Gunmakers) Ltd, and then in 1967 came the move to the present address of 7 Bury Street.

Churchills are perhaps best known for the 'Churchill XXV', the light 25 inch barrelled game gun, introduced by Robert Churchill.

The following gun numbers and dates have been kindly given by Churchill (Gunmakers) Ltd. They cover the period from 1891 to 1900, when many of the pigeon guns, on which E. J. Churchill's early fame rested, were built.

1891 commenced with	No 156	(July 20, 1891)
1892 October . . .	No 339	
1893 March . . .	No 384	
1894 February . . .	No 480	
1895 January . . .	No 569	
1896 January . . .	No 655	
1897 January . . .	No 761	
1898 January . . .	No 923	
1899 January . . .	No 1047	
1900 January . . .	No 1156	

COGSWELL & HARRISON

The firm of Cogswell and Harrison was first established in 1770 under the name of Essex, a relation of the Benjamin Cogswell who was in business around 1844 at 224 The Strand.

The firm became Cogswell and Harrison in 1860, and in 1874 Edgar Harrison joined the business. In 1879 the branch at 141 New Bond Street was opened, then in 1882 the Harrow factory and range were opened, and on the death of his father in 1887, Edgar Harrison took control.

In 1894 a large place in Gillingham Street was acquired where there was the only gunmaker's shooting range in central London. The factory in Gillingham Street near Victoria Station was the centre of Edgar Harrison's notable achievement in making sound machine made guns at a reasonable price.

In 1917 the branch at 168 Piccadilly was opened and the one at 226 The Strand closed. Later during the depression in the 1920s the branch at 141 New Bond Street was closed. In 1912 and 1924 Edgar Harrison was Master of the Gunmakers' Company.

Cogswell and Harrison continue in business today at 168 Piccadilly.

JOHN DICKSON AND SON

The business of John Dickson and Son was established by the first John Dickson in 1820, in the High Street of Edinburgh. He was succeeded by his son, also highly skilled, and in 1842 the business was transferred to 63 Princes Street.

At Princes Street the third John Dickson worked continuously for sixty-five years, until larger premises became necessary and the business moved to its present location at 21 Frederick Street.

In 1938 the company took over the old established business of Mortimer & Son, who were known to be in existence in 1740, and in 1947 they took over the business of James MacNaughton & Sons and eventually in 1962 the business of Alex. Martin Ltd, and more recently in 1967 the businesses of Forrest & Son of Kelso and Wm. Garden Ltd, of Aberdeen.

In their early years the firm earned a reputation for fine muzzle-loading sporting guns and rifles, and it is interesting to note that the firm continued to build percussion and even flintlock guns into the early 20th century, for an eccentric customer called Charles Gordon. Some hundreds of these guns were built for him, many of them in fine cases containing every possible piece of equipment.

John Dickson and Son are perhaps best known for their famous 'Round Action' hammerless ejector gun, so named because of the rounded shape of the action body. The 'Round Action' patented about 1880 has the lockwork attached to the trigger plate and the ejector mechanism added about 1886 is contained within the action body.

The following gun numbers and dates have been kindly given by John Dickson and Son.

YEAR	GUN NUMBER	YEAR	GUN NUMBER
1812–54:	1–1500	*1886*	. . . 4000
1860	. . . 2000	*1892*	. . . 4500
1864	. . . 2500	*1898*	. . . 5000
1870	. . . 3000	*1903*	. . . 5500
1878	. . . 3500		

GEORGE GIBBS OF BRISTOL

The gunmaking business started as J. and G. Gibbs at 4 Redcliffe Street in 1835. It became exclusively the business of George Gibbs in 1842, first at 142 Thomas Street, then at Clare Street and finally at 39 Corn Street. The factory was built in 1873, the date of the Gibbs and Pitt patent gun of which some 10,000 were built.

In 1865 the firm acquired the sole right of boring Metford rifles, which they held for fourteen years. The Metford ·461 rifling was combined from 1870 with the famous Farquharson action to make the match and sporting rifles for which the firm were especially noted.

The great hunter and explorer Sir Samuel Baker had his powerful first rifle built by Gibbs in 1841 and the famous hunter Frederick Selous used and had the highest opinion of the Gibbs ·461 rifle.

George Gibbs senior died in 1884. Gibbs's match rifles gained notable successes in the 1880s and 1890s.

STEPHEN GRANT

In 1860 Stephen Grant was the managing partner of Boss & Co. after the death of Thomas Boss and in 1866 he established his own business at 67A St James's.

Stephen Grant was a man of great experience and skill in the building of soundly constructed traditional guns and rifles of the highest quality. He was wary of new ideas, until time and trial had established their true worth. He was entrusted to build six big-game double rifles for the use of H.R.H. The Prince of Wales (afterwards King Edward VII) on his visit to India in 1875, and also received orders and warrants of appointment from the Royal Houses of France, Spain, Germany, Austria, Hungary, Russia, Persia, Turkey and some Indian Maharajahs.

In 1889 the firm became known as Stephen Grant & Sons and when in 1898 Stephen Grant died the business was continued by his sons Stephen and Herbert Edward.

In 1920 the firm moved to 7 Bury Street and in 1925 Joseph Lang

& Son were taken over, and the firm became known as Stephen Grant and Joseph Lang Ltd.

There followed a series of take-overs: 1930 Harrison and Hussey, 1932 Charles Lancaster & Co., 1935 Watson Bros, 1939 F. Beesley, 1944 Edward Paten and Son (Shooting and Fishing Agents) which was sold to Strutt and Parker in 1959.

In 1960 Henry Atkin was amalgamated to form the present firm of Atkin, Grant and Lang Ltd, of 7 Bury Street, St James's.

With the firm, during the period in which the above gunmakers were either bought out or amalgamated, was W. R. H. Robson who first joined his father, William Robson, in Stephen Grant and Sons in 1923. He was made a director in 1925, and on his father's death in 1946 he became Chairman and Managing Director.

Roy Robson, as he is known to his fellow gunmakers, was Master of the Gunmakers' Company in 1950 and 1959, and from 1957 to 1964 the fourth President of the Gunmakers' Association (reconstituted in 1962 as the Gun Trade Association).

He also took a particular interest in the benevolent societies connected with the gun trade, being a trustee of the Gun and Allied Trades Benevolent Society for many years and Chairman of the 'Long Sufferers' Association in 1960. He retired in 1964.

The following dates and gun numbers relating to Stephen Grant have been kindly given by Atkin, Grant and Lang Ltd, their records starting in 1867.

YEAR	GUN NUMBER	YEAR	GUN NUMBER
1867: about 2480		*1885*: about 5450	
1870: ,, 3000		*1890*: ,, 6100	
1875: ,, 3900		*1895*: ,, 6700	
1880: ,, 4750		*1900*: ,, 7300	

W. W. GREENER

W. W. Greener's father William Greener set up in business in his native town of Newcastle when in 1829 he returned from London where he had been working for John Manton. William Greener applied himself to improving percussion muzzle-loading guns and rifles, a most important invention being the expanding bullet for use in muzzle-loading rifles.

In order to be close to the source of gunmaking materials W. Greener moved to Birmingham in 1844. His criticisms of the Birmingham Proof House did much to bring about the changes embodied in the Gun Proof Act of 1855.

The Birmingham business prospered, W. Greener's guns and rifles becoming well known at home and abroad, particularly in South Africa where he supplied many two-groove 'Cape Rifles'. His position in the trade was recognised when he was appointed to make guns for Prince Albert and in the Great Exhibition of 1851 he received the highest award 'for guns and barrels perfectly forged and finished'.

In 1835 his first book *The Gun* appeared, followed by the *Science of Gunnery* in 1841 and an enlarged edition of the latter in 1846.

In his last work *Gunnery in 1858* he was scathing in his criticism of the new breech-loaders; he lived and died a muzzle-loading man.

His son, William Wellington Greener, on the contrary, devoted himself wholeheartedly to the improvement of the breech-loader. Perhaps the best known of his many innovations was the top cross bolt of 1865 which was combined with the Purdey bolt in 1873 to form the very strong well known 'Treble Wedge Fast' breech action.

W. W. Greener, although not the inventor, will always be associated with the development and vigorous exploitation of choke boring. Some of Greener's early hammerless and ejector guns resembled in many respects the famous Anson and Deeley actions, for Greener was ever quick to recognise an important invention.

As an author W. W. Greener surpassed his father; his best known book *The Gun and its Development* was first published in 1881 and ran to nine editions. Other books included *Modern Shot Guns, The Breech-Loader* and *Choke Bore Guns*.

In the 1890s W. W. Greener claimed that his sporting gun factory in St Mary's Row, Birmingham, was the largest in England and the only one in which gun barrel forging was carried on.

His son H. Greener had by then joined his father in the business which, apart from the address at St Mary's, Birmingham, was also carried on at 68 Haymarket, London from 1879 and 19 Paragon Street, Hull.

In 1916 the London business moved to 29 Pall Mall and in 1920 the firm became W. W. Greener Ltd and was continued by W. W. Greener's sons Harry and Charles E. after their father's death in 1921. Charles E. Greener became the second President of the Gunmakers' Association in 1930.

In 1933 the London business moved to 40 Pall Mall and after the death of Harry in 1929 and Charles in 1951, the business was continued by H. Leyton Greener, son of Harry, until it was sold in 1965 to Webley and Scott Ltd.

HOLLAND AND HOLLAND LTD.

The history of Holland & Holland began in 1835, when it was founded at 98 New Bond Street by Mr Harris J. Holland a sportsman with considerable experience of general game shooting, and also well known as a fine shot at trap pigeons at the Red House and Hornsey Wood.

His nephew Mr Henry Holland served a six-year apprenticeship in the workshops, and took over the general management from his uncle around 1875. In 1877 the firm became Holland and Holland. On the death of Mr Harris J. Holland in 1895 the business came into the hands of Mr Henry Holland, who directly made Mr Froome a partner, as a mark of his appreciation of the value of Mr Froome to the business.

Mr Froome, who was apprenticed to the firm around 1855, was of very great service in helping to establish the firm's reputation for fine quality rifles of all kinds. His remarkable ability enabled him to set new standards in the accurate sighting in of double rifles, and it was in great measure due to his ability that Holland and Holland were able to win so decisively the Rifle Trials arranged by Mr Walsh in 1883. Although most of the top makers did not take part in these rifle trials, because they had much to lose by failure to win and little to gain from winning, Holland and Holland had such confidence in the shooting of their rifles and in Mr Froome who did the shooting that they took the risk and carried the day, winning in all classes from rook rifles to 4 bore elephant rifles.

In 1886 Mr Holland was successful in the production and sale of Colonel Fosbery's rifled choke, ball and shot gun, which Holland and Holland named the Paradox. This marvellously versatile gun quickly replaced the old smooth bore, ball and shot gun.

In the 1890s Holland and Holland were specialising in cylinder bored shotguns throwing 135 to 140 pellets in a 30-inch circle at 40 yards (load 1⅛ No 6 shot). The well known 'Royal' hammerless action of 1889 was further improved by the addition of the ejector mechanism of 1893 and the single trigger mechanism of the late 1890s. The Harrow Road factory was opened in 1897 and in 1899 the firm became Holland and Holland Ltd.

Well known from the 1890s was Holland and Holland's extensive shooting ground named 'The Badminton' by permission of the Duke of Beaufort.

In 1903 Henry Holland became Master of the Gunmakers' Company and in 1912 the first President of the Gunmakers' Association. He died in 1930 and was succeeded by Colonel J. E. D. Holland, D.S.O., M.C.

Messrs Holland and Holland, at 13 Bruton Street since 1960, continue the tradition established in the 19th century of building a wide variety of best quality sporting guns and rifles.

CHARLES LANCASTER

Charles Lancaster of 26 York Street, Gloucester Road (his workshop was in Tichfield Street), was well known for the finely finished and bored barrels that he supplied to the trade in the great days of John and Joseph Manton, to whom he sold many barrels bearing his initials C.L.

Some of the barrels used in the early guns of James Purdey were also by Lancaster. In the words of Colonel Peter Hawker: 'Lancaster, who has raised many gunmakers to the head of the trade by allowing them to put their names to what was his work in all essential parts of the barrels, has long since started for himself. This I advised him to do if ever Joe Manton retired. I may now safely say that no man stands before him.'

It was in 1826 that he set up as a gunmaker at 151 New Bond Street, building percussion guns and rifles of the highest quality. His first Royal Appointment was to the Prince Consort in 1843 and the three succeeding generations of the Royal Family continued their patronage.

Lancaster died in 1845 and the business was continued by his sons Charles William and Alfred.

Between 1846–52 a few Lancaster two-grooved rifles were issued for use in the Kaffir war.

In 1851 the Lancaster oval bore rifling was introduced and also exhibited at the Great Exhibition and in 1852 Lancaster's shooting grounds at Wormwood Scrubs were opened and claimed to be the first in London.

In 1852 came the base fire cartridge and gun and in 1856 Lancaster oval bore percussion rifles were issued to sappers and miners.

Alfred Lancaster set up on his own at 27 South Audley Street in 1859 and in 1886 moved to 50 Green Street.

In 1878 Charles William Lancaster died and his business was taken over by his pupil Henry Alfred Alexander Thorn, the business becoming Charles Lancaster & Co. in 1879.

In 1882 Thorn tried out a few Spencer pump action guns, fitted with his own Damascus barrels, the actions imported from America. In his hammerless guns Thorn favoured back action locks and continued to use best quality Damascus rather than steel barrels.

The first edition of *The Art of Shooting* by 'Charles Lancaster' was published in 1889, running to many editions and still in print.

In 1897 Thorn introduced his 'Pigmy' cartridges which, although unsuccessful, anticipated the 2-inch gun and cartridge of thirty years later.

In 1904 the firm moved to 11 Panton Street and became Charles Lancaster Ltd. In 1925 they moved to Mount Street and in 1932 to 7 Bury Street on being purchased by Stephen Grant and Joseph Lang Ltd.

One of the best known of the Lancaster guns is the famous light game gun the Lancaster 'Twelve-Twenty'.

The following numbers relating to Charles Lancaster have been kindly given by Atkin, Grant and Lang Ltd. These apply to best quality guns and rifles.

YEAR	GUN NUMBER	YEAR	GUN NUMBER
1826 . . . 100		1879 . . . 4924	
1830: about 600		1880 . . . 4949	
1840: „ 1200		1881 . . . 4982	
1850: „ 2100		1882 . . . 5079	
1860: „ 3200		1883 . . . 5186	
1861 . . . 3400		1884 . . . 5359	
1862 . . . 3540		1885 . . . 5497	
1863 . . . 3693		1886 . . . 5627	
1864 . . . 3805		1887 . . . 5764	
1865 . . . 3914		1888 . . . 5926	
1866 . . . 3999		1889 . . . 6136	
1867 . . . 4087		1890 . . . 6406	
1868 . . . 4183		1891 . . . 6671	
1869 . . . 4271		1892 . . . 6988	
1870 . . . 4328		1893 . . . 7189	
1871 . . . 4401		1894 . . . 7360	
1872 . . . 4477		1895 . . . 7548	
1873 . . . 4562		1896 . . . 7709	
1874 . . . 4644		1897 . . . 7940	
1875 . . . 4714		1898 . . . 8132	
1876 . . . 4769		1899 . . . 8353	
1877 . . . 4833		1900 . . . 8529	
1878 . . . 4892		1901 . . . 8700	

JOSEPH LANG

Joseph Lang, who had worked for Alexander Wilson of 1 Vigo Street and from 1812 of 14 Tichbourne Street, Piccadilly, established himself in business in 1821 at 7 Haymarket, producing guns and rifles of the highest quality. It is of interest that he married the daughter of James Purdey the elder.

In 1826 he advertised the entire stock of Joseph Manton who had gone bankrupt, and in 1827 he opened his Shooting Gallery, 21 yards in length.

Around 1850 he did much to make the lemon and white pointer fashionable and suggested Field Trials.

In 1851 he exhibited at the Great Exhibition and there saw the Lefaucheux breech-loading gun. He introduced his own version of the pinfire gun in 1852 and in 1853 he moved to 22 Cockspur Street.

In 1880 Lang's son Edward was trading as Joseph Lang and Son at 88 Wigmore Street and in 1881 at 89 Wigmore Street. In 1890 he moved to 10 Pall Mall and while there introduced the curious 'Vena Contracta' gun invented by Horatio Phillips, shooting editor of *The Field*. This gun fired a 12 bore cartridge but the barrel tapered into a 20-bore in the first nine inches.

Lang's son James set up on his own in 1887 at 33 and later 64A New Bond Street, then in 1888 at 18 Brook Street. In 1891 he became James Lang & Co. and moved to 162 New Bond Street and in 1895 became Lang & Hussey Ltd.

In 1898 the businesses of the two brothers were amalgamated to form the firm of Joseph Lang and Son Ltd which was bought out by Stephen Grant and Sons in 1925.

The following dates and gun numbers relating to Joseph Lang have been kindly given by Atkin, Grant and Lang Ltd, their records starting with 1858.

YEAR	GUN NUMBER	YEAR	GUN NUMBER
1858: about 2085		*1880:* about 6000	
1860: „ 2332		*1885:* „ 7031	
1865: „ 2970		*1890:* „ 7546	
1870: „ 3916		*1895:* „ 8150	
1875: „ 5180		*1900:* „ 9100	

JOHN MANTON

John Manton was born in 1752, the son of John Manton of Grantham (1725–1802). He was apprenticed to John Dixon of Leicester in 1766 and around 1775 was working for John Twigg of Piccadilly. He learned much of the art of building double guns from Twigg, becoming his foreman. In 1781 he opened his own establishment at 6 Dover Street where the business remained until it closed down in 1878.

He soon achieved a high reputation for the building of fine guns, rifles and pistols and achieved Royal patronage. In 1814 he took his son George Henry (born 1789) into partnership and thereafter traded as John Manton and Son. In 1833 William Hudson became a partner and in 1834 John Manton died.

The business was continued by George Henry Manton with his nephew Gildon Manton (born 1820) as partner.

In 1854 George Henry Manton died followed by Gildon in 1856 and in 1867 his widow sold out to the foreman Charles Roe, who carried on the business until it closed down in 1878.

John Manton's apprentices, apart from his famous brother Joseph, included John Blanch and Staudenmayer.

JOSEPH MANTON

Joseph Manton was born in 1766, the third son of John Manton of Grantham. He was apprenticed to Newton of Grantham and then joined his elder brother John.

In 1792 he established his own business at 25 Davies Street where in 1816 he patented his pelletlock and in 1818 invented his tube lock. He soon became famous mainly for the quality of his double guns.

In 1819 he moved to premises at 11 Hanover Square, the shop door being at 314 Oxford Street. In 1822 his sons Frederick and Charles were working for him and he traded for a short time as Joseph Manton and Sons.

In 1825 Frederick was sent out to establish Manton and Co., 10 Lall Bazaar, Calcutta and in this year Joseph was imprisoned for debt.

In 1826 he was declared bankrupt and his entire stock sold. In 1827 he restarted at Marylebone Park House, New Road but in 1828 he was again in prison and closed down. In 1832 he traded at Burwood Place, Edgware Road for fourteen weeks and in 1834 was trading as Joseph Manton and Son (John Augustus) at 6 Holles Street, Cavendish Square.

In 1835 Joseph Manton died aged 69 and in 1838 the business was sold to Henry Egg who advertised as 'Successors to Joseph Manton and Son'. In 1841 a branch was opened at 1 Piccadilly which in 1843 remained the firm's only address. From 1851 to 1880 the firm was continued by Henry Egg only.

In 1846 William Robert Wallis bought Manton & Co., Calcutta and in 1850 he bought the business of Samuel Nock at 43 Regent Circus, trading under both names at 116 Jermyn Street. In 1878 he retired and the business was continued by his sons.

The Calcutta business moved after 1837 first to 63 Cossitollah and later to the present address of 13 Old Court House Street.

JAMES PURDEY AND SONS LTD

James Purdey, the founder of the present firm of James Purdey and Sons Ltd, was born in 1784. He was the son of James Purdey born 1732, who was a gunmaker in the Minories, a street near the Tower of London which had a number of gunmakers in it in the 17th and 18th centuries.

James Purdey served his six year apprenticeship with Thomas Ketch Hutchinson, commencing in 1797, and then worked for Joseph Manton as a stocker and finisher from 1803 to 1806, when he left to become Forsyth's 'leading man', or manager, working on the building of early percussion guns.

In 1814 Purdey set up business on his own in Princes Street, Leicester Square. After some early struggles, he is said to have been helped by the patronage of Lord Henry Bentinck, a story supported by the fact that Purdey wrote under a photograph of Lord Henry, taken years later, 'My first and best customer. J.P.'

He had prospered sufficiently by 1826 to take over Joseph Manton's old premises (Manton having gone bankrupt) at 314 Oxford Street. He is said to have changed the number of this address for superstitious reasons, presumably he did not want the same number as the unfortunate Joe Manton. He first used the number 315 Oxford Street but after a very short time, perhaps because of some objection to his use of this number, he changed it to 314½ Oxford Street, which remained his address until 1882.

In 1843 James Purdey, known as 'the younger' (1828–1909) was apprenticed to his father, and in 1882 the business moved to Audley House, 57 and 58 South Audley Street, as a result of collaboration with the Duke of Westminster. This building with its famous Long Room, steeped in past and present associations, is the centre of today's thriving business.

The factory where new guns are built and old ones maintained is at Irongate Wharf, Paddington.

James Purdey was primarily concerned with the era of the percussion cap muzzle-loader. He built some fine flintlock guns in his early years in Princes Street, many of which were later converted for the percussion cap, and so examples are very rare. Early in the 1820s he was producing fine percussion guns of the type that were to become general, that is they had the hollow nozzle or nipple over which a primed copper cap fitted.

The early use of the percussion cap, the ability to build guns and rifles of the highest quality and finish, which were at the same time strong and durable, gained for Purdey a reputation which has endured and has been built upon by succeeding generations.

James Purdey was noted in his later years for his work on double game rifles of the higher velocity two-groove type that replaced the old standard 16 bore firing an ounce ball and 1½ drams of powder. According to W. W. Greener, Purdey produced, in 1856, rifles of the two-groove type, of 40 and 50 bore, firing a heavy charge of powder, to which he gave the name of 'Express train'. The term 'Express' has since been used for a rifle having sufficient velocity to give a long point blank range and low trajectory.

Both the James Purdeys were much in attendance at the fashionable pigeon shooting: the elder at The Red House Club, Battersea and Hornsey Wood House and the younger at 'The Gun Club', Notting Hill.

Purdey's son, James Purdey the younger, took over the business in 1863 when his father died. He was at the head of the business during the period of tremendous activity that saw the transition from the pinfire gun to the hammerless ejector and from the two-groove muzzle-loading rifle to the breech-loading Express rifle.

Following such important inventions as those of the Purdey bolt and the hammerless action, James Purdey the younger was the first to use Sir Joseph Whitworth's fluid compressed steel tubes.

During this period, the firm of James Purdey and Sons built guns for many of the greatest game shots of the day, including Lord Ripon, Lord Walsingham, Lord Huntingfield, Maharajah Duleep Singh, Sir Henry Stonor, Lord Hill and A. Stuart-Wortley.

The following list of royal patrons headed a bill for a pair of guns dated 1899:

> Makers to Her Majesty The Queen, H.R.H. The Prince of Wales, H.R.H. The Duke of York, H.R.H. The Duke of Cambridge. H.I.M. The Emperor of Russia. H.I.M. The German Emperor. H.M. The King of Italy. H.M. The King of Spain. H.M. The King of Portugal. H.R. & I.H. The ArchDuke Franz-Ferdinand of Austria.

The firm became known as James Purdey and Sons in 1879, that is James Purdey the younger and his sons Athol Stuart (1858–1939) and Cecil Onslow.

In 1882 for a short time before the move to Audley House the firm had premises at 287 to 289 Oxford Street. About 1925 the firm became a limited company and about 1929 Athol Purdey's sons James Alexander (1891–1960) and Thomas Donald Stuart (1897–1957) took over; Tom Purdey, as he was always known, becoming Chairman and Managing Director.

The firm of James Woodward was bought out in 1949. Tom Purdey became the Third President of the Gunmakers' Association in 1951 and in 1954 President of James Purdey and Sons Ltd with Lord Sherwood as Chairman and C. H. Lawrence, M.B.E. as Managing Director.

C. H. Lawrence, or Harry Lawrence as he is generally known, has long been associated with the history of Purdeys, both his father and uncle having worked for the firm. Harry Lawrence's father left Purdey's to go to India and on returning worked for J. Woodward for a time; however he returned to Purdey's and became Manager of the Factory in 1912.

Harry Lawrence, after serving his apprenticeship with Purdey's from 1914 to 1921, worked as an actioner and also gained a thorough knowledge of all aspects of gunmaking. During the war he developed a precision tool business working on Government contracts; his services in this field were recognised by the award of the M.B.E.

He has been Chairman of the Proof House Committee since 1954 and was Master of the Gunmakers' Company in 1954 and 1962, something of a Purdey tradition for between 1841 and 1969 Purdey family or Purdey directors have been Masters of the Gunmakers' Company 24 times.

The present directors are Lord Sherwood (Chairman), V. B. J. Seeley, C. H. Lawrence, M.B.E. (Managing Director), A. J. R. Collins, C.V.O. and the Hon. R. B. Beaumont, present Master of the Gunmakers' Company.

The following dates and gun numbers have been kindly given by James Purdey and Sons Ltd.

YEAR	GUN NUMBER	YEAR	GUN NUMBER
1814–25:	974	1857 . . .	5268–5443
1826 . . .	975–1149	1858 . . .	5444–5542
1827 . . .	1150–1324	1859 . . .	5543–5747
1828 . . .	1325–1549	1860 . . .	5748–5997
1829 . . .	1550–1874	1861 . . .	5998–6271
1830 . . .	1875–1999	1862 . . .	6272–6422
1831 . . .	2000–2247	1863 . . .	6423–6671
1832 . . .	2248–2421	1864 . . .	6672–6871
1833 . . .	2422–2497	1865 . . .	6872–7121
1834 . . .	2498–2697	1866 . . .	7122–7420
1835 . . .	2698–2773	1867 . . .	7421–7646
1836 . . .	2774–2848	1868 . . .	7647–7896
1837 . . .	2849–3098	1869 . . .	7897–8246
1838 . . .	3099–3223	1870 . . .	8247–8322
1839 . . .	3224–3298	1871 . . .	8323–8646
1840 . . .	3299–3473	1872 . . .	8647–8821
1841 . . .	3474–3623	1873 . . .	8822–9096
1842 . . .	3624–3698	1874 . . .	9097–9288
1843 . . .	3699–3848	1875 . . .	9289–9505
1844 . . .	3849–3998	1876 . . .	9506–9648
1845 . . .	3999–4048	1877 . . .	9649–10153
1846 . . .	4049–4098	1878 . . .	10154–10440
1847 . . .	4099–4223	1879 . . .	10441–10800
1848 . . .	4224–4348	1880 . . .	10801–10900
1849 . . .	4349–4473	1881 . . .	10901–11082
1850 . . .	4474–4599	1882 . . .	11083–11342
1851 . . .	4600–4720	1883 . . .	11343–11669
1852 . . .	4721–4844	1884 . . .	11670–12036
1853 . . .	4845–4944	1885 . . .	12037–12171
1854 . . .	4945–5093	1886 . . .	12172–12530
1855 . . .	5094–5167	1887 . . .	12531–12875
1856 . . .	5168–5267	1888 . . .	12876–13150

YEAR	GUN NUMBER	YEAR	GUN NUMBER
1889 . . .	13151–13468	1895 . . .	15135–15362
1890 . . .	13469–13662	1896 . . .	15363–15726
1891 . . .	13663–14000	1897 . . .	15727–16095
1892 . . .	14001–14520	1898 . . .	16096–16420
1893 . . .	14521–14851	1899 . . .	16421–16736
1894 . . .	14852–15134	1900 . . .	16737–17078

JOHN RIGBY AND CO.

Rigby of Dublin, established 1735, was a name well known in the era of the flintlock. A silver medal records the following: 'Independent Dublin Volunteers, Reward of Merit, Presented to John Rigby, March 25, 1781, being the best shot in the Grenadier Company of the Independent Dublin Volunteers.' Also a pair of silver cups were presented to him in 1816 by the contractors for small arms in Dublin, 'As an acknowledgement of his exertions in the interests of his trade'. The development of rifles of the highest quality and a close connection with the design and manufacture of government arms was to be a dominating feature of the firm's activities in the 19th century.

William Rigby succeeded to the business in 1819 and subsequently entered into partnership with his younger brother John Jason Rigby. Rigbys were pioneers in the forging of Damascus barrels, the distinctive style being a fine pattern deeply etched to bring the harder metal into relief. Also of note during the percussion period were the over and under combined rifle and shot guns, and their use of back action locks with a third bent to raise the hammer a fraction above the percussion cap; this was for convenience in carrying and to prevent the cap from being detached.

On the death of his father in 1858 the business came into the hands of John Rigby who achieved the distinction of being appointed to the post of Superintendent of the Royal Small Arms Factory at Enfield in 1887.

In 1860 John Rigby invented the method of forming cartridge cases from coiled sheet brass, the type being similar to that adopted four years later by Colonel Boxer as the service cartridge for use in Snider rifles.

Rigby long range rifles were successful in competition with other makers in the second stage of the Queen's Prize in the 1860s. Captain Horatio Ross, the great rifle shot, used Rigby rifles, and it was with one of these that he won the Cambridge University Long Range Cup in 1867. In 1878 John Rigby led the Irish Eight to victory with the highest score ever made at Wimbledon up to that time, and he also won numerous other trophies for rifle shooting.

On the introduction of cordite for the ·303 service rifle it was found that Metford's rifling would not stand up to sufficient wear for service needs. Mr Rigby's answer was the five groove rifling in which the grooves and lands were of equal width. This type of rifling was also used for ·303 sporting rifles.

While Mr John Rigby was occupied at the Enfield factory, the firm of John Rigby & Co. of St James's Street, W.1 (from 1866) and the factory at Ham Yard were managed by his son Mr Ernest John Rigby who had been five years in the Birmingham Small Arms factory before managing the family business, showed his competence with the rifle by winning the Albert Cup and shooting for the Irish Eight at Bisley.

Though Rigby's turned out many fine sporting guns, it is for a wide variety of excellent sporting rifles that the firm is best known. John Rigby & Co. pioneered the modern, high velocity, Nitro Express rifle. In 1897 they introduced the very first ·450 calibre Cordite rifle. It fired 70 grains of Cordite and a 480 grain bullet that developed a muzzle energy of close to 5,000 ft/lb. Until then Big Game rifles had been mostly 8–12 bore, firing 5–10 drams of black powder. Later, the ·470 cartridges were developed, and their ·416 Big Game magazine rifle.

About 1892 the Dublin business was sold to Messrs Truelock and Harris, and in 1900 the firm became John Rigby & Co. Ltd of London only.

In 1916 John Rigby died and the business was continued by his sons Theo and Ernest John, Master of the Gunmakers' Company in 1914.

In 1955 the firm moved to 32 King Street and in 1963 to 28 Sackville Street, W.1, where business is carried on today.

The following gun numbers and dates, kindly given by John Rigby & Co., relate to best quality double guns and rifles and also best single and magazine rifles.

YEAR	GUN NUMBER	YEAR	GUN NUMBER
1822	5341	1870	13416
1825	5745	1875	14227
1830	6667	1880	15076
1835	7640	1885	15660
1840	8531	1890	16106
1845	9487	1895: about	16410
1850	10171	1900: ,,	16700
1855	10634	1905: ,,	17250
1860	10986	1910: ,,	17550
1865	12418		

WEBLEY & SCOTT LTD

In 1898 the Birmingham wholesale arms manufacturers Messrs Scott and Webley amalgamated to form the Webley & Scott Revolver and Arms Co. Ltd. With Mr T. W. Webley as managing director they became the largest wholesale arms business in Birmingham, the London branch being at 78 Shaftesbury Avenue.

Apart from Government contracts for the famous Webley revolver they had for years supplied a considerable proportion of the London and provincial gunmakers with guns which of course bore the names of a variety of 'gunmakers'. In the case of some London makers whose guns were supplied by Webley & Scott the barrels were London proved so that they bore London proof marks in order to help the illusion that they were London made guns.

Webley and Scott did not apply to sporting guns the mass production methods used for revolvers; the reason being that it was considered that sportsmen's requirements were too diverse to make it a practicable proposition. As many of the gunmakers who were supplied by Webley and Scott required variations to suit their particular style or to suit their customer's requirements, a standard gun was not practicable.

Improvements were made to gun barrel steels to the extent that Mr Webley considered the Webley & Scott steel as good as the Krupp steel with the advantage that it stood up better to brazing.

Messrs Webley & Scott Ltd of Handsworth, Birmingham 21, bought out W. W. Greener in 1965 and continue today to manufacture a variety of weapons including fine sporting guns.

WESTLEY RICHARDS AND CO. LTD

The firm of Westley Richards and Co. Ltd was established in 1812 by Mr William Westley Richards. At their factory in High Street, Birmingham they specialised in good quality, ready made guns, large numbers of which were sold through the London agency (started in 1815) managed by the famous 'Bishop of Bond Street' at 178 New Bond Street. 'Uncle' William Bishop was a great character as well known to those sportsmen who wished to raise some ready money on a gun as to other gentlemen who profited by obtaining a good gun at a moderate price. This roomy figure was invariably seen clothed in black, a large white apron on, his long shirt cuffs turned back, and on his head, and never seen off it, his high silk hat. Also part of the scene were his dogs and the bust of Colonel Peter Hawker who had written favourably of Westley Richards' guns in his famous book. William Bishop served the firm for 56 years.

The consistent good quality of Westley Richards' guns, coupled with Hawker's and the Bishop's recommendations did much to establish the early reputation of the firm.

However, far from resting upon this reputation gained in the days of muzzle-loaders, they were destined to take a leading part in transforming the early breech-loaders into efficient hammerless ejectors. At the head of the business during this period was Westley Richards' son who joined the firm in 1855. Apart from his interest in gunmaking he was a keen hunting man, keeping many horses at his home Ashwell Hall, Oakham. He later became High Sheriff of his county.

Westley Richards assisted Whitworth in the development of his rifle and also Captain Minié in the design of the first Enfield rifle. Other notable developments were their breech-loading carbine of 1858, their solid drawn brass cartridge case, their falling block mechanism of 1868 that anticipated the Martini action, and some help with the bolthead of the Lee-Metford rifle.

In the development of breech-loading sporting weapons Westley Richards had a record that is remarkable. Patented in 1858 and improved in 1862 was their top lever fastening connecting with the 'doll's head' extension. In 1875 came the superb Anson and Deeley hammerless action, notable for its strength and economy of parts (Anson was a foreman and J. Deeley Managing Director). To this was added in 1884 the first efficient fore-end ejector mechanism, and in 1898 a further refinement was added to the famous boxlock action when the locks were rendered detachable by the simple expedient of unclipping the under plate. Added in the 1890s was a double trigger which effectively prevented a double discharge (a most useful addition to a heavy double rifle), and in 1901 a selective single trigger mechanism. Fine sporting rifles were produced from muzzle-loading rifles with the hollow based expanding bullet to a variety of high velocity breech-loading rifles, including the ·318 Accelerated Express, ·425 Magnum Express ·and ·476 calibre. After 1910 some double rifles were built on the over and under principle.

A. H. Gale managed the London agency on the death of William Bishop and Leslie B. Taylor succeeded John Deeley in 1899 as Managing Director. John Deeley, who had been Managing Director from 1872, remained as Chairman until his death in 1913, and George Dawson Deeley was then appointed chairman.

The London agency moved to Conduit Street where it was known as the Westley Richards (Agency) Ltd, then on being bought by Holland and Holland Ltd it was moved to 13 Bruton Street.

Westley Richards & Co. Ltd continue business from Grange Road, Bournbrook, Birmingham 29.

The following gun numbers and dates have been kindly given by Westley Richards and Co. Ltd. These 'five figure' numbers include most of the best quality double guns and rifles. The Company explain that there are so many series of numbers for other types and qualities of weapons, some with prefixes like 'O' and 'T' which were in use for varying lengths of time, that it would not be practicable to give these.

YEAR	GUN NUMBER	YEAR	GUN NUMBER
1869	12000	1908	17000
1877	13000	1924	18000
1884	14000	1935	18500
1893	15000	1957	19000
1901	16000		

JOHN WILKES

John Wilkes is probably the oldest London gunmaking firm to remain continuously in the hands of the original family. At their premises in Beak Street they carry on today in much the same manner as the traditional 19th-century gunmakers, in that shop and workshops are at the same address and all the family are practising gunmakers.

The first John Wilkes recorded was established in Birmingham in 1830, specialising in military and sporting guns. In 1879 the son, also John Wilkes, came to London and entered into partnership with James Dalzeil Dougall at 59 St James's Street. He stayed until Dougall died and the business was sold in 1893, setting up on his own in Lower James Street, W.1.

In 1919 a move was made to Gerrard Street and in 1924 came the last move to 79 Beak Street. In 1968 John Wilkes, working in the shop until the last, died aged 82. The business is carried on by his sons, John and Tom Wilkes, who continue the family tradition of building to order best quality sporting guns and single and double sporting rifles.

JAMES WOODWARD

In 1827 James Woodward joined Charles Moore and they traded as Moore and Woodward. Charles Moore, the son of William Moore, had established himself at Regent Circus in 1800, he then moved to 77 St James's Street in 1824. In 1833 Moore and Woodward moved to 64 St James's Street, then in 1851 became James Woodward and in 1872 James Woodward and Sons (James and Charles; there was also a grandson Charles L. Woodward).

In 1877 Woodward's hammerless gun was introduced and in an advertisement of 1882 James Woodward and Sons described themselves as express gun and rifle manufacturers of 64 St James's Street, their factory being at 1 Blue Ball Yard.

J. Woodward & Sons built finely finished guns and rifles with a particular elegance and refinement of design. Perhaps their most important contribution was their over and under gun first introduced in 1913, followed by an improved model in 1921; this over and under gun is certainly one of the best designed and most graceful of the type.

In 1937 the firm moved to Bury Street and in 1949 was bought by James Purdey and Sons Ltd.

The following dates and numbers for James Woodward's guns and rifles have been kindly given by James Purdey and Sons Ltd. The records start from No 3268.

YEAR	GUN NUMBER	YEAR	GUN NUMBER
1874–79:	3268–3717	1910–15:	6045–6433
1880–85:	3718–4102	1916–21:	6434–6637
1886–91:	4103–4608	1922–27:	6638–6832
1892–97:	4609–5230	1928–33:	6833–7014
1898–1903	5231–5712	1934–39:	7015–7153
1904–09	6713–6044	1940–48:	7154–7184

MR W. R. H. ROBSON'S NOTES ON LONDON GUNMAKERS

(*Some sources of information from books are indicated by giving the author's name in brackets.*)

ADAMS, Robert
 1858: Henry Street, Bermondsey.
 1859: 76 King William Street.
 1866: 46 Pall Mall.
 c. 1882: Adams & Co., 32 Finsbury Pavement.

ANDREWS, Charles E.
 1900: 15 Swallow Street.

BAKER, Thomas Kinslake
 1838: 1 Stonenther Street (Hawker).
 1844: also Bury Street.
 1850: St James's Street.
 1851: 88 Fleet Street.

——Frederick Thomas
 1858: also 21 Cockspur Street.
 1899: 88 Fleet Street and 29 Glasshouse Street.
 1908: 29 Glasshouse Street.

BARTON, John

 1800–32: (Glendinning).

 1812–16: 14 Haymarket (Hawker).

 1818: 15 James Street, Haymarket.

J. BEATTIE

 1882: J. Beattie were at 104 Queen Victoria Street, advertising their 'Acme' hammerless gun.

J. BLANCH & SON

 Established 1809.

 1825: at 39 Fish Street Hill.

 1900: at 29 Gracechurch Street, where they had been for many years. They built some very attractive game guns.

BOZARD & CO.

 1885: 33 New Bond Street.

 1896: 8 Bennet Street.

 1898: 4 Panton Street.

 1908: 8 Craven Street, Strand. (Also the address at this time of W. MOORE & GREY.)

BREECH LOADING ARMOURY CO. LTD

 1866–8: 4 Pall Mall.

COLT, Colonel Samuel (1814–62)

 1835: established at Hartford, Connecticut, to manufacture his single-barrel pistol with revolving cylinder.

 1851: at London Exhibition.

 1853: 1 Spring Gardens.

 1854: Thames Bank factory, Pimlico, opened.

 1857: 14 Pall Mall.

 1864: Colt's Patent Fire-Arms Manufacturing Co.

 1892: 26 Glasshouse Street.

 1894: also 15A Pall Mall to 1908 or later.

G. H. DAW

 In 1882 G. H. Daw and Co. (established 1780) were at 67 St James's Street, London, S.W., and 57 Threadneedle Street.

 George Daw was responsible for introducing the central fire cartridge and gun in 1861.

DOUGALL, James Dalzeil, FSA, FZS

 1760: established ('Purple Heather').

 1857: published *Shooting Simplified.*

 1864: 59 St James's Street.

 1865: 2nd edition of *Shooting Simplified* with chapter on the Dougall lock-fast gun.

 1875: Shooting, its appliances, practice and purpose.

 1883: 8 Bennet Street.

1888: James Dougall & Sons.

1893: business bought by Charles Ingram, 10 Waterloo St., Glasgow. Many years at 23 Gordon Street, Glasgow.

EGG, Durs (1750–1834) (Glendinning)

Established in the reign of George III (1760–1820).

1777: already well established (Neal p. 8).

1797: made gun for Prince of Wales and possibly received the warrant.

1812: 132 Strand (Blanch).

1824: 1 Colonnade, Pall Mall (Hawker).

1834: died.

1838: (Son John? or D.I.) 10 Opera Arcade, removed from 20 Haymarket (Hawker).

1850: 4 Pall Mall (Hawker).

1866–8: Breech Loading Armoury Co. Ltd were at this address.

1875: Egg business and premises taken over by Watson.

EGG, Joseph (brother of Durs) 1780 (Glendinning)

1816: 1 Piccadilly (Hawker).

1838: sons Charles and Henry trading as Egg & Sons. They bought the lease and business of Joseph Manton & Son and advertised as 'Successors to J. Manton & Son' (Neal).

1844: C. & H. Egg (Hawker).

1851: Henry Egg.

1870–80: Henry William Egg.

EVANS, William

from Purdey

1883: 95A Buckingham Palace Road.

1885: 4 Holden Terrace, Pimlico.

1888: 4 Pall Mall Place.

1896: 63 Pall Mall.

1944: bombed out and at 67A St James's to date.

FAIRMAN

1850: 68 Jermyn Street.

1853–68: 23 Jermyn Street.

FORSYTH, Rev Alexander John, M.A., LL.D.

1768: born 28th December.

1791: succeeded father as Minister of Belhelvie, Aberdeenshire.

1807: invented the percussion lock.

1812: in business as Forsyth & Co., 10 Piccadilly, with James Purdey as manager.

1816: 8 Leicester Street.

1843: died 11th January.

1851: firm showed in Great Exhibition.

1852: business closed (Blanch).

GYE & MONCRIEFF
1876–85: 60 St James's Street.
1886–87: 44 Dover Street.

HANCOCK, W. J. & CO.
1891: 308 High Holborn.
1896–99: also 5 Pall Mall Place.

HARRISON & HUSSEY LTD
Claud Harrison (many years with Cogswell & Harrison) Chairman and
Manager Director, and H. H. Hussey started 1919 at 41 Albemarle
Street.
1922: Hussey had left.
1929: 20th June, Claud Harrison died.
1930: 7 Bury Street on purchase by Stephen Grant & Joseph Lang Ltd.

HARRISS, Henry Joseph
1895–98: traded as Joseph Lang & Son at 10 Pall Mall.
1899: 9 Carlton Street.

HELLIS, Charles
1884: established.
1894: 21 Shrewsbury Road.
1897: 119 Edgware Road.
1905: died. Business continued as Charles Hellis & Sons and carried
on by the two following generations until acquired by Henry Atkin
in 1956. Although many Hellis guns were made, the firm was probably best known for its extensive trade in cartridges.

HENRY, Alexander
1869–72: 39A Kingdom Street (Edwin H. Newby, agent).
1877–86: 118 Pall Mall.
1887–93: 31 Cockspur Street.
1894–98: 23 Pall Mall.
1899: 13A Charles Street, Haymarket. This notable rifle maker was
also at 12 South St Andrew Street, Edinburgh.

HUSSEY, Henry Joseph
Late assistant manager to Holland & Holland.
1894: joined James Lang & Co. Ltd, 102 New Bond Street.
1895: name altered to Lang & Hussey Ltd.
1898: appointed Managing Director.
1899: started as H. J. Hussey Ltd, 81 New Bond Street.
After 1908: Ryder Street.
1914: with son H. H. Hussey as Hussey & Hussey Ltd, 88 Jermyn
Street.
1918: died and business closed.

1919: H. H. Hussey and Harrison joined in Harrison & Hussey Ltd, but left about 1921 and joined Ogden Smiths, St James's Street, adding his name to theirs.

Died *c.* 1935.

A wonderful connection had been built up by Harrison & Hussey in a short time, but as it was decided not to continue the business it was acquired by Stephen Grant and Joseph Lang Ltd in 1930.

JEFFERY, W. J. (born 1857)

Established 1885 at 60 Queen Victoria Street.

?1897: 13 King Street, St James's.

1909 (March): died and succeeded by brother Charles.

1909: in August, Jeffery Ltd.

1915: 26 Bury Street and other two addresses closed.

1920: Charles Jeffery died; nephew of Jeffery, Pearce, continued.

1927: 9 Golden Square.

1955: 5B Pall Mall.

1960: bought by Holland & Holland Ltd and moved to 13 Bruton Street.

LING, William

1838: 16 Church Street, Soho.

1844–62: 61 Jermyn Street (Hawker).

LITTLE, G. & Co.

1889–96: 63 Haymarket.

LONDON ARMOURY CO.

1857: Railway Arches, Henry Street, Bermondsey Street.

1864: 36 King William Street.

1875: 54 King William Street.

1884: 118 Queen Victoria Street.

1888: 114 Queen Victoria Street.
31 Bury Street.

c. 1939: 10 Ryder Street.

MALEHAM, Charles H.

In 1882 Charles H. Maleham of Sheffield was at 20 Regent Street, Waterloo Place, London.

MANCHESTER ORDNANCE AND RIFLE CO.

1865: 28 Pall Mall.

MOORE & GREY

1818: William Moore & Co., 43 Old Bond Street (3 doors from Piccadilly).

1838: William Moore, 78 Edgware Road.

1844–53: William Moore and W. Grey, 78 Edgware Road (Hawker 1844).

1854: William Moore & Co., now Wm Grey and Son.

1854: W. Grey & Son (late Wm Moore & Co.) (Hawker).

1854–72: Wm Moore & Co., 43 Old Bond Street.

1873: Wm Moore, Grey & Co., 43 Old Bond Street.

1874–78: Wm Moore & Grey.

1879–95: Wm Moore & Grey Ltd.

1896: 165 Piccadilly.

1908: 8 Craven Street, Strand (also the address at this time of Bozard & Co.)

and also 11 The Arcade, Aldershot.

mid 1920s: bought by Cogswell & Harrison Ltd.

MORRIS

1883: Morris's Aiming and Sighting Apparatus, 63 Haymarket.

1887: 7 and 9 St Brides Street.

1888: The Morris Tube Ammunition and Safety Range Co. Ltd.

1889: 11 Haymarket.

MORTIMER JACKSON & SON

1790–1820: (Glendinning).

1812: 21 St James's Street.

1826: 34 St James's Street.

John Blanch was apprenticed to him and married his daughter. 3 years with John Manton.

MURCOTT, Theophilus

1854: Essex Street, Strand (Hawker).

1861: 68 Haymarket.

1870: Patented his double hammerless.

1878: premises (and ? business) taken by Greener.

NEEDHAM

Henry

1851: 4 Vine Street, Regents Park (Blanch).

1854–56: 5 Meards Court, Wardour Street.

William

1844: 26 Piccadilly.

1850: introduced his breech-loader.

Wm & Joseph: 1852

Joseph & Co.: 1854

Joseph & Henry: 1870

1874: introduced his ejector.

1876: 53 Piccadilly.

1879: 1A Wilton Place, Knightsbridge.

1880: 6 Park Side, Knightsbridge.

NOCK, Henry (1741–1804)

1772: 12 Ludgate Hill.

1787: invented his patent breech.

1802: Master of Gunmakers' Company.

1805: see under Wilkinson.

NOCK, Samuel

1800: apprenticed to his father, Henry.

1812: 180 Fleet Street.

1826: 43 Regent Circus.

1836: Master of Gunmakers' Company.

1850: business bought by Wm Robt Wallis, proprietor of Manton & Co., Calcutta.

1853–62: 116 Jermyn Street.

PARKIN, E.

1857: 3 Marylebone Street, Piccadilly.

PARKIN, Thomas

1861: 3 Marylebone Street, Piccadilly.

PATON, Edward & Sons

1860: already established at 44 George Street, Perth, and Highland Club Building, Inverness.

1871: 108 Mount Street, Grosvenor Square.

1883: 99 Mount Street, Grosvenor Square.

Later Shooting and Fishing Agents only, at 88 and 35A St James's Street and 5 St James's Place.

1929: 37 Bury Street.

1944: bought by Stephen Grant & Joseph Lang Ltd to form with their own Agency, Grant & Woodward (established 1884), the firm of Paton, Grant & Woodward at 7 Bury Street.

1959: Paton, Grant and Woodward sold to Strutt & Parker, Lofts & Warner.

PERKES, Thomas

1882: 70 Osnaburgh Street.

1890: 14A Castle Street East.

1893: also at 119 Jermyn Street.

1895: 18 Cork Street.

1896–98: Perkes, Adams & Co., 15 Swallow Street.

PRITCHETT, Samuel

1800, 1812: Master of Gunmakers' Company.

1812: 37 Chambers Street, Goodman's Fields.

1844: 59 Chambers Street.

1854: also 7 Poultry.

1855: also 138 St Mary Axe.

1856: 59 Chambers Street, 18 St Mary Axe and 86 St James's Street.

1857: Chambers Street, St James's Street and 24 Great Prescot Street.

1864: Chambers Street, Great Prescot Street and 4 St James's Street.

REILLY, E. M. and Co.

1882: E. M. Reilly and Co. were at 277 Oxford Street, 16 New Oxford Street, London, and Rue Scribe, Paris.

RIVIERE, Isaac

1818: 28 Piccadilly.

1844–51: 135 Oxford Street (Hawker).

SEARLE, Thomas

1869–71: 23 Jermyn Street.

SILVER & CO.

1882: S. W. Silver & Co. were at 67 Cornhill.

SMITH, George

1859: 40 Davies Street.

1867: 16 Davies Street.

1868: 104 New Bond Street.

1870: 82 New Bond Street.

1871: 10 Davies Street.

1872: 253 Oxford Street.

1874: 3 Park Lane.

1885: 110 Mount Street.

1888: 3 Angel Ct, King Street.

1891: 4 Stafford Street.

1897: 153 Piccadilly.

STAUDENMAYER, Samuel Henry

Apprenticed to John Manton and one of the finest rifle borers of the time.

1812–18: 35 Cockspur Street (London Directory 1812 but Hawker in 1816 says No 53).

1810–32: (Glendinning p. 190) 32 Cockspur Street (Hawker 1825).

STORM'S BREECH-LOADING ARMS DEPOT

1864–65: 121 Pall Mall.

SYLVEN, Thomas

1864: 33 Leicester Square and 10 Panton Street.

1865–80: 44 Bedford Street.

TATHAM, Henry

1820–40: (Glendinning p. 190).

1810–12: Tatham & Egg, 37 Charing Cross (London Directory).

1826: 24 Pall Mall.

1844: 37 Charing Cross (Hawker).

1854–60: 37 Charing Cross (Hawker).

1857–58: also 3 Opera Arcade.

THORN, William

1874–76: 4 Pall Mall.

TOLLEY, J. & W.

1882: J. & W. Tolley of the Pioneer Gun Works, Birmingham, and 1 Conduit Street, London, W, specialised in wildfowl guns.

WALLIS, John

1859–64: 116 Jermyn Street.

WATSON, Thomas W.

1875: 4 Pall Mall.

1885: Watson Bros.

1895: 29 Old Bond Street.

1930: 13A Pall Mall.

1935: 7 Bury Street.

Besides a very fine general connection, they made a speciality of small bore guns for ladies and boys.

WHITWORTH & CO. LTD

1866: 28 Pall Mall.

1871: Sir Joseph Whitworth & Co.

1880: 24 Great George Street.

1888: 2 Victoria Mansions.

WILKINSON

1772: Henry Nock started at 12 Ludgate Hill.

1787: invented his patent breech.

1802: Master of the Gunmakers' Company.

1804: succeeded by his apprentice and foreman James Wilkinson (died 1825), whose sister-in-law Dinah Wilkinson (died 1834) had daughters Caroline and Charlotte who married respectively Charles and John Augustus, the youngest children of Joseph Manton.

1825: succeeded by his son Henry, trading as James Wilkinson & Sons at 27 Pall Mall.

1850: Wilkinson & Son

1850–54: at 27 Pall Mall and at 18 St Mary Axe (Hawker).

1861: Henry succeeded by manager John Latham.

1874: Ceased making guns.

1888: The Wilkinson Sword Co. Ltd.

c. 1909: 53 Pall Mall.

1939: ceased selling guns, but continued their world-renowned trade as sword cutlers, commenced shortly before Crimean War, garden tool makers and later, razor blade makers.

Wilkinson Sword Ltd.

1955: 16–17 Pall Mall.

WILSON, Thomas & Co.

1869: 15 Cockspur Street.

1870–71: 2 East India Avenue and 5 Lime Street.

The following provincial gunmakers were listed by G. T. Teasdale-Buckell in his book *Experts on Guns and Shooting*, published in 1900 by Samson Low, Marston & Co. Ltd.

Amliac, Anglesey: W. Jones.

Aberdeen: C. Playfair & Co.

Andover: E. Chamberlain.

Ashford, Kent: Leeson.

Barnstaple: Mrs A. Gale.

Bedford: W. Darlow.

Beccles, Suffolk: Harry Tilney.

Belfast: William Hunter.

Belfast: J. Braddell & Son.

Blackburn: James Gregson.

Blairgowrie: J. Crockard & Son.

Blanford: Arthur Conyers, 59 East Street.

Boston: E. C. Slingsby.

Brampton, Cumberland: W. Milburn.

Braintree: G. T. Bartram, Bank Street.

Bridgwater: S. Norris & Son.

Bristol: G. Gibbs.

Brigg: G. H. Hockey.

Brighton: L. Weston.

Bournemouth: A. H. Lightwood.

Bury St Edmunds: John A. Scotcher.

Cambridge: Gallyon & Sons.

Canterbury: J. Fox.

Cardiff: S. Chambers.

Carmarthen: G. Giles.

Clitheroe: J. Baldwin.

Chelmsford: W. A. Leech.

Cheltenham: McLoughlin & Sons.

Cheltenham: E. C. Green.

Chester: H. Monk.

Chippenham: J. B. Warrilow.

Church Brampton: A. H. Rutt.

Cirencester: C. R. Holland.

Cockermouth: G. P. Graham.

Colchester: John S. Boreham.

Cork: T. W. Murray & Co.

Corhampton: Manning & Vicery.

Cromer: C. Francis.

Darlington: J. F. Smythe.

Devizes, Wilts: A. E. Cole & Co.

Derby: John Fry, Sadler Gate.

Derby: Charles Rosson.

Dorchester: C. Jeffrey.

Driffield: J. Conyers.

Dublin: Trulock & Harris.

Dumfries: J. Mitchell & Son.

Dundee: J. R. Gow & Son.

Durham: G. Robson.

Edinburgh: J. Dickson & Son, 63 Princes Street.

Edinburgh: Fraser.

Edinburgh: Alexander Henry & Co.

Exeter: S. A. Agnew, 79 South Street.

Eynsham: E. J. Gibbons.

Framlingham: B. Norman.

Gainsborough: Charles F. Liversidge.

Glasgow: J. D. Dougall & Son.

Glasgow: A. Blaw.

Glasgow: C. J. Annan.

Gloucester: F. S. Fletcher, 158 Westgate Street.

Gloucester: Charles F. Green.

Grays: W. P. Walker.

Guildford: Samuel R. Jeffrey.

Hereford: B. E. Ebrall.

Hereford: Philip Morris.

Holbeach: J. C. Hardy.

Honiton: Matthew Bros.

Honiton: H. J. Materface.

Horncastle: G. H. Wilson.

Hull: W. W. Greener.

Huddersfield: W. Golden.

Inverness: J. Graham & Son.

Inverness: Hugh Snowie & Son.

Ipswich: Frank A. Bales.

Jedburgh: Greenbank & Son.

Kelso: G. Forrest & Son.

Kilmarnock: W. McCririck.

King's Lynn: L. G. Clough, 52 High Street.

Knaresborough: C. Hall.

Landport, Portsmouth: George Newnham.

Launceston, Cornwall: T. Symons.

Leamington: John Hobson.

Leeds: Linsley Bros.

Leicester: Clarke & Son, Gallowtree Gate.

Leighton Buzzard: R. Farmer.

Lewes: Gerald Lloyd.

Leyburn: R. Campbell & Son.

Limerick: A. Nestor.

Lincoln: Wallis Bros.

Lincoln: J. R. Hanson.

Liverpool: W. Richards, 27 Old Hall Street.

Liverpool: George Higham.

Liverpool: Hooton & Jones.

Liverpool: Williams & Powell.

Liverpool: Messrs Blissett & Sons.

Long Stratton: J. Brewster.

Louth: J. P. Hodgson.

Luton: J. J. Langley.

Malton, Yorks: J. W. Anderson.

Manchester: William Griffiths.

Manchester: J. Percy, 48 King's Street, W.

Marlborough: H. A. Turner.

Newark: Smith & Sons.

Newcastle-on-Tyne: W. R. Pape, Collingwood Street.

Newton Abbot: J. Clarke & Son.

Newport, Isle of Wight: Wood & Tame, 114 Pyle Street.

Newton Stewart: J. Erskine & Son.

Northampton: Rowland Hill.

Norwich: E. Wilson.

Nottingham: T. Knight.

Nottingham: J. Frampton.

Nottingham: S. Jackson.

Oban: C H. Bishopp.

Oswestry: J. G. Benbow.

Oswestry: George G. Higham.

Oxford: S. G. Venables.

Oxford: F. E. Webb.

Perth: R. Lees.

Plymouth: F. H. Edwards, 2 George Street.

Plymouth: Jeffreys & Son.

Pocklington, Yorks: H. Conyers.

Portsmouth: Cole & Sons.

Portsea: J. Marks.

Preston: William Richards.

Reading, Market Place: T. H. Turner.

Reepham, Norwich: E. Gibbs.

Retford, Nottingham: F. West.

Repton: W. Hodgson.

Saffron Walden: F. R. Furlong.

Scarborough: F. Rhodes, 5 North Street.

Sevenoaks: T. E. Kither.

Sheffield: C. H. Maleham.

Shepton Mallet: G. Chambers.

Sittingbourne, Kent: W. G. Palmer.

Shrewsbury: Samuel Smallwood.

Shrewsbury: C. W. Ebrall.

Skipton: C. S. Griffiths.

Sleaford: W. M. Hooton.

Southampton: John Patstone.

Southampton: Cox & Clarke, 28 High Street.

Southampton: Cox & Macpherson.

Stirling: D. Crockart.

Stowmarket: T. A. Dadley.

Swaffham: Johnson & Son.

Taunton: George Hinton.

Thetford: G. E. Bond.

Tiverton, Devon: William Thorn.

Torquay: J. H. Mountstephen.

Tonbridge: P. Powell.

Tring: G. Grace.

Truro: T. H. Tims.

Ulverston: Tom Parkinson.

Wakefield: B. Boston.

Warrington: T. Dainteth.

Windsor: A. E. Cole & Co.

Windsor: T. C. Hill.

Winchester: Hammond Bros.

Woolwich: H. Andrews.

York: T. Horsley & Sons.

The following notable Birmingham gunmakers not otherwise mentioned are added with their addresses around 1900:

William Ford, 41 Whittall Street, St Mary's, Birmingham.
William Jones, Established 1826, 75 Bath Street, St Mary's, Birmingham.
William Powell & Son, 13 Carr's Lane, Birmingham.

CHAPTER ELEVEN

The Shooting of Muzzle and Early Breech-loaders

As some collectors of the guns and rifles of this period will desire to shoot them, a few words on the subject may be of service, first as regards muzzle-loaders and then breech-loaders.

Before attempting to shoot muzzle-loading guns and rifles there are some obvious precautions to be taken. If the gun or rifle is of good quality and in original condition it may be safe to use, but in order to be quite sure, it is best to take the weapon to a practical gunmaker who can take out the breech and make a thorough examination of the barrel. Such an examination is all the more necessary if the weapon has suffered from usage or neglect, and here it should be stressed that some barrels that have had rust pits struck off on the outside and have been rebrowned and also had the bores lapped, may have lost quite a lot of metal; they may look right and are therefore more dangerous. Such a weakness can soon be discovered if the thickness of barrel walls is measured. In the event of such a weakness a gunmaker will advise sending the weapon for re-proof for use with black powder or that it be kept as a non-shooter.

Assuming that the gun to be used is found in good order or has been reproved, the next most important step is to find out the correct load of powder and shot and obtain or make accurate measures. A guide to the loads of shot guns is contained in chapter 1, but if the gun happens to be cased there may be some indication of the intended load. If in the slightest doubt it is wise to keep to the lighter loads and to No 6 size black powder rather than No 2. No 2 Black is a fast burning powder and should not be used with heavy loads or in guns larger than 12 bore. No 6 Black will in any case give much better results in a duck gun, and should also be used in all rifles.

Powder loads for rifles were generally smaller than might be expected, for example, $1\frac{1}{2}$ drams of No 6 was the standard load for a 16 bore deer rifle, throwing a 1 oz ball. Two-groove rifles were designed for heavier loads; sometimes these were engraved on the rifles, or if cased they were usually provided with measures or the loads were written inside the lid. As has been previously mentioned a rifle, and a double rifle in particular, was sighted for an exact load and this must be used if the rifle is to shoot correctly.

Now to the actual loading: assuming that the bores are wiped clean of excess oil and a couple of caps have been fired to clear the breech, the safest and most accurate way to load is to fill a measure with the powder and tip this into the muzzle, while holding the gun or rifle upright. This will prevent the danger of a flask blowing up should there be a piece of smouldering tow or rag in the breech after the first shot (such as an odd strand of rag or tow having been left in after cleaning).

In loading a shot gun a thick felt or fibre wad is rammed firmly down on the powder and after the measure of shot has been poured down it is followed by a card wad. This card will be easier to ram gently home if it has a small hole in the centre to let the air through; sometimes the old wad cutters had small notches in the side to make little air channels.

When loading a rifle designed for normal ball, this ball should be carefully placed in the centre of a greased linen or soft leather patch of the appropriate thickness and carefully rammed home. Here it should be stressed that it is of the utmost importance that the ball is firmly down on the powder; this can be very difficult if after several shots the bore has become foul, but to fire the rifle with a gap between powder and bullet can give a dangerously high pressure in the breech and could result in a burst. If the bullet cannot be rammed down then it must be withdrawn by screwing a strong worm into it, but if very firmly wedged it may be a job for a gunsmith: moral, if the bore is getting tight stop shooting. A thick wad rammed down before the ball can be a help in cleaning the bore and ensuring a gastight seal. Information about the powder load and bullet for particular rifles can probably be best obtained from the various muzzle-loading rifle clubs which enthusiasts could join.

The percussion cap should fit tightly on to the nipple, otherwise in a double-barrelled gun the explosive force of the first cap fired may blow off the second. If the exact size of caps for particular nipples are not available then slightly larger caps can be gently squeezed in a bit at the base to make them grip.

In loading a double gun particular attention must be taken to see that one barrel is not double loaded, either for powder, shot or both; a mark on the ramrod showing the place level with the muzzle, when correctly loaded, is a useful safeguard. When one barrel only has been fired the percussion cap of the loaded barrel should be removed before the fired barrel is reloaded.

In damp or cold weather the fired barrel or barrels should be reloaded at once while the barrel is still warm and before the residue of the powder absorbs moisture.

When the shooting is over there comes the task of cleaning the gun. For washing through the barrels a plastic bucket is ideal as it does not scratch the barrels and this should be filled with cold water with a little washing up detergent in it. The breech ends of the barrels are placed in the bucket, the barrels are gripped by the muzzle end and with the other hand the water is pumped up and down with the aid of a rod with tow wound round the jag or with a close bristle brush. Having changed the water and got the barrels thoroughly clean, the next stage is to get them quite dry. This can be tackled in two ways: firstly by pouring hot water through them and then wiping out inside to remove all surplus moisture and, by working a towed jag up and down, blow the moisture from the breech while it is still hot. Or secondly the surplus moisture can be wiped out of the barrels and blown out from the breech as before and then the drying process completed in an airing cupboard or other suitable warm place. Only when certain that there is no moisture left, should the barrels be oiled, and here some discretion should be used; a thin film of oil is all that is required for the bores and just a little in the breech. If too much oil is used it runs out and soaks into the wood and has in any event to be removed before the gun can be used again.

If the gun is to be put away for some time or has become excessively fouled it will be wise to remove the nipples carefully with the appropriate key and clean and oil the screw threads. Also if there should be persistent fouling or leading in the barrel this can be moved with a copper wire brush or a brass turk's head.

Having dealt with the barrels, the lock plate, the hammer, and in particular the inside of the hammer head cup, should be brushed clean and oiled. It is also as well to check the inside of the lock in case any corrosive matter has penetrated and wipe it over with a lightly oiled rag.

After a day or two it is wise to check the barrels and give them a further brush through and oil with a wool mop.

Apart from such useful items as a powder flask, shot pouch and powder and shot measures, useful additional items are the shot chargers containing a load of shot in each end, handy for quick reloading in the field and a cap dispenser which saves quite a lot of fumbling with loose caps.

Essentials are the correct nipple key and a stout double worm for withdrawing gun charges and a strong single-pointed screw-shaped worm for withdrawing a lead ball from a rifle. If much shooting is to be done with a gun, a loading rod with its smooth ball-shaped end can save a great deal of wear and tear on the fingers, making loading marvellously easy compared with grasping the thin end of a ramrod.

Muzzle-loading can be great fun and relatively inexpensive, but every precaution should be taken to ensure safety and there must be no question of trying to work out equivalent smokeless powder loads.

Early breech-loaders were of course all black powder proved and if they are in good order and in proof they may well be safe to use with black powder cartridges. Pinfire cases are of course difficult to obtain and rather too scarce to use now, so it is probable that most of those who wish to shoot with early breech-loaders will prefer centre-fire guns.

Assuming then that a collector wishes to shoot with one of his early hammer guns the first thing to do is to take it to a practical gunmaker and ask him to examine the gun and measure the barrel walls as well as the diameter of the barrels 9 inches from the breech. If the gun is in proof (that is the inside of the barrel has not been enlarged more than 10 thousandths of an inch from the proof size), and the barrel walls are of the correct thickness, the action tight and so on, then the gunmaker may well advise that the gun is all right to be shot with its intended black powder load. If however there is any doubt then the gun can be sent for reproof for use with black powder.

Should it be desired to use a gun with modern nitro cartridges then the advice of the gunmaker can be sought as to the likeliness of its passing nitro proof. The decision about submitting a valuable collector's item to nitro proof will depend on the strength and condition of the gun, its value and how much it is desired to use it with nitro cartridges.

If it is a valuable item and there is any doubt about it standing up to the strain of the proof charge then it is probably best to keep the gun as a collector's item, and perhaps for the odd shots with cartridges reloaded with a light black powder charge. A less valuable or stronger hammer gun can then be submitted for nitro proof. A great deal of pleasure can be derived from shooting with a hammer gun that was in its day a 'best' gun; the greatest care should be taken of these, because good examples are scarce and are likely to be more highly prized in the future.

It should be noted that a police permit is required to buy black powder, which is normally granted in all bona fide cases for use in muzzle-loading shotguns or black powder proved breech-loading shot guns, provided that the owner has a Shot Gun Certificate.

If it is the intention to use any muzzle-loading rifles or pistols or any other weapon, normally exempt from a Firearms Certificate when possessed as a collector's item only, then it becomes necessary to have a Firearms Certificate. The firearms must then be used on approved ranges or such safe places as may be approved.

Some Terms Explained

ACTION: The mechanism for opening and closing the gun.

ACTION BODY: The iron or steel body that contains the above.

ACTION FACE: The part of the action body that fits against the breech ends of the barrels and through which the strikers operate.

BEND: The angle at which the stock is set down from the line of the barrels.

BENT: The notch in the tumbler that takes the sear when the gun is cocked.

BREAK-OFF: The false breech that the barrels of a muzzle-loader hook into, and from which they 'break off' when the barrels are removed from the stock. The term is sometimes used for the equivalent part of a breech-loader.

CAST OFF: The angle at which the stock is set away from the shooter in order to bring the barrels in to the line of his eye.

CAST ON: The angle at which the stock is set towards the shooter in order to bring the barrels out to the line of his eye.

COMB: The top ridge of the stock.

CROSS PIN: The pin or bolt in the front of the action body on which the barrels hinge open.

FENCES: In a percussion gun the shields round the nipples. In a hammer gun the carved curves round the strikers. In a hammerless gun the top and sides of the standing breech.

FORE-END: The detachable forward grip under the barrels which usually houses the ejector mechanism.

HAMMER: The external or internal arm that hits the striker, or percussion cap. The arm that held the flint on a flintlock was called the cock, hence the terms half cock—full cock—to cock—cocked, etc., which were applied to the percussion gun, hammer gun and later to the combined tumbler and hammer of the hammerless gun.

HEEL PLATE: An iron, horn, composition or rubber plate fitted to the shoulder end of the stock.

HUTS: Breech plugs.

JAG: The brass top of a cleaning rod jagged to retain tow for cleaning.

SEAR: The arm in the lock that fits into the bent to hold the tumbler at cocked.

STOCK: The wood that fits the gun to the shoulder.
   Full stocked: the wood fitted to the full length of the barrel.
   Half stocked: Stocked to the forward grip.

Top strap: An extension from the rear of the action body to strengthen the grip of a heavy gun or rifle.

Trigger plate: The plate on which the trigger work is set.

Tumbler: The part of the lock which has the cocking bent (or bents in a muzzle-loading or early breech-loading gun) and in a hammerless gun the tumbler also serves as the internal hammer.

Turk's head: The brass or steel wire head for a cleaning rod used for removing hard fouling from barrels.

Bibliography

Remarks on Rifle Guns, Ezekiel Baker, London 1825.
The Oakleigh Shooting Code, Tom Oakleigh, London 1838.
The Modern Shooter, Captain Lacy, London 1842.
Tiger Shooting in India, Lieut. W. Rice, London 1857.
Gunnery in 1858, W. Greener, London 1858.
The Shot-gun and Sporting Rifle, J. H. Walsh (Stonehenge), London 1859.
The Dead Shot, Marksman, London 1862. 3rd edition.
The Wild Fowler, H. C. Folkard, London 1864. 2nd edition.
The Sporting Rifle, Lieut. J. Forsyth, London 1867.
The Hunting Grounds of the Old World, H. A. Leveson, London 1868.
Modern Breech-loaders, W. W. Greener, London 1869.
The Gun and its Development, W. W. Greener, London 1881.
A Hunter's Wanderings in Africa, F. C. Selous, London 1881.
The Modern Sportsman's Gun and Rifle, J. H. Walsh, London 1882.
The Badminton Library: *Shooting*, Lord Walsingham and Sir R. Payne-Gallwey, London 1887.
The Badminton Library: *Big Game Shooting*, Several authors, London 1896.
Letters to Young Shooters, Sir R. Payne-Gallwey, London 1890.
Fur and Feather Series, A. Stuart-Wortley, London 1893, 4, 5.
Experts on Guns and Shooting, G. T. Teasdale-Buckell, 1900.
A Century of Guns, H. J. Blanch, London 1909.

Books still in print:

The Art of Shooting, Charles Lancaster, first published 1889, 13th edition 1962, Messrs Atkin, Grant and Lang Ltd, London.
The Modern Shotgun, Major Gerald Burrard, Herbert Jenkins Ltd, London 1931.
English Guns and Rifles, J. N. George, The Stackpole Co., Pennsylvania 1947.
The Mantons: Gunmakers, W. Keith Neal and D. H. L. Back, Herbert Jenkins Ltd, London 1967.
Sporting Guns, Richard Akehurst, G. Weidenfeld and Nicolson Ltd, London 1968.
Royal Sporting Guns at Windsor, H. L. Blackmore, H.M.S.O., London 1968.

Acknowledgements

The author wishes to thank the following for their valuable contributions:

Mr W. Keith Neal for his kind help and encouragement and in particular for providing so many excellent photographs of guns in his collection.

Mr W. R. H. Robson for generously making available his notes on London gunmakers.

The following gunmakers have kindly helped with their histories and numbers:

Atkin Grant and Lang Ltd, Boss & Co Ltd, Churchill (Gunmakers) Ltd, John Dickson & Son Ltd, Holland & Holland Ltd, James Purdey & Sons Ltd, John Rigby & Co Ltd, Westley Richards & Co Ltd and John Wilkes.

The author and publishers thank the following for access to guns in their collections:

W. Keith Neal Esq.: Plates 9, 10, 11, 21, 22, 23, 24, 25, 26, 27, 28, 31, 32, 33, 34, 35, 37, 38, 39, 40, 41, 59, 64, 65, 68, 69, 70, 71, 72, 73, 74, 75, 76, 77, 82, 84, 85. Photographed by owner.

J. Roberts & Son: Plates 7, 8, 12, 13, 36, 42, 43, 63, 67, 78, 79, 80, 81, 86. Photographed by Mike Brown Studios.

Frank Anderson Esq.: Plates 30, 44, 50, 83. Photographed by Chris Crosthwaite.

Gordon Colquhoun Esq.: Plates 53, 54, 55, 57, 60, 62. 53–55, 60 photographed by C. O'Brien Esq.; 57, 62 by Chris Crosthwaite.

From author's collection: Plates 1, 2, 3, 4, 5, 6, 14, 15, 16, 17, 19, 45, 46, 47, 48, 49, 51, 52, 56, 61. Photographed by Chris Crosthwaite.

The author and publishers also thank the following: Wallis & Wallis for plate 66, Westley Richards & Co Ltd for plate 87, J. Purdey & Sons Ltd for plate 88, John Wilkes for plate 89, and Atkin Grant & Lang Ltd for the frontispiece and figure 43.

A special word of thanks to my wife for her great help as secretary, typist and proof reader.